Cold War Genres

Cold War Genres

Local and International in Hindi Literature

Gregory Goulding

SUNY
PRESS

Photograph by the author.

Published by State University of New York Press, Albany

Printed in the United States of America

For information, contact State University of New York Press, Albany, NY
www.sunypress.edu

Library of Congress Cataloging-in-Publication Data

Name: Goulding, Gregory, author.
Title: Cold war genres : local and international in Hindi literature / Gregory Goulding.
Description: Albany : State University of New York Press, [2024]. | Includes bibliographical references and index.
Identifiers: LCCN 2024005570 | ISBN 9781438499598 (hardcover : alk. paper) | ISBN 9781438499604 (ebook) | ISBN 9781438499581 (pbk. : alk. paper)
Subjects: LCSH: Hindi literature—20th century—History and criticism. | Literary forms.
Classification: LCC PK2038 .G68 2024 | DDC 891.4/309—dc23/eng/20240422
LC record available at https://lccn.loc.gov/2024005570

For Emma

Contents

Acknowledgments ix

Note on Transliteration and Translation xv

Introduction 1

1 A Stream of Pure Sanskrit Curses: Caste, Knowledge, and Critique in the Long Poem 27

2 Realism, Romanticism, and the (Lower) Middle Class: The Problem of Aesthetic Process 67

3 Muktibodh's Prose Fiction and the Question of the Real 97

4 The Long Poem between Genre and Form 127

Conclusion: The Afterlives of Muktibodh 169

Appendix: Full Translations of "Brahmarākṣas" (The Brahmin Demon) and "Aṃdhere meṃ" (In the Dark) 197

Notes 241

Works Cited 273

Index 291

Acknowledgments

It is hard to imagine how many people helped in the writing of this book, let alone who to thank. Any omissions should be considered entirely the fault of the author.

Vasudha Dalmia has been the beating heart of my scholarship, at times producing pressure, at times relieving it. Over the years she has been a steadfast supporter as my project took shape. The members of my dissertation committee—Lawrence Cohen, Robert Kaufman, and Michael Mascuch—have each contributed their voice and influence to my writing and thinking in ways that I remember almost every day. Colleen Lye and Martin Jay supported my work at critical early moments, and I continue to think of them as models for the kind of academic writing I try to produce.

Before I began my graduate studies, I first began learning Hindi with Gabriela Ilieva. She saw through the chaos of a nineteen-year-old's mind to a stubborn, abiding interest in the languages of North India that set me on this path. I was fortunate to be able to study with committed and deeply knowledgeable language instructors in Lucknow, Jaipur, and Pune through the American Institute of Language Studies, and I would especially like to thank Swami ji, Vidhu ji, Neelam ji, Sayeed ji, Sujata Mahajan, Shantanu Kher, and Supriya Sahasrabuddhe. In Berkeley, I continued my language study with Usha Jain, with whom I read for the first time many of the works that are fundamental to this project. I was deeply fortunate to spend a year reading modern Marathi poetry with Philip Engblom, whose patient but tireless reading continues to form a model for my own teaching.

During my research, primarily in Delhi and Bhopal, I was offered help and friendship from many librarians, scholars, and lovers of literature—far more, in fact, than I could list, and testament to the comment to this literature that I hope to honor. I would like to thank Ashok Vajpeyi for his assistance and guidance at the beginning stages of my work. I would also like to thank Rashmi Vajpeyi, the director of Natrang Pratishthan, for allowing me access to their extensive archives, as well as Shiv Narayan Khanna for his assistance in my research. I would also like to thank the staff of the library for their help and company during my time there. I would like to thank the Center for the Study of Developing Societies for hosting me as a visiting scholar, and especially Ravikant for his support and assistance. Sanjiv Kumar, over several meetings, welcomed me into the literary world of Delhi. Pravin Kumar discovered me reading in the CSDS library, and quickly became a dear friend.

In Bhopal, Nirmala Sharma took me into her home and made me part of her own unique community in Bhopal. It is in no small part due to her kindness and friendship that I remember the city so fondly. Udayan Vajpayee unhesitatingly offered his time and help to me upon my arrival in that wonderful city, and our conversations guided my subsequent research. Basant Tripathi and Manoj Rupda, without hesitation, showed me what felt like all of Nagpur, introducing me to associates of Muktibodh as well as to literary figures. Uday Prakash hosted me in Amarkantak at a formative moment, and our conversations gave me a new perspective on my research. I would also like to thank the following for taking the time to meet with me and share their knowledge of Muktibodh and Hindi literature: Rajesh Joshi, Rameshchandra Shah, Madan Soni, Chandrakant Devtale, Dudhnath Singh, and Vinod Kumar Shukla. The staff of Bhopal's Sapre Sangrahalaya library welcomed me to their archive and facilitated my research: I especially would like to thank director Mangala Anuja, who offered me every assistance. My work was also facilitated by the staff of Bharat Bhavan in Bhopal, the Hindi Sahitya Sammelan in Allahabad, and the Nehru Memorial Museum and Library in Delhi.

I would like especially to thank Ramesh Muktibodh, the eldest son of Gajanan Madhav Muktibodh, who took me into his home in Raipur and introduced me to a host of literary figures in Raipur and Rajnandgaon. He brought me into his family, and showed me the small city where Muktibodh spent his last years, including his former home on the grounds of Digvijay College. I gained a new sense of responsibility to the memory of his extraordinary father, and I can only hope that I have done some small justice to it in this work.

I am indebted to so many who, over the years, helped me in ways big and small, and form that massive network of friends and colleagues that makes the study of South Asia such a paradoxically intimate and friendly space. Rahul Parson and Preetha Mani were with me at the start, and I can't imagine better companions for the journey. Preetha has been my mentor, my friend, and one of the sharpest and most critical readers of my work. Luther Obrock has always been, and continued to be, a sparkplug of ideas, the truest audience for all the tangents that escape my work. I am grateful to many other friends and colleagues who assisted this project and lent support in various ways: Talia Ariav, Alessandro Battistini, David Boyk, Yigal Bronner, Laura Brueck, Allison Busch, Elizabeth Chatterjee, Nandini Chatterjee, Padma Chirumamilla, Jennifer Clare, Vinay Dharwadker, Jatin Dua, Jennifer Dubrow, Rotem Geva, Asher Ghertner, Nikhil Govind, Shounak Ghosh, Jason Grunebaum, John Stratton Hawley, Samuel Hodgkin, Thibaut d'Hubert, Joya John, Wade Johnson, Mahmood Kooria, Carola Lorea, Manjita Mukharji, Projit Mukharji, Mike Munz, Nitin Narain, Anjali Nerlekar, Francesca Orsini, Vasudha Paramasivan, Abhijeet Paul, Frances Pritchett, Sean Pue, Sanne Ravensbergen, David Shulman, Ulrike Stark, Carolien Stolte, Emilia Roza Sulek, Sanjukta Sunderason, Margherita Trento, and Rebecca Whittington. My deepest thanks to them all, and my apologies for any whom I failed to name. I had expected to include in this list of friends Pranav Karol, but he passed away as I completed this manuscript. A master of Delhi and someone who made friends in an instant, I am one of the many whose world is smaller without him in it.

Friends and Colleagues in Philadelphia and at the University of Pennsylvania shaped me as a scholar. I met Debjani Bhattacharya and Adam Knowles in Leiden, but our friendship will always be tied to Philadelphia. My departmental colleagues Daud Ali, Lisa Mitchell, and Davesh Soneji have supported me more than I could have imagined. Daud has been a mentor and friend, and has offered support at some of the most difficult moments of this project. Megan Robb has been a comrade in the study of Hindi and Urdu, and a friend as we have both grown up at Penn. Kashi Gomez has been the ideal colleague and best of office neighbors. Working with Laura Flippin made a joy of a famously difficult job. I am deeply grateful for the support of colleagues Oscar Aguirre-Mandujano, Courtney Brennan, Jamal Elias, Cam Grey, Rachael Hickson, Suvir Kaul, Sonal Khullar, Ania Loomba, Mark Lycette, Afsar Mohammad, Rahul Mukherjee, Kevin Platt, Teren Sevea, Fatema Shams, Emily Steiner, Kok-Chor Tan, Emily Wilson, Heather Williams, and Alexandra Zeiger.

I have been extremely fortunate to be able to work closely with graduate students at such an early stage of my career, and I cannot thank enough the students of SAST at Penn. I would particularly like to thank Anirudh Karnick, Ayesha Sheth, Mustafa Menai, Zain Mian, Nudrat Kamal, Apurva Desai, Akhil Veetil, Anju Biju, and Noor Habib. I hope that all of you will see something of your impact in this book, and I am so excited to see what you will do. I would also like to thank Shaashi Ahlawat, Matthew Chemplayil, Rama Godse, Daniel Lapinski, Kaustubh Naik, Sneha Chowdhury, and Diana Zhang, as well as all of the students who attended my graduate seminars.

Dissertation research that shapes this book was conducted with the assistance of the Fulbright-Nehru IIE Student Research Fellowship and the Social Science Research Council's International Dissertation Research Fellowship. Between finishing my dissertation and beginning my position at Penn, I was supported as a Research Fellow in the International Institute for Asian Studies at Leiden University. Modified portions of chapter four appear in "'My Unwritten Novel': The Long Poems of Gajanan Madhav Muktibodh between Genre and Form" published in *Comparative Literature* in September 2021. I have also presented parts of this work at the Annual Conference on South Asia at Madison in 2010, 2015, 2017, and 2019, the annual meeting of the American Comparative Literature Association in 2011 and 2015, the Princeton South Asia Conference in 2015, the Princeton Hindi/Urdu Workshop in 2018, the annual conference of the Association of Asian Studies in 2018, and the AMESALL Seminar Series at Rutgers University in 2021. I am grateful for the support of these institutions, and for the feedback from colleagues I have received over the years.

My primary editor at SUNY Press, James Peltz, has been unstinting in his support. I would also like to thank Caitlin Bean and Aimee Harrison, as well as the three anonymous peer reviewers of the manuscript. Finally, thanks to my copy editor for his perceptive and careful reading of the manuscript.

My parents, Teresa and Christopher Goulding, have supported me with an unshakable confidence for which I am deeply grateful. I am thankful for the friendship and support over the years of Daniel Borkan, Daniel Brueckenhaus, Ryann Croken, Andrew Dailey, Christopher Limone, Laura Llamado, Rochelle Lo, Molly Lubin, Christopher and Eliza Rafferty, and Maya Schenwar.

Important editorial assistance at all hours has been offered by Tabs, Mortimer, Phil, Geraldine, Spot, and Sidewinder. Pilsie, with her infinite capacity for judgment and sense of justice, would no doubt find this work deeply lacking, but was with me for every word. Her perfect life seemed to coincide with that of this manuscript; if I could, I would trade it for her in an instant.

Emma Kalb has believed in the value of this project when I wasn't sure I could, and together we have come through to the other side. I can only hope that this book has some of her brilliance and commitment.

Note on Transliteration and Translation

Like all scholars of South Asian literatures, I must confront "the war between the good and the better." I have included transliterations from the Devanagari to roman script for all quotations from poetry, but not from prose. My goal in this is to make the sounds of the poetry quoted reasonably accessible to those without access to the language or script. Otherwise, I have used diacritics when quoting words from the original language, except in the case of proper names or words that have been adopted in English.

In my transliteration of words originally written in the Devanagari or Nastaliq script, I have followed the current American Library Association/Library of Congress standards for romanization, with the following regular exceptions. In place of r̥, for vocalic r (ऋ) I use ṛ, which is identical to the romanization used for the retroflex flap (ड़/ढ़). For the nasalized vowel (ँ), for purely stylistic reasons I use, in place of ṁ, ṃ.

All translations from Hindi or Marathi are my own. For reasons that will be elaborated upon, I have chosen to translate all of Muktibodh's poetry in the lower case, including proper names and the first-person pronoun. In addition, following what is becoming convention, English words in the original Hindi have been rendered in translation with italics, unless they are words, such as *ṭren*, that have become Hindi words themselves, related to English only through etymology.

Map 1. Map of modern India with relevant cities in Central India. *Source*: Created by the author.

Introduction

hāy! hāy! tolstoy
kaise mujhe dīkh gae
sitāroṃ ke bīc-bīc
ghūmte va rukte
pṛthvī ko dekhte.
śāyad, ṭolsṭoy-numā
koī vah ādmī
aur hai,
mere kisī bhītarī dhāge kā ākhirī chor vah,
anlikhe mere upanyās kā
kendrīya samvedan
dabī hāy-hāy-numā,
śāyad, ṭolsṭoy-numā.

oh tolstoy
how do you appear before me
amidst the stars
roaming and pausing
as you view the earth.
perhaps, like tolstoy
a certain man
another,
the far end of a thread within me,
the central perception
of my unwritten novel
like a strangled, smothered cry
perhaps, like tolstoy.

—Muktibodh, "Aṃdhere meṃ" (In the dark)[1]

The apparition of an imposing male figure, a global guru; the expansion of that figure to cosmic significance as he looks down from the vantage of the stars; and a thin mental thread joining this cosmic man to another, terrestrial figure. This passage—taken from "Aṃdhere meṃ," the most well-known poem written by Gajanan Madhav Muktibodh and a central work in modern Hindi literature—features an element that will appear in various forms: the unwritten novel that, paralleling the cosmic guru of Tolstoy, is tied to but impossibly distant from the speaker.[2]

Muktibodh refers to the *kendrīya saṃvedan*, or "central perception," of this unwritten novel. The word *saṃvedan* indicates both perception, as in sonar and other forms of remote sensing, as well as sensation, with its necessary component of *vedan*, meaning pain. The idea of individual sensation at the heart of poetics is, not surprisingly, a key motif of Muktibodh's writing.[3] But why is this central perception a novel? Were the poem to present a more generic symbol of artistic production and expression, we might expect a lyric poem—*kavitā*—in its place. Instead, expression is bound up as part of the larger, all-encompassing genre of the novel. This passage presents the unwritten novel as the unachievable ideal of a certain kind of artistic expression, beginning with the moment of lyric potentiality, that ties its threads to the larger world, and even the cosmic plane on which Tolstoy roams. As such, the novel occupies a special, privileged place in this passage, one that demonstrates a problem of genre, and the relation between poetry and prose, which will be central to the argument of this book.

Muktibodh, who died in 1964 at the age of 47, never completed a novel. Although an early, short novel may have been written and lost, and a short story "Vipātra" (The Antagonist) is sometimes classified as a novella, there is nothing in Muktibodh's oeuvre to suggest that novel-writing was an essential part of his practice.[4] Despite this, references to the novel, whether as a nonexistent ideal or as an actual goal in the case of his nonfiction writing, appear frequently, almost from the beginning of his career. In 1943, he presents the novel as a desideratum, comparing it with the "image of life," possible in a poem.[5] Fifteen years later, the novel remained both out of reach and dialectically twinned to the poem. In "Aṃdhere meṃ," the novel becomes a lost horizon, an unachievable unity with the cosmic guru.[6]

This book argues that Muktibodh's attachment to the novel—and, more generally, to the idea of prose narrative—is a key to understanding the most unique development of that work: the series of long, fantastic poems written from 1957 to Muktibodh's death in 1964, which are central to his legacy today. Muktibodh is one of the most canonized and debated figures in postindependence Hindi literature, and his reception has frequently hinged on the interpretation of these long poems, with critics variously reading them as expressions of lower-middle-class anxiety in the Nehruvian era, or as a retreat from the political goals of the earlier progressive period.[7] I argue, however, that the long poem can also be read as a unique formal response to the literary debates of the early Cold War world that, even as they repeated a pattern of debates between realism and modernism that in a South Asian context can be traced to the 1930s, took on special importance in the long 1950s of Hindi literature.[8]

Considering the long poem as a question of genre, with a special relation to the novel, illuminates a larger series of debates in Hindi literature, in turn showing how Hindi literature—and South Asian literary cultures in other languages—responded to the problems of twentieth century literature. As I will argue, the involvement in these debates in Hindi literature is visible not only on the surface, at the high point of Nehruvian internationalism, but also at the level of literary form. The unwritten novel of "Aṃdhere meṃ" therefore turns our attention to the larger problem of genre in twentieth-century literature that is the ultimate horizon of this book.

Despite being universally referred to as long poems, or *lambī kavitāeṃ* in Hindi, they are not especially long; *Aṃdhere meṃ* is approximately 1,200 lines, and none approach the length of what are considered important long poems in modernist and postmodernist Anglophone literatures, such as *Paterson, The Maximus Poems,* and *The Changing Light at Sandover.*[9] Accordingly, Muktibodh's long poems do not explicitly evoke the novel, and neither do they attempt to take up an epic form such as *kāvya,* despite frequent comparison. If, like *The Wasteland,* these long poems can be read as extensions of lyric form, it was in part in response to their historical moment: I argue that Muktibodh's long poems, in their particular approach to image, fragment, lyric form, and narrative, can illuminate the Cold War politics of genre and literary form that was central to Muktibodh's thinking and to Hindi literature in the 1950s. These long poems insist on bending the potential of *kavitā* into the space of narrative totality.

Fundamentally, therefore, this is a study of literary innovation in Hindi poetry during the early Cold War, which forefronts experimentation with genre, and the intersection of the lyric within a larger space of genre, in its analysis of a specific body of work. As such, it addresses itself to several fields: the study of Hindi literature in the twentieth century; the space of vernacular literatures in the literary internationalism of the 1950s; and the history of genre in modern literature in the era of realism and modernism debates. In each of the spaces in which it aims to make its intervention, its originality lies both in forefronting poetry in conversation with prose, and in its thesis that Muktibodh's long poems should be read as a unique response to problems of Hindi literature in the Nehruvian period. In its focus on this relatively small body of work, it aims to illuminate a dynamic visible throughout Cold War literary history of tension between literary genre, form, and narrative. In this introduction, therefore, I will frame Muktibodh's long poems in the context both of modern Hindi literature and the literary history of the Cold War. Through looking at him across these two scales of literary history, I hope to show how they might point to a fuller understanding of the dynamics of Muktibodh's work and its reception.[10]

The Central Outsider

One of the most well-known figures in Hindi literature, whose writings have been a continuous subject of critical debate for more than fifty years, Gajanan Madhav Muktibodh forms a natural subject for a study of postindependence poetry. But the long history of Muktibodh's reception is accompanied by the elevation of his life story and character, creating an image of the small-town, lower-middle-class prophet that is inseparable from any consideration of his writing. As I will argue, Muktibodh played no small part in creating this narrative, and his own conception of himself, as articulated in his autobiographical criticism, played an essential role in his critique of the Cold War literary world. No study, therefore, can ignore Muktibodh's biography, and the impact that it had in the Hindi world after his death.

Muktibodh lived for most of his life in what are today the states of Madhya Pradesh, Chattisgarh, and Maharashtra, in the center of modern India.[11] The son of a police inspector, he moved often, and spoke Marathi at home despite writing in Hindi; his brother, Sharaccandra Muktibodh, became a prominent writer in Marathi, most likely because his initial education took place in that language.[12] He first came to prominence in Hindi as a part of the seminal group collection of poetry, *Tār saptak* (A Heptad of Strings). This 1943 anthology of seven poets, edited and introduced by Sachchidananda Hirananda Vatsyayan "Agyeya," is seen as the initial moment of Hindi modernism, a dividing line between a poetry that, even as it became politically engaged in the progressive movement, still drew largely from *chāyāvād* and its aftermath, and a new poetics of free verse, increasingly conversational language, and attention to the everyday life of the emergent middle class.[13]

Although Muktibodh's participation in *Tār saptak* remains an essential part of his biography, and established his name as a major young poet, his most important poems—and those that are at the center of my study—were written towards the end of his life, when he had achieved a degree of financial stability as a teacher in the small town of Rajnandgaon, after working for most of the 1950s in Nagpur. In Nagpur, Muktibodh worked in a variety of journalistic positions, both for All-India Radio and, briefly, as an editor of a now-defunct newspaper. Nagpur looms large over the poetry he wrote in Rajnandgaon; the city, then the capital of a pre-1957 Madhya Pradesh and still the largest city in the region, is described in several of the poems I will discuss in this book. Muktibodh's vision of Nagpur as a dark, nightmarish place of political violence, paranoia, and social oppression, most famously articulated in his famous poem "Aṃdhere meṃ" (In the Dark), presents an indelible image of the regional cities of Hindi, removed from both the cosmopolitan environment of the large metropolitan cities and any hint of rural authenticity. Instead, the milieu of Muktibodh's writing presents the defining image of the lower middle class, which became, from the 1970s onwards, a key element of his reception. The disillusionment of the late 1960s and

1970s, and the political repression of the Emergency, were prefigured in Muktibodh's dark vision from the heart of Nehru's India.

In part because he achieved a measure of financial stability only in the final seven years of his life, but also due to the factors I will discuss in this book, his first book of poetry, *Cāṃd kā muṃh ṭeṛhā hai* (The Moon's Face Is Crooked), was only published as he lay in a coma in AIIMS hospital in Delhi before his death in 1964.[14] Although the long poems in that book were already becoming well-known—Ashok Vajpeyee had pronounced "Aṃdhere meṃ" the *Wasteland* of Hindi in 1960—his death launched both the poems and the figure of Muktibodh himself into the public conscience.[15] The rebellious, marginalized figure in the small cities, struggling to express the anxieties rising beneath the optimism of Nehruvian India, became indelibly linked with the long, strange poems attached to him. This combined image, in turn, became a crucial way through which Hindi criticism explained this period to itself, and debated the legacy of postindependence literature.[16]

This book does not claim to be either a study of Muktibodh's life or a comprehensive guide to his works.[17] As the only English-language monograph focusing on this writer, as well as one of the very few English-language academic monographs on the subject of postindependence Hindi poetry, I do feel a responsibility to represent this large body of work to an audience largely unfamiliar with it. *Cold War Genres* builds off of multiple generations of criticism in Hindi, which have, through analyzing Muktibodh, dealt with the historical shift from the optimism of Nehruvian, nonaligned India to the disillusionment of Naxalism and the Emergency of the 1970s.[18] This body of work has also seen Muktibodh as exemplary of a problem of genre, narrative, and poetic image, that illuminates the way in which Hindi engaged with the global politics of literature in the Cold War. For that reason, it is essential to understand how this work relates to recent scholarship on the internationalism of the twentieth century.

Cold War Vernaculars

Cold War Genres makes, in its title, a claim that requires some substantiation: that a study of a single author, without the kinds of international circulation and intervention of government agencies in literature and culture that might be associated with the Cold War, can form a contribution to the study of its literary history. Even among his contemporaries, Muktibodh was little traveled, and he remains undertranslated today.[19] But it is arguably through this isolation and perceived marginalization that the influence of the Cold War becomes most distinct and visible in Hindi literary history, because it demonstrates how the dynamics of the Cold War and the literary internationalism of the 1950s were received and refracted from the perspective of Hindi literature.

Hindi literature, in its complex and uneven incorporation into a world system, brings up both problems relating to Cold War literary history and theoretical problems of the structures of global literary history. Hindi is typically considered and framed as a vernacular language. In the mid-twentieth century, however, Hindi was seen as a hegemonic language in the new Republic of India, and alongside the other constitutional languages of India it was involved in new processes of translation and exchange.[20] Associated both with new institutions of literature and culture and with their participation in new international associations, writers in Hindi were newly able to participate in networks of global literature.[21] This affected not only the lives of the writers who were able to travel, but also the larger literary world through their writings and the new conception of the world that resulted from them. How is the idea of the vernacular shaped by the very different context of Cold War internationalism, and how, more generally, is this project shaped by the language order of the twentieth-century world?

Fundamentally, this project is shaped by the concept of the vernacular language and literature in twentieth century South Asian literature. Essentially, this idea frames a distinction between English, as a "cosmopolitan" language linking communities across South Asia and the world, as opposed to "vernacular" South Asian languages, of which Hindi might be considered the most prominent.[22] According to such a model of thinking, a cosmopolitan English is often contrasted with a language, such as Hindi, that is oriented towards the local and authentic.[23] Writers in the vernacular might be further categorized depending on the extent to which they participate in international networks. For instance, within the space of Hindi, a writer who would be seen as cosmopolitan, such as Agyeya, would be seen as such insofar as he participates in cosmopolitan literary culture through travel, knowledge of English, and general connection to intellectual spaces.[24]

A writer such as Muktibodh, on the other hand, is more often seen in terms of his local impact on Hindi poetry. Indeed, Muktibodh's biography of a series of low-paying jobs outside of the major metropolitan eras of the Hindi-speaking world, the perceived difficulty of his poetry, and the conspicuous lack of opportunities for cosmopolitan travel such as those enjoyed by his contemporaries such as "Agyeya," means that Muktibodh's work is often seen, outside of its importance to left aesthetics and the lionization of Muktibodh himself, as an example of an authentically localized voice in Hindi.[25] But Muktibodh, deeply rooted in a specific geographic space but engaged with issues of the cosmopolitan, in ways that shape the formal structure of his work, prompts a reconsideration of the boundaries between cosmopolitan and vernacular in South Asian literature.

To the extent that the international perspective of Muktibodh is discussed, it is in the context of his political commitments to the left in India, and the resulting debate over how these commitments shaped his literary perspective.[26] The debate, usually referred to as one between *prayogvād*, "experimentalism," and *pragativād*, "progressivism," was a frequent subject of Muktibodh's own writing.[27] This debate, as it evolved in the decades after his death, is an important aspect of how his work is remembered, and indeed becomes a means through which Hindi criticism reassessed the literature of the period. But as a range of critics have noted, writers frequently defied the later perception of a literary world split between these two poles.[28] Rather than limit its interpretation to a position in these debates, however, *Cold War Genres* sees Muktibodh as a means both to historicize them as expressions of global aesthetic debate in the Cold War and to consider how the historical framing of these debates in Hindi intersects with a range of other problems.

The study of the Comintern and the Cold War internationalism that followed it—the Comintern having been formed in 1932 and dissolved at the beginning of the Second World War, and the beginning of the Cold War roughly coinciding with the independence of India in 1947—has been reframed by recent scholarship as interventions in world literary history. This scholarship has, broadly, followed two paths. The first has focused on questioning the perceived division between realism and modernism, and reread the debates associated with it. This work has historicized Cold War aesthetic debate within the longue durée of literary criticism and empire, and argued that the familiar debate between realism and modernism can be seen not simply as a paradigmatic question within left aesthetics, but as constitutive of the imperial world system in the nineteenth and twentieth centuries.[29] As this book will argue, debates in Hindi that are seen as split between realism and modernism have to be read as a constellation of questions that take in colonial discourses of literature, Zhdanovite politics of social realism, and reformist movements in nationalist India.[30] This suggests an expansive approach to the literary history of the Cold War that includes this larger scope of realism.

The second strand has focused primarily on the Cold War in the context of what became known as the Third World. Recent decades have seen a transformation in understandings of the Cold War, from viewing the conflict largely as an opposition between the two world powers of the United States and the USSR, to conceiving of it as an extension of the imperial era and global, postcolonial realignment, whose military aspects played out primarily in what was at the time considered the Third World.[31] Parallel to this, scholars of literature have begun to revise a literary history that focuses primarily on a single system of world literature, in favor of what Katerina Clark has called, in reference to the Comintern, the "literary international," and in which, as Monica Popescu has shown in her recent literary history of Cold War Africa, writers had to navigate a complex, multipolar field of cultural politics.[32] This research has also taken into account the important role played by institutions, such as the Congress for Cultural Freedom (CCF), that were explicitly or, in the case of the CCF, implicitly sponsored by government agencies, and that had profound effects on the shape of seemingly autonomous aesthetic and cultural debates.[33] This influence, as some scholars have argued, goes so far as to shape even the disciplinary structure of literary studies today, so that Bhakti Shringarpure has argued that postcolonial literature, and "postcolonial studies" as an institutional formation, is deeply shaped by Cold War era ideas of the divorce between literature and politics.[34]

But the emphasis of new Cold War literary studies on Africa also illuminates a revealing gap in this scholarship. The vast majority of this work has focused on literature in metropolitan languages—English, Russian, and to a lesser extent French and Portuguese.[35] Although the axiomatic multilingualism of India is shared across Africa and other locations of the Third World, language politics presents an essential difference for the study of Cold War literary history in India.[36] The linguistic diversity of India, because it affected the processes of translation, the nature of circulation and influence, and the ways in which writers engaged with global debates, shapes the terms through which we understand the essential issues of Cold War literature. The problem of linguistic comparison is often cited as a core issue in the idea of a literary history of India.[37] During the Cold War, however, both the approach of the Indian government towards language and the different conceptions of language and translation in competing world systems further complicate any attempt to formulate a uniform literary history. For instance, recent work by Laeticia Zecchini has shown how PEN International helped to develop a largely Anglophone literary network; the resulting flow of influence from the United States was thus, necessarily, filtered through English.[38] Relatedly, whereas the Congress for Cultural Freedom sponsored literary magazines in the assumed national languages of Brazil, France, and other countries, the primary CCF magazine in India, from 1955 onwards, was the English-language *Quest*.[39] Soviet approaches to translation require further study, but initial work on the history of Progress Publishers by Rossen Djagalov and Peter Kalliney indicates that Soviet ideas of language and approaches to translation were radically different and less centered on Anglophone literary networks. [40]The result is that, in terms of a literary history of circulation and print culture, editors and publishers in Indian language often formed unique translations of concepts such as that of the Third World, and of the literary space that such a concept entailed.

The conjunction between the revisiting of realism-modernism debates and the increasing attention to the literary history of the Cold War makes clear the benefits of a study of nonmetropolitan literary cultures during the period. Recent work by Francesca Orsini has begun to explore the print culture of the Cold War world in Hindi, and particularly the ways in which the intersection of evolving discourses of nonalignment and the Third World came to inform preexisting concepts of the world in the 1950s, 1960s, and 1970s.[41] This book, in its focused study on the late works of a single author, aims to illustrate, through a case study, the potential intervention of looking at Hindi literature during the Cold War. A more focused literary study can demonstrate the ways in which writers were shaped by Cold War literary culture not necessarily when engaging directly with the geopolitics of the time, but rather at a more intimate, everyday level.

The Cold War, of course, is far from the only category through which this book will consider Muktibodh's work, and I do not wish to argue that Hindi literature during this time was determined by international politics. This book emphasizes the engagement of Muktibodh's long poem with international debates on literary form, but the work is equally shaped by dynamics specific to the Hindi-speaking world in the twentieth century. But considering this work through the lens of Cold War internationalism reframes Hindi aesthetic debate, and Muktibodh's innovative responses to it, as part of a larger literary history. In this history, literatures seen in the category of vernacular can be viewed as participating in global Cold War aesthetic debate in particular ways. Muktibodh's work, which might otherwise be seen as that of an "outsider" artist, can be properly read as engaged in a reimagination of the universal and its relation to literary genre.[42] Similarly, the explicit internationalism of a period that is noted in Hindi literary history for being split into right and left "camps," shows how global literary debate, expressed within a specific literary culture, transforms those debates, as questions of realism in Hindi refract a deeper, specific history of genre, literary form, and the depiction of society in North Indian literature, from the nineteenth through the twentieth century.

The Stakes of Literary Form

Although, as I will show, Muktibodh frequently discussed the Cold War world, *Cold War Genres* argues that the importance of this figure and his work to Cold War literary history lies not—or at least not only—in the thematic object of his work, but rather in the formal innovation of his long poems. It is with these long poems, and through the process by which they came to be made, that the influence of Cold War literary debate can be seen most clearly in Muktibodh's work, and it is this formal innovation that makes him such a crucial figure in Hindi literary history. My analysis therefore has to be situated in an understanding of literary form.

A major methodological commitment of this work is to read poetry across genre; rather than seeing it as an isolated body of work, *Cold War Genres* reads Muktibodh's long poems as constantly in communication with other genre formations, and especially across the boundaries between prose and poetry which are crucial both to left aesthetic debate as well as to Hindi literary history. In both the larger context of Cold War literary culture and study, and in the context of Hindi in particular, poetry tends to be a neglected subject. For this reason, this book can claim to be one of the few studies of modern literature in South Asia, or of Cold War literature, to focus on poetry in particular.[43]

Current research on world literature, in its emphasis on the novel, tends to exclude other genres. Most importantly for my study, it tends to exclude the short lyric poem. The Warwick Research Collective, in their claim that the peripheral realism of the novel best registers the world system, embraces the seeming centrality of the novel.[44] Pheng Cheah's recent *What Is a World*, even as it claims the capacity of postcolonial literature to critique the dominant global system, similarly relies upon the novel both for its formal ability to engage with a global social totality, and for its association with postcolonial modernity.[45] In doing so, these works build on an understanding of the novel as having a special relationship to modernity.[46] Critiques of this approach often present a different genre, claiming that its global circulation and its implications are unjustly overlooked. Jahan Ramazani's work on the lyric presents the lyric in terms of the novel, placing its importance, in part, on the different contrasting "canonical attributes" of the lyric, such as its brevity, self-reflexivity, and subtlety.[47] Ramazani's continued exploration of the global lyric is invaluable for thinking about the lyric's particular transnational capability, but it does not resolve the question of the novel's importance, and the relation between discourse around the novel, and its effect on other genres.

The novel, meanwhile, is central not only to ideas of twentieth-century world literature, but also to key analyses of south Asian literary history. In part, this is because of a history in which the realist novel was explicitly promoted in colonial India as a literary genre associated with social progress and modernization, but which early novelists perceived as explicitly foreign, requiring a range of adaptations.[48] Meenakshji Mukherjee's pathbreaking *Realism and Reality* established the framework for thinking of the novel in India as a combination of adaptation from local prose forms, such as the *dastān* of Northern Indian Persianate literature, and social reform–oriented efforts towards depicting new forms of domestic life, piety, and gender reform.[49] The novel, because it was so strongly associated with these ideas and with a depiction of a dynamic, changing social world, became bound up with the idea of an Indian nation and a sense of political subjectivity that was part of it. At the same time, however, the novel drew from a range of popular narrative forms.[50] The result was that, even as the novel became one of the most popular forms of literature in the late nineteenth century, it continued to be shaped by the unique circumstances of North Indian literature.

Across South Asia, following independence the short story became in several ways a more prominent genre than the novel.[51] In Hindi, this moment is most strongly associated with the *naī kahānī* (new story) group of writers, and the journal of the same name, which presented a new literature of middle-class urban life after independence.[52] Unlike the lyric, the short story, as a prose genre, relates in oblique ways to discourses of the novel, both in Hindi and in other contexts.[53] If *naī kahānī* writers developed sophisticated theories of the short story and its role in postindependence literature, for Muktibodh, the short story was sublimated within a larger conception of prose literature.

If prose was presented and thought of as an essentially modern form, poetic genres, and especially the brief lyrics that were prominent in the nineteenth century, became categorized as morally decadent and essentially backward.[54] The Sanskrit *kāvya,* which became symbolic of classical literature as a whole, stands out as an exception; the *kāvya* was often presented as a precursor to the novel and as the redeeming genre of Indian literary history.[55] The result was that the modern lyric was shaped by a range of generic influences, including both the short poetic forms that predominated in Braj and Urdu poetry during the nineteenth century and the complex discursive field of realism, progress, and narrative form that constituted Hindi literature as a whole.

My goal is not to sideline or dismiss the long history of the novel and its discussion, its unique importance to theories of world literature, or its claim to represent, in its form, social totality. Rather, I intend to incorporate and consider the ways in which the novel interacts with other generic forms, and how the discourse around the novel and its capacities informs literary innovation elsewhere. The focus of this book therefore is rooted in the history of the lyric in Hindi, but I take "lyric," in the broadest sense, as a starting point for considering genre amid a range of formal stances and decisions. In doing so I draw from recent debates on the lyric as form and genre that have questioned a single generic definition of the lyric, and have attempted to historicize the modern lyric as a distinctly modern genre, one often created through retroactive analysis. Jonathan Culler's 2015 *The Theory of the Lyric* argued that the lyric could be defined, transhistorically, in its emphasis on address by a speaking subject.[56] A different group of scholars have emphasized that the definition of the lyric is historically contingent, taking its present form only in the nineteenth century. Virginia Jackson and Jopie Prins, in their anthology *The Lyric Theory Reader*, have compiled a historiography of lyric theory that, in contradistinction to Culler, presents the lyric as a mutable term, one that is formed into a genre through processes of literary criticism as much as an essential poetics, and whose antiquity was a result of that criticism rather than fact.[57] The novel, however, looms over this recent theory as well, with Jackson and Prins acknowledging the influence of a prior theorization of the novel as genre.[58] My contention in this book is that the novel, and the idea of the novel, is essential to understand the ways in which the poem is conceptualized and imagined in modern literature, in ways that become particularly visible in the history of Hindi poetry.

The combined factors of the novel as a preeminent genre in the discourse of Indian literature and the general instability of genre itself combine to create a fraught landscape for understanding poetry. In this circumstance, the need is to understand how specific literary instantiations respond to these pressures. Given the amount of information we now have on literary history, circulation, and print culture, and on discourses of realism and modernism, a case study could demonstrate how literary innovation responds. A central part of the argument of this book, therefore, is that individual moments, even as they cannot be reduced to the outcome of historical trends, are created in conversation with them, and that understanding these moments of innovation can help us reflect on those trends.

But this book is not interested in merely correcting a gap in the present literature. Instead, it sees the problem of poetry and genre as constitutive of literary history. In the long poems that form the center of this study, literary form itself is shaped by these debates, and by Muktibodh's understanding of them. Muktibodh did not write his long poems out of an attempt, for instance, to shape the ideals of *kāvyā* towards modernity; that was in part the criticism he made of Jayshankar Prasad's *Kāmāyanī*, a *chāyāvād* work that explicitly was modeled on *kāvyā*.[59] Nor could one argue that he extended the lyric out of a response to the fragmentation of modern life. Rather, throughout his career he saw his work as existing in tension with questions of narrative, image, subjectivity, and political commitment, which was bound up for him in the question of genre.

In this sense, my study will depart from a prevailing opinion of Hindi literary criticism that Muktibodh's long poems were an attempt to constellate the diverse and incoherent experiences of the middle class in Nehruvian India. Although they are also that, I aim to demonstrate that the long poems constitute a unique response to a common problem of literature wherever these literary debates were most vociferous. In this sense, I view Muktibodh's long poems as running parallel to works and bodies of literature, such as those described by WrEC, that were shaped by similar problems of politics and literature.[60] Understanding these problems in turn, however, requires an understanding of the contexts of Hindi literature that are inseparable from this history.

Hindi Literature

As stated earlier in this introduction, Hindi in its modern form stands apart in South Asian literary history. Many of the organizing themes I have discussed so far—the intersection of Cold War literary history with nonmetropolitan languages, the complicated trajectories of genre in modern South Asian literatures—are common to other South Asian languages, and indeed common to literary modernity. Hindi stands out, however, in its relation to the nationalist movement, and its role in articulating an idea of India centered on the majoritarian upper castes of the "Hindi heartland" of North India.[61] In this book, the history of Hindi shapes the formation and content of the long poem and Muktibodh's work as a whole, including the formal structure of the long poem, Muktibodh's approach to language, and the way in which his work was received as articulating a crisis of India as a whole.

Modern Hindi emerged, over the course of the nineteenth century, as a literary language distinct from other, more established literary languages of North India.[62] Even as writers in Hindi borrowed from the preexisting literary cultures of North India in a range of ways, they often perceived and treated Hindi as a fundamentally new language, the creation and development of which could be framed in political terms. This was especially pressing in the case of poetry; unlike prose literatures, which had relatively little precedent and thus were less easily comparable to older literary cultures, poetry in the new language of standard Hindi often needed to prove its necessity.[63] Even as late as the *chāyāvād* period in the 1920s, which forms the most important background to later writers such as Muktibodh, writers felt the need to frame their works in terms of the newness of *khaṛī bolī*, the term used to describe the new variety of Hindi in which they wrote. "We are unacquainted still with *khaṛī bolī*, Sumitranandan Pant would write in the preface to his 1926 volume *Pallav* (Flowerbud), "and so the touch of these words doesn't thrill us; they seem to us stale, flavorless."[64] Muktibodh's poetry, I argue, builds on this sense of newness; although his initial poetic training was with *chāyāvād* poetics, his long poems would frequently draw from obscure, Sanskrit-derived vocabulary, mixing together mythical and technical language in a way that critics would often find obscure.

The impact of left politics and thought on this paradigm from the mid-1930s onwards should be understood in this context. The 1936 foundation and initial meeting of the All-India Progressive Writers Association (AIPWA) was a benchmark in its organization of prominent writers across languages, but it was also a part of a series of developments, such as the formation of the All-India Peasant's Union, and the emergence of a left-leaning bloc in the Congress, that would eventually split into the Socialist Party following independence.[65] These changes were accompanied by the new visibility of the Soviet Union in the 1930s, which included not only an awareness of widely publicized Soviet policies and industrial developments, but also the new availability of Russian writers from the time, most notably Maxim Gorky, and to a lesser extent Mayakovsky.[66] As a result of this combination of local and international trends, Hindi poetics was impacted by a reframing of familiar concepts of reform and nation-building towards an explicitly left-oriented set of messages and a newly internationalized perspective.[67]

On an aesthetic level, however, later literary critics in Hindi, such as Ramvilas Sharma and *Hans* editor Prithvi Raj Chauhan, would argue that truly progressive, or *pragatiśīl*, poetry, did not and should depart significantly from the formal poetics of *chāyāvād*. By the late 1930s, writers such as Harivansh Rai Bachchan (1907–2003) would become a model for what was called "late *chāyāvād*," which replaced the confident, romantic nationalism of earlier *chāyāvād* poets with what Vijaydevnarayan Sahi would call an "irresistible compulsion."[68] Progressive poetry, by writers such as Kedarnath Agrawal (1911–2000), would depart thematically but not stylistically from this model, in contrast, both with the most prominent examples of Urdu progressive literature, such as the writers of *Aṅgāre*, and from the *janvādī* (populist) literature promoted by left Writers of the 1970s.[69]

This was the environment in which *Tār saptak*, the anthology of poets that first brought Muktibodh to attention in the Hindi world, was published in 1943. Its editor was already a prominent poet and novelist, but the other contributors were, at the time, relatively unknown young poets. Its release is understood to be a watershed in modernism in Hindi—even if this status has been repeatedly questioned, in terms of both its novelty and the modernism of its participants.[70] Indeed, the poetry of its participants shows the marked influenced of *chāyāvād* diction and free verse forms, and its place at the center of literary history probably stems from the later importance of the seven writers, and the debates that surrounded them over the 1950s. But within ten years of the publication of *Tār saptak,* the literary landscape of Hindi had changed utterly. In contrast with the Indian languages with which Hindi has always been in conversation, namely, Marathi, Bengali, and Urdu, on a stylistic level, a consensus around *chāyāvād* poetics had been maintained over about two decades.[71] But by the end of the 1940s, free verse and an emphasis on everyday speech had become the norm. Thematically, as well, modernist poets in Hindi began to question what was perceived as the individualism of *chāyāvād* poets. Instead, the poetry of what were at the time called *prayogvādī,* or experimental, poets, emphasized not emotional experience but the perception of the world, and the formation of a new, modernist poetics to describe that perception.[72]

If the retrospective importance of *Tār saptak* resulted from the importance of its collaborators, this was also accompanied by an institutional sea change in how Hindi literature was produced, distributed, and rewarded. In the 1920s and 1930s, the most important Hindi literary journals were largely published by writers or editors as labors of love; well-known journals such as *Sarasvati* and *Hans* operated on small budgets and were subject to a range of restraints, such as colonial censorship.[73] They were also, as I emphasized when discussing *chāyāvād* poetics, sublimated to the national project. But on every level, this uniformity would fracture over the course of the 1940s. By the 1950s, the landscape of Hindi journals, newspapers, and magazines, was vast and well-financed, with publications produced from a range of institutional sources. These included not only major publishers, such as Gyanpith Prakashan and Rajkamal Prakashan, but also the Indian government itself.[74] That Indian government also created several new institutions of culture, such as the Sahitya Akademi, which directly funded Hindi literature.[75] Although small, self-funded journals certainly still existed—some of Muktibodh's most important works would be published in *Vasudhā,* which was published by Harishankar Parsai out of Jabalpur—they were, during the Nehruvian period, part of a larger ecosystem of literature.

Along with the changes created by the newly independent state, modernism in Hindi was also deeply shaped by the inception of the Cold War. Again, because Hindi was so naturally poised to be the recipient of national institutions of culture, it was also impacted by international trends that shaped literature. Soviet-sponsored journals and literary organs proliferated, as did accusations of American interference in culture. These positions would harden into a perception of two camps. On one side, *prayogvād* (experimentalism), which came more and more to be referred to as *nayī kavitā* (new poetry) after the foundation of an eponymous journal in 1953.[76] The other side of progressive literature shifted from being called *pragatiśīl*, to a slightly derogatory *pragativād* (progressivism), which put more of an emphasis on the "-ism" of the term, and its accompanying sectarianism.[77] Although, as we will see, writers never fit along these lines perfectly, the perception of their being two different, opposed bodies of literature would become especially dominant over time. Agyeya, the editor of *Tār saptak* as well as two sequel anthologies, would become especially identified with the term *prayog*, which he used to describe the literature of the first anthology. By the 1970s, he would be openly accused of collaboration with the CIA, due to his brief involvement with the CIA-backed Congress for Cultural Freedom.[78]

On an aesthetic level, the impulse towards individual experience was solidified into a sophisticated set of aesthetic points by writers associated with *nayī kavitā*. The most important of these were Lakshmikant Varma and Vijaydevnarayan Sahi. Together, they developed the idea of the *laghu mānav*, or minor man. Lakshmikant Varma proposed the term as opposing the perceived grandiosity of progressive literature; to the archetype of a heroic great man, Varma posed an individual who perceived and analyzed the world, based on his own individual experience. In *Nayī kavitā ke pratimān*, Varma's book-length study and one of the earliest major studies of Hindi modernism, Varma posited that the minor man was in fact the true realism, as opposed to the progressive conception of it, because he dwelled in real contemporaneity, rather than an imaged, utopian future.[79] His chief criticism of progressivism was that, in sublimating experience to a political project, it left no room for anything that could reasonably called attention to the real world.

Vijaydevnarayan Sahi is the most important of the school of literary critics who ultimately were connected to the socialist wing of the Congress Party and the ideas of Rammanohahr Lohia, which is today represented by the Samajwadi (Socialist) Party. As an active politician, lawyer, and scholar of English, as well as an editor for *nayī kavitā* and founding member of the *parimal* group,

Sahi was at the center of not only what is remembered as *nayī kavitā,* but of the school of thought of critics who distanced themselves from the Progressive movement and (in the Cold War parlance of the time) from the Communist International that they saw as controlling it.[80] Unlike other critics, such as Lakshmikant Varma and Dharmvīr Bhāratī, who for the most part were concerned with directly criticizing progressive writers and their aesthetic choices, Sahi formulated a literary history that connected the literature, and its debates, of the 1950s, to the larger story of Hindi's formulation during the nationalist period. Although Sahi only published occasionally, and his essays were only later collected outside of journals, Sahi's historical perspective makes him one of the most influential critics of this period; as Ram Vilas Sharma would later point out, his ideas were adopted wholesale in the work of Namwar Singh.[81]

In his 1960 essay "Laghu mānav ke bahāne hindī kavitā par kuch bahas" (Some Provocations Regarding Hindi Poetry Prompted by the Minor Man), Sahi presents his most detailed idea of literary history, and the role of the *laghu mānav* in the formation of *nayī kavitā*. Two points distinguish Sahi's treatment of the *laghu mānav* here from that of Lakshmikant Varma's. First, the *laghu mānav* is here presented as in the past, with the essay opening with the question, "Has the *laghu mānav* truly died?"[82] That is, from the early 1960s, the aesthetic goals of the previous decade were already appearing out of date. Sahi's idea of the *laghu mānav* is this for reason already more critical than that seen in Varma, because it implies an essential incompleteness to the idea, although, because the essay was incomplete, that incompleteness was never elaborated. The second point is that whereas Varma defines the *laghu mānav* in terms of his idea of ideal literature, Varma's idea of reflected experience, Sahi historicizes the idea, linking the concept of the *laghu mānav* to the decay of the ideals of the *chāyāvād* period. As he puts it, the poetry of the 1930s, typified by Harivansh Rai Baccan, was seized by a crisis of purpose, an "irresistible compulsion," leading the following generation of poets to place experience at the center of their work.[83] Sahi argues that the poets of the *Tār saptak* anthology and their descendants, that is, the modernists of the 1950s, were the first generation of poets in Hindi to examine their world without the assumption of an ethical compulsion that rules the world.[84]

In the *laghu mānav* concept of reflected experience and contemporaneity, as well as in the social realism being put forth by left progressive critics, claims of objective perception were paramount. At times, it seemed as if modernist critics were arguing not over the idea of objectivity but over the role of the social in that objectivity. More stridently polemical critics such as Lakshmikant Varma claimed for *nayī kavitā* the title of realism, or *yathārthvād*, making the argument that the progressives, in their presentation of a left ideal, were in fact neglecting to engage with the actual reality presented by experience. Critics on the left counterposed that *nayī kavitā* and *Parimal* critics were themselves engaged in a solipsistic self-reflection, a critique that would eventually harden into Ramvilas Sharma's idea that these poets were slipping into existentialist angst.[85] Through the 1950s, however, the discourse was less internationalized, and dominated more by Anglo-American modernism, on the one hand, and Soviet-era social realism, on the other.

This was the environment in which Mutkibodh worked, and he intervened in all of the major debates that I have outlined. Muktibodh's long poems, I will argue, are as deeply engaged with prose genres—and the idea of prose, or *gadya*, itself—as they are with the Hindi short poem, or *kavitā*. Through the influence of parallel experiments in Marathi free verse, Muktibodh created new techniques to introduce nonrealist narrative into his poems. In so doing, he not only expanded the scope of the poem in Hindi, but he also introduced elements of the fantastic, drawn from popular literature and myth, that could not easily be accommodated within realist fiction. Thus, even as they are shaped by its history, Muktibodh's long poems demand to be viewed outside of the framework of the Hindi poem, and to be understood instead within the larger ecosystem of Hindi literature as a whole.

Reading these long poems in this way, and bringing them into conversation with the larger questions of literary debate during the Cold War, establishes a crucial moment in which Hindi literature was imagining its place in the world. Analyzing the ways in which Muktibodh's work responded to a multiscalar matrix of literary problems shows how it serves as an example of the ways in which modern Hindi was uniquely situated in an imagination of the world during the Cold War. Rather than seeing Muktibodh as a solitary genius, or even an outsider artist as he was at times portrayed, I view Muktibodh as a key example of Hindi modernism's engagement with the Cold War world.

Structure of the Book

Cold War Genres centers Muktibodh's long poems, but it is not organized solely around their analysis. Instead, it builds its argument through considering the evolution of these long poems in the context of Muktibodh's other work, and the interactions of that work with the larger milieu of Hindi literature and international literary debate. In this analysis, the long poems emerge from problems most visible in prose fiction and criticism, which themselves can be viewed as experiments in literary genre. Through bringing together this range of his work, therefore, the book aims not only to provide a fuller picture of Muktibodh's literary contribution, but also to exemplify a central idea of the book that poetry needs to be seen from the perspective of a literary history across genres.

The first chapter begins with an analysis of a single poem in order to show how the long poem was able to address questions of Brahminical systems of education and rationality that are at the heart of Muktibodh's poetry, and to illustrate the centrality of his work to the larger historical context of Nehruvian India. Muktibodh's poetry and fiction is filled with demons, scientists, and ghosts, elements that, in their fantastic excess, confound any neat analysis of his work, and are at times treated by Hindi critics as scandalous. In this chapter, these nonrealist elements reveal a rich archive of engagement with questions of science, education, and caste in Nehruvian India, and argues that the exploration of these questions in Muktibodh's work constitutes one of his most important contributions to South Asian literature. Despite prominent scenes of science and frequent references to popular genre literary tropes of detective fiction, Northern Indian narrative traditions of *qissā* and *dāstān*, and folklore and mythology, nonrealistic elements in Hindi literature have largely been neglected by secondary criticism, influenced in part by discourses of literary realism and social reform during the colonial period. I argue that the nonrealist elements of these works are in fact central to understanding the engagement of modern Hindi literature with the internationalism of the Nehruvian era. Not only do these long poems, in their incorporation of narrative form, challenge the structure of the *naī kavitā* lyric, but they also connect the social critique of Hindi poetry to the overarching question of science, education, and technology in Nehruvian India, and to discourses of rationality and development in the larger Cold War world. While raising these points, this chapter acts as a tour of the long the poem and its features, and a guide to the concerns of the book as a whole.

The second chapter considers how the international debate around questions of literary realism is transformed in the local context of small-town 1950s India. Why did realism, as an idea, assume the centrality that it did in the criticism of twentieth-century Hindi, and what role did it play in the aesthetic practices of Hindi modernist writers? Even as the discourse of realism in Hindi connected to the global practice of literary realisms, this chapter argues that realist practices are shaped by the specific context of their articulation. It takes as its central example Muktibodh's critique of realism. Muktibodh's critique of realism, for instance, reworked romantic aesthetics and insisted on the realist value of nonrealist works of art, resulting in a theory of realism that can be fruitfully compared to Bertolt Brecht's remodeling of realist tenets. However, while it is possible to argue that Brecht and Muktibodh shared similar ideas about social antagonisms and literary ethics, I argue that Muktibodh's aesthetic thought, including ideas of poetic process rooted in a romantic theory of the imagination, must be analyzed in terms that emphasize the specificity of his experiences as a lower-middle-class, small town, intellectual in postindependence India. His critique of realism and defense of nonrealist modes of art, including the fantastic and the allegorical, was rooted in his experience of life in these small, provincial cities. In arguing for this specificity, I insist that such a focus on location actually sharpens our understanding of the force and terms of global literary debates during this period.

The third chapter considers how Muktibodh's short stories become a site of literary experimentation through looking at how questions of realism play out in this crucial literary genre. It argues that this experimentation was driven by the problems of lower-middle-class life described in the previous chapter. The resulting intersection between the short story and other narrative forms, such as the parable, articulates the problems of lower-middle-class experience that otherwise escape the structure of the realist short story. The short story forms one of the most prominent bodies of postindependence literature in South Asia, often exceeding the novel in popularity and influence. In Hindi, the *naī kahānī*, or "new story," emphasized individual experiences that could be generalized to describe the life of the newly urbanizing middle class. Muktibodh, who expressed a complicated, ambivalent relationship to the short story, created a body of prose fiction that tests generic boundaries. His short stories are a series of parables of modern life set within accounts of middle-class frustration, crises of masculinity, and bureaucratic suffocation. I examine these stories, showing how they situate the problem of realist form in the social context of postindependence life. By calling attention to the tension between the parable and the short story as differentiated but parallel forms, I argue that Muktibodh's short stories serve as a critique of the genre of the realist short story in light of his depiction of lower-middle-class life, and that this generic experimentation is a necessary precondition for understanding his modernist long poems.

The fourth chapter analyzes the formal structure of Muktibodh's long poems, considering the form's antecedents and the ways in which it responds to a tension in Hindi literature between genre, narrative, and poetic image. The modernist long poem, in its engagement with the questions of narrative and realism that were central to the critical debates of the 1950s, emerges in this chapter as a key location for literary experimentation in Hindi. Therefore, I argue that the history of the Hindi long poem should be read not within the history of poetry, but as an outcome of the questions over literary realism and genre that were discussed in the previous two chapters. I trace the genealogy of the long poem in both the history of debates over realism and genre—which include the novel, short story, and free verse—and the revival of classicist, neo-epic forms in early twentieth century South Asia. The poetic landscape of modern Hindi was shaped by the rejection of lyric poetic genres that dominated the nineteenth century, and the search by writers for new poetic models. I argue that because the modern poem, unlike the novel and the short story, was not dominated either by a single narrative mode or a single idea of lyric subjectivity, it was open to a greater degree of formal experimentation. The experimentation and referentiality of the long poem, by incorporating a range of narrative elements within the lyric subjectivity of postindependence poetry, functions as a response to the problem of realism and the representation of postcolonial Indian society. Rather than view Muktibodh's long poem solely in terms of the history of poetry in Hindi, this chapter argues that they must be historicized with reference to a wide range of literary forms across multiple languages, particularly modern Marathi literature. It claims that Hindi literature must be seen in relation to other literary cultures of South Asia and as part of a global network of modernist literatures during the twentieth century. A history of the long poem, therefore, reveals a multilingual history of a form that cuts across generic boundaries and addresses some of the most pressing critical questions of twentieth-century literature.

The conclusion examines Muktibodh's legacy in Hindi literature and criticism. Beginning with the event of his death in 1964, it takes up two crucial moments of debate. It shows how Muktibodh became central to Hindi criticism after his death as the interpretation of his long, phantasmagoric poems, and his biography as a member of the lower-middle-class in the small towns and cities of Central India, came to exemplify the antinomies of postindependence life and seemed to crystalize a key tension between modernist and realist poetics in Hindi. At the same time, Muktibodh's posthumous reception intersected with new trends in the institutionalization of literature in the late 1970s, as his work became the subject of state support, leading to a fierce struggle over his legacy between Congress-aligned critics associated with the new arts center of Bharat Bhavan and Marxist critics working in a series of small underground journals. Muktibodh's reception is one of the most important examples of aesthetic debate in a modern South Asian language and remains a touchstone of literary history in Hindi. Through revisiting this complex history of reception, interpretation, and institutionalism, the chapter considers how the aesthetic questions of the 1950s were transformed through their memory in criticism in the 1970s as writers debated the meaning of the decade after independence.

This book features, throughout, extensive translations from Muktibodh's poetry and prose writings. In addition to the traditional academic translator's dilemma of accuracy versus readability, this presents a challenge; Muktibodh is known in Hindi as a difficult writer, both in his subject matter and his language, which often features obscure, Sanskritized vocabulary. As a result, he is at times described as difficult or even impossible to translate into English.[86] The existence of this book implies that I do not hold this belief; at times, in fact, I find that his writing, in departing entirely from the conventions of Hindi, flows smoothly into English. Instead, I have found that Muktibodh presents a challenge to translation style that is a variation on the question of whether to bring the foreign language into the target language: How does one translate awkwardness?

Frequently, Muktibodh's writings are written in such a way that, in the original Hindi, they appear strange and difficult to read; as I will discuss, even some of his closest associates, themselves noted poets, found this to be the case. A great deal of this awkwardness derives from the combination of the syntax of his long, paratactic sentences and his use of enjambment and short line length. The result is that following the movement of his thought can be difficult—most likely intentionally. But this also forms an essential part of his poetics, and of my analysis.

I have chosen to translate this dissonant, angular quality of his writing as much as possible, and particularly to try to preserve the syntax of his logic. At times this requires some liberties with the poem that I would otherwise avoid; for instance, in order to create a logical connection between two words that, in the original, would be joined by a rhyme, I may choose to use some kind of resonance between English words, or even, in the following chapter, to bring in a wordplay that does not exist in the original Hindi. My goal above all is to bring across both the strangeness and difficulty of Muktibodh's writing, as well as the excitement and startling beauty that they can produce. Muktibodh, in his original Hindi, "is almost too interesting to read"; and as much as I hope this book forms a contribution to contemporary questions of literary history, it also takes up the impossible task of communicating some of his qualities to a new readership.[87]

Chapter One

A Stream of Pure Sanskrit Curses

Caste, Knowledge, and Critique in the Long Poem

śahar ke us or khaṇḍahar kī taraf
parityakt sūnī bāvṛī
ke bhītarī
ṭhaṇḍe aṃdhere meṃ
basī gaharāiyāṃ jal kī . . .
sīṛhiyāṃ ḍūbī anekoṃ
us purāne ghire pānī meṃ . . .
samajh meṃ ā na saktā ho
ki jaise bāt kā ādhār
lekin bāt gahrī ho.

that way from the city towards the ruins
an abandoned, silent, bāvṛī;
inside,
in the clammy dark
settled depths of the water . . .
some steps, drowned
in the surrounding stagnant water,
like the point—
you can't get to the bottom of it
but it's deep.[1]

The stanza begins with movement "that way," *us or*, towards a generalized, unclear place: the ruins, described as if they are a part of any city outskirts, like a warehouse district, or cantonment area. In these generic ruins lies something specific: a *bāvṛī*, a sunken stepwell famous in the dry northwest of India, including Rajasthan and Malwa.[2] The steps disappear into the stagnant water before, in the final lines of the stanza, a sudden shift into the internal: the steps are swallowed in darkness, their depth like a point, or *bāt*, unknowable but deep. The stanza thus moves both outwards and inwards, evoking both narrative story and personal, lyric experience, a dual movement that is characteristic of Muktibodh's work as a whole.[3]

The lines are short and heavily enjambed, although the enjambment preserves more of its syntax in its original Hindi than in my translation. In the first five lines, for instance, the third line is a postpositional phrase that would normally follow and modify the preceding word to form "the well / inside."[4] In my translation, I have resorted to the use of a semicolon and a two-clause structure in order to preserve the logical flow of the lines, and to give the reader in English some sense of the movement of this stanza from the city, to the ruins, to the "settled depths" of the stepwell.

The feeling of abrupt, jagged transition, of a sentence of statement that refuses to finish, but which uses enjambment, syntax, and rhyme in order to create a propulsive narrative energy, is a trademark of the long poems; I refer to it as a paratactic style. Muktibodh's long poems tend to present narrative even as it is resisted and fractured. And although Muktibodh's style is understood to be free verse, he belongs to a generation of writers who had, in their education and early careers, been deeply exposed to metrical forms. In the fourth chapter of this book, I will discuss the influence of Marathi and Hindi meter and poetics on the long poem; for now, I will note that the carefully composed lines of Muktibodh's free verse are an essential aspect of his construction of the long poem.

These lines are the first stanza of "Brahmarākṣas" (The Brahmin Demon; hereafter written as "Brahmarakshas"). First published in 1957 and included, in a revised form, in *Cāṃd kā muṃh ṭeṛhā hai* (The Moon Has a Crooked Face) in 1964, this is one of Muktibodh's most canonized and well-known poems.[5] The poem's narrative is a journey into this well, and the presence within it of the ghost of a Brahmin, called a *brahma-rākṣasa*, literally "Brahmin Demon." It describes his intellectual arrogance and false belief that the world is seeking his wisdom, before turning to his past, presumably when he was living, as a researcher of mathematics. The poem is divided into two halves, the second of which, I will argue, echoes and transforms the imagery and themes of the first.

The story of this poem, with its themes of satire, guilt, and anxiety, and the formal structure introduced through its first stanza, illustrate some of the problems of Muktibodh's work that this book aims to address. These problems include the formal question of why these long, fantastic poems take the shape they do, and how they address larger problems of literature in the Cold War world, as well as thematics of the intersection of class, caste, and an imagination of the world in newly independent India. Because this poem—which is, in fact, relatively concise, almost belying its categorization as a "long poem"—illustrates these themes neatly, in the first chapter of this book I will examine it, as a précis or prolegomenon to the problems discussed in following chapters.

This chapter addresses two issues: first, an explanation of the long poem as a form and genre, how it operates, and the comparable problems of theme and form that we will explore; second, this specific poem, and its highly representative issues of education, caste, science, in postindependence India. Finally, this chapter will ask why these themes are so particularly suited to this poem, and how they relate to poetic form. The concern of "Brahmarakshas" with the fate of the postindependence intellectual is ultimately inseparable from its poetic form, and the capacity of that poetic form to bring together myth, popular literature, and the linguistic capabilities of modern Hindi.

What Is a Long Poem?

Although Hindi criticism is mostly unanimous in the idea that Muktibodh's long poems are at the center of his legacy, it is less clear on what the long poems actually are. Are they "an unending poem"?[6] Or do they form "a grim, terrifying museum of still images," as put by Shamsher Bahadur Singh?[7] Should they be defined solely by their length, or is the title "long poem" simply a useful shorthand to describe the poems, written from roughly 1957 to 1964, that demonstrate a break from prior practice? Or should his poetry be read, as it is put in the encyclopedia of Hindi literature *Hindī sāhitya koś*, as "if not the thing itself, then the yeast of poetry"?[8] If we consider the long poem either in the context of an Anglo-American modernism to which Hindi is often compared, or to the literary context of Hindi in the twentieth century, the long poems of Muktibodh escape satisfying categorization.

At the most basic level, Muktibodh's long poems are usually understood to be the poems written from roughly 1957 to his death in 1964, which range in length from about 200 to 1300 lines. These poems all feature some kind of narrative, usually presented in the first person, that describes a journey through a fantastic landscape. These narratives usually culminate in an invocation of revolution, and an emergence of a *guru* figure, who will make possible the utopian moment.

Difficulty in defining Muktibodh's long poems reflects a long-standing problem of defining longer poems within modernism. In Anglo-American modernist literary history, despite the importance of T. S. Eliot's *The Wasteland*, the long poem has often generated consternation, both among critics and among writers. This is because the long poem, in its length and its emphasis on narrative, seems to go directly against the emphasis in modernism on the single, nonnarrative image. As a result, critics have argued, "everything argued against the writing of the long poem . . . even the poems that were written."[9] Writers of modernist long poems attempted to make what Dickie has called an "extended lyric," which would draw out the focus on image and singular experience, even as the poems, often framed as "public poetry," attempted to create a major, longer form, distinguished from both the modernist lyric and the epic.[10]

Muktibodh's long poems present many of the challenges common to the modernist long poem, even as they depart from the model of the genre in several important ways. Muktibodh's long poems, with their dark, fantastic tone, planetary invocations, and self-lacerating speakers, certainly bear comparison with Eliot's early career works such as *The Love Song of J. Alfred Prufrock*, as well as *The Wasteland*.[11] Similarly, Muktibodh's long poems, in their extension of the lyric out of an interest of political commitment, may echo the impulse of modernist long poems towards the "public poem."[12]

As I will discuss in the fourth chapter, the problem of lyric image and narrative possibility was indeed crucial to Muktibodh's own thinking about the long poem. The poems themselves, as in the example I discuss in this chapter, are not at all averse to narrative. But they do not fit, either, with the return to story described in postmodern poetry. Unlike the postmodern long poem, Muktibodh's long poems feature a dreamlike, first-person journey that is more reminiscent of the romantics than the ironic, fractured narrators that followed modernism. At the same time, these narratives frequently do engage with tropes drawn from myth and genre literature, in a manner similar to late modernist/postmodernist long poems.[13] We might also consider that the long poems of Muktibodh, in their reference to various genre tropes (science fiction, myth, horror, folktale), are taking up a postmodern method coming out of works such as *The Changing Light at Sandover* or *Gunslinger*.[14] In those works, the use of narrative is complicated by a postmodernist distrust of a stable narrator.[15] Similarly, Muktibodh saw a tension between his idea of the modernist lyric image narrative structure, which he almost exclusively depicts as the novel. But the strategy of his long poems is strikingly different from that of these major modernist figures; rather than use pastiche and irony, it reverts to a romantic sincerity, inspired and framed through political commitment, and its use of myth is driven as much by the forbidding of the fantastic within Hindi literature as it is by the forbidding of narrative within lyric.

When we turn from the Anglo-American literary history to consider their place within their own literary context, Muktibodh's long poems still resist categorization. The association of Muktibodh with *Naī kavitā* means that, similarly to the case with the modernist long poem in English, his works are strongly associated with the problem of lyric experience. In his own writing, as I will discuss, he saw the long poem as "an extended lyric," writing towards the end of his life that they were becoming more and more "massive," or *vistṛt*. The poems themselves can seem, at times, to present a series of discrete images that resist narrative form. As my reading of "Brahmarakshas" will show, however, Muktibodh's long poems are too deeply invested in the politics of story and social commitment to resist narrative in this way. The roots of his use of genre, I will argue, lie elsewhere—in an effort to accommodate what he sees as a pressure of social totality and political commitment with personal expression.

The most obvious comparison would be to *kāvya*, the narrative verse genre that is at times translated and compared to "epic." Sanskrit *kāvya*, which was extensively theorized and contained a great number of rules and expectations regarding narrative theme, poetic meter, and language, was extensively adapted into modern Hindi and other South Asian languages.[16] These neo-*kāvya* texts, including Jayśaṇkar Prasād's *Kāmāyanī* or Dinkar's *Urvaśī*, addressed modern themes but still took pains to maintain *kāvya* traditions, especially in their claims towards mythical subjects. Muktibodh would comment extensively on these neo-epics, in particular *Kāmāyanī*, and his works are, at times, compared to them.[17] The grand themes of his works, and their frequent discussion of myth in some form or another, further this comparison.

A comparison to *kāvya* would be natural. But Muktibodh, in his discussion of *Kāmāyanī*, explicitly rejected the attachment to myth, and he underlined the allegorical relation of his works to real life in a way that was incompatible with *Kāvya*. His works would furthermore, in their particular narrative structure, reject the closure that is frequently considered necessary in *kāyvā*.[18] The ambiguous engagement with *Kāvya* points to a final reference point for understanding the long poems. What is different is that Muktibodh's long poems are drawing from post-*Chāyāvād* and *naī kavitā* traditions of the lyric, seen through Muktibodh's own political commitments. That is, they are deeply concerned with the status of the lyric "I" and its relation to the social, in ways that depart from any Hindi attempts at a neo-*kāvya*.[19]

Having considered the spectrum of genre possibilities in which to take the long poem, we can provisionally conclude that it is a poem that is longer than a lyric, features an autobiographical voice but engages with the social through dramatic, kaleidoscopic dream-narratives, and is written in free verse without a larger linking structure. The challenge, in part, is to maintain awareness of the range of possibilities brought up by the problem of narrative in modernism, and the parallel problems of literature in Hindi, without allowing any of these problems to overdetermine our understanding of the poem.

To examine this, I will devote the remainder of this first chapter to examining "Brahmarakshas," one of Muktibodh's most celebrated long poems—but also one of the shortest. The shorter length of this poem allows me to translate and discuss it in its entirety, and to discuss through this the typical aspects of the long poem. As I will show, this poem also shows the ways in which Muktibodh's long poems bring in genre elements, and how the combination of these elements comments on particular aspects of postindependence life. This poem features a guru figure, which also highlights the concerns and anxieties around caste that are highly animating elements of Muktibodh's work.

The Brahmarakshas appears several times in Muktibodh's work besides this poem, most prominently in a short story, "Brahmarākṣas kā śiṣya" (The Pupil of the Brahmarakshas), which states explicitly that the Brahmarakshas is doomed to life after his death until he has passed on his teachings. The figure of the Brahmarakshas goes back as far as the post-Vedic Brahmana texts and the *Mahābhārata;* in the classical Sanskrit tradition, the Brahmarakshas is created by various means, but primarily through violating expectations of Brahmins, such as restrictions on food or sexual relations with other caste groups. By all accounts, Muktibodh's idea of the Brahmarakshas as cursed by failing to pass on his teachings appears to be original, and since his invention of the Brahmarakshas as tortured teacher, it has become a dominant and popular image in Hindi literature.[20]

In all its iterations in myth and literature, the Brahmarakshas is a terrifying figure—and it is far more so in this poem. Much of the criticism of the Brahmarakshas sidesteps this aspect to describe the work as a satire and tragedy of the postindependence intellectual. In this analysis, the Brahmarakshas takes on an entirely symbolic role, with the "tragedy" being his failure to put his vast knowledge into action.[21] The pedagogical aspect of the poem is reduced to a question of praxis, thus limiting the extent to which the figure can speak to larger questions of education, caste, and epistemology.

In this way, the Brahmarakshas is central to Hindi literary history as a symbol of the fate of the postindependence intellectual. In its predominant reading, however, the critical capacity of the Brahmarakshas in this poem is not totally explored, because despite the figure of the Brahmarakshas being traditionally predicated on caste violations, the caste status of this figure is not discussed. This is especially crucial given that, for both Muktibodh and the

Indian left in general, the question of caste, and the upper-caste status of CPI ideologues in particular, is such a vital issue.[22] For these reasons, in this chapter I will explore the figure of the Brahmarakshas with an eye towards these critical capacities, showing how it is attentive towards the interlinked problems of knowledge, caste, and politics, in ways that foresee not only the cynicism of the disillusionment period, but also the caste-critique of left politics in India generally.

I will be discussing a single long poem. But this poem can be broken up into three sections: the well, the demon, and the scientist. Each of these sections is distinct in its use of tone, imagery, and literary trope. Each section also connects to a different reading of the poem as a whole, as well as a different aspect of my argument.

The well, which forms the setting of the poem and dominates the first few stanzas, takes up the first section of my discussion. Why did Muktibodh choose a very particular location—a stepwell or baoli, common to Western India—for this poem? What particular ideas and resonances are drawn upon through this setting? And why does the poem begin, as it does, by evoking both the past, and an irresistible attraction to it? Through a discussion of this opening section, I aim to show how Muktibodh made use of a wide range of materials to form his setting, as well as to underline the importance of Muktibodh's conception and imagination of the past to the work as a whole.

The next section takes us to the Brahmarakshas himself—one of the great creations of modern Hindi, a multivalent, nightmarish creature. I will read the Brahmarakshas through not only this poem but Muktibodh's other writings, where the Brahmarakshas appears in similar but arguably distinct ways. As we shall see, these other iterations of the Brahmarakshas give us a sense of how we might read the Brahmarakshas of the poem. They also ask us to extend our reading of the first section, because in asking us to incorporate a biographical reading of the poem, they also force us to consider the idea of Brahminical learning being evoked here. This reading foregrounds caste and a conception of caste privilege. The chapter will also explore and contend with here the ways in which the Brahmarakshas has been understood in Hindi literary history, primarily as a symbol of the dilemmas of the middle class. I will also show how this understanding of the Brahmarakshas can be deepened by attention to its complex sources, as well as its specific development throughout Muktibodh's work.

Finally, in the last section I will address the abrupt shift in this poem towards the seemingly disconnected narrative of a researcher. In a turn away from the mythic and Brahminical, the poem suddenly tells a redemptive story of the Brahmarakshas as mathematician, whose legacy is to be carried forward by the speaker of the poem, who takes up a central position after remaining in the background throughout the earlier sections of the poem. Thinking about the Brahmarakshas as researcher and scientist also, in bringing us full circle, return to the question of the Nehruvian era's emphasis on the "scientific temper."[23] Is such a "temper" being evoked here? And, if so, can we now consider such a turn without considering the earlier iteration of the Brahmarakshas, with its strong undercurrent of Brahminical resentment? And if that is the case, what does that say about the contemporary to which this poem is addressed?

The Well

bāvṛī ko gher
ḍālem̥ khūb uljhī haim̥,
khaṛe haim̥ maun audumbar
va śākhom̥ par
laṭakte ghughuom̥ ke ghom̥sle
parityakt, bhūre, gol.
vigat śat puṇya kā ābhās
jangalom̥ harī kaccī gandh mem̥ baskar
havā mem̥ tair
bantā hai gahan sandeh
anjānī kisī bītī huī us śreṣṭhatā kā jo ki
dil mem̥ ek khaṭke-sī lagī rahtī.
bāvṛī kī in mum̥ḍerom̥ par
manohar harī kuhnī ṭek
baiṭhī hai ṭagar
le puṣpa-tāre-śvet.
uske pās
lāl phūlom̥ kā lahaktā jhaum̥r—

merī vah kanher . . .
vah bulātī ek khatre kī taraf jis or
aṃdhiyārā khulā muṃh bāvṛī kā
śūnya ambar tāktā hai.

surrounding the stepwell
its branches tangled
stands a silent *audumbar* tree.
on its branches
owl's nests hanging
abandoned, brown, round.
the sensation of a hundred virtuous deeds long ago
has settled into a wild, green, raw smell
and hangs in the air
forms a suspicion
of some unknown, dissipated greatness:
a rattle catching in the heart.
leaning over the lips of the well
on its elegant green elbows
sits a *ṭagar* valerian
with its white star-shaped blossoms.
next to it
a flash of red flowers—
my own oleander . . .
it calls me to danger
where the well's dark open mouth
stares up at the empty sky.[24]

For all Muktibodh's reputation as a rough, difficult poet operating at a cosmic scale, these stanzas show a soft, intimate side to Muktibodh's work; the *audumbar*, a tree often haunted, and here presented with empty owl's nests, shifts, in the following two stanzas, to a verdant, vegetal space. The two flowers are presented, familiar, as close to the speaker; the image of the *ṭagar* tree leaning with its elbows over the lips of its wells creates a light touch, introducing an element of the anthropomorphic that seems out of place in the expected darkness of the setting. The lightness of these lines, the use of primary colors, and the sharp turn away from a more familiar sense of a ruin as an abandoned or ruined place stand out from the rest of the poem.

The lines call and echo each other, with the triplet line of "abandoned, silent, baoli" repeated in the "abandoned, brown, round" nests of owls hanging from the fig. But as the lines move forward, they are dominated not by scrub but by flower—the small, white, star-shaped blossoms of the Valerian tree, and the oleander. The poisonous oleander flower, in turn, implies the danger and temptation that gradually tinge the scene, and pulls the reader's attention towards the dark entryway at the center of the poem.

This brings us to the "sensation of a hundred virtuous deeds," and the evocation of the past. Setting the poem in ruins, underlined in the first lines, creates a relationship to history that the poem will need to reconcile, even if the directionality of the first line ironizes this relationship somewhat. But the poem has no other choice, given the deeply fraught politics around the idea of the past, of ancient history, in Hindi literature. A key aspect of Muktibodh book-length criticism of Jayshankar Prasad's *Kāmāyanī* revolves around criticizing the idea of "Vedic India" in Hindi poetry.[25] The revivalism of the classical past, already suffusing this poem, is rooted not in the structure of the well itself but in the miasma that rests at its surface. The idea of the past in this poem is not a standing monument, to which the speaker must be reconciled, but a sensual premonition: a "rattle in the heart" or a "wild, green, raw smell."

The poem draws the reader into an enclosed, hidden space. The stepwell appears in the poem as a ruined space, with steps disappearing into stagnant waters, but the final lines of the first stanza pull at some deeper, unrevealed meaning. The depth of the well is compared to the *bāt kā ādhār*, a point of conversation—something unfathomably deep. The introduction of that speaker is itself subtle: up to the point at which they claim ownership or familiarity with the oleander, everything is descriptive, the narrator undisclosed. With the speaker's appearance, the descriptive is recast as experiential: What are the rattling memories of greatness, and a past of virtuously acquired merit, the *vigat śat pūṇya*? The symbolic language of the well as an open mouth, and the lushness of the speaker's approach to it, opens up, but does not insist upon, a range of psychological and personalized readings, all of which involve the speaker's interaction with the well. The lushness and depth of the well, and its inherent relation to the heavens, introduces an element of ambiguity that, I will argue, is essential to our reading of the entire poem, because it implies an interrelationship between these elements, rather than the static, symbolic presence of a single location.

These lines also introduce the active presence of the speaker. It is only with the final stanza that we have a speaker who takes up an active place in the narrative world of the poem, with the line "my own oleander." But the speaker's interaction with the scene has been gradually increasing. When, finally, the eye of the poem moves towards the well itself, it is in the context of the speaker, who perhaps has already left the city, moved through the surroundings, and reached the vegetation surrounding the lip of the well.

Who is this speaker? Hindi scholarship has taken the speaker of all these poems to be synonymous with the author.[26] All of his long poems, with only a few exceptions,[27] are written in the first person, and as I discussed in the introduction, the mythos of Muktibodh's life is a large part of his appeal and reception since his death. This poem is arguably particularly personal, with the figure of the Brahmarakshas appearing throughout Muktibodh's work and often explicitly compared to himself.

"Brahmarakshas" is in some ways typical of the dynamic of Muktibodh's voice. As with "Aṃdhere meṃ," and many other works, the poem revolves around a relationship between a student and a teacher—in this case, as we shall see, the Brahmarakshas himself. In other works, the "guru" figure is more abstract, or is replaced with a friend, who occupies a similar role—in one poem, memorably lifting the poet up on his shoulders.

This stanza displays an attitude towards voice and address that complicates the more romantic pronouncements of other poems. The speaker here evokes a specific self, but is fuzzy around the edges—What is his relationship to the oleander? One could almost call this voice playful as it relishes the lush vegetation around the well. That intimacy, however, means that the speaker here implies a personal relationship with the space, one underlined, of course, by the symbolism of the well, at once haunted and inviting, promising some kind of mental underground relationship with whatever it contains.[28]

Despite the insistence of this first-person voice, and the personal touch, there are complications to reading the voice of this poem in terms of the speaker beyond those familiar to any post-romantic reading. As we will see, both in this chapter and the following, Muktibodh's depiction of himself was crucial to his larger conception of the lower middle class; in some of his most important writing on the subject, he dramatizes a version of his own life in order to make a point about what he sees as an evolving fracture of the middle class in postindependence India. That performative self is visible in these stanzas, if more subtly, in the implied connection between the abandoned, overgrown ruins, their past greatness becoming a mere "rattle in the heart," and the speaker. That implied relationship becomes crucial with the introduction, in the following stanza, of the hero of this poem.

The Brahmin Demon

bāvṛī kī un gahrāiyoṃ meṃ śūnya
brahmarākṣas ek paiṭhā hai,
va bhītar se umaṛtī gūṃj kī bhī gūṃj,
harbaṛāhaṭ śabd pāgal se.
gahan anumānitā
dūr karne ke lie pratipal
pāp chāyā dūr karne ke lie, din-rāt
svacch karne—
brahmarākṣas
ghis rahā hai deh
hāth ke pañje barābar,
bāṃh-chātī-muṃh chapāchap
khūb karte sāf,
phir bhī mail,
phir bhī mail!!
aur . . . hoṭhoṃ se
anokhā stotra, koī kruddh mantroccār,
athvā shuddh sanskṛt gāliyoṃ kā jvār,
mastak kī lakīreṃ
bun rahīṃ
ālocnāoṃ ke camakte tār!!
us akhaṇḍ snān kā pāgal pravāh . . .
prāṇ meṃ samvednā hai syāh!!

a brahmarakshas has penetrated
into the voidblack depths of the baoli;
up from within resounds, echoing against itself,
a mad, babbling sound.
the great reckoner
every moment
scrubbing at
the shadow of offense—day and night
to cleanse—
the brahmarakṣas
scrapes his body
with the claws on his hands, smooth,
slapping water across arms chest mouth
cleaning and cleaning
and yet
still filthy
still filthy!!
and . . . from his lips
an amazing stotra, some enraged recitation—
or perhaps a flood of pure Sanskrit obscenity,
brows knotted together into
glittering strands of criticism!!
in the insane streaming waters of that unbroken
bath . . .
the sensitivity of life itself blackens![29]

The eye of the poem shifts abruptly from the speaker, standing above, below the earth, and inside the well. Here, attempting endlessly to remove impurity, lies the *Brahmarakshas*, one of Muktibodh's most original, complete inventions, bringing the specter of caste privilege to bear over his entire oeuvre.

The figure of a Brahmarakshas itself long precedes Muktibodh's work. The Brahmarakṣas is first attested in a Brahmana text, before appearing in the *Mahābhārata*. There, and in later Puranic texts, the Brahmarakshas is the demonic form of a Brahmin after his death, who has been condemned for a range of caste violations, such as restrictions on food or sexual relations with other caste groups.[30] In these stories, the Brahmarakshas takes on a more generic sense of a monstrous, corrupted figure, which carries through into contemporary understandings of the word.[31]

Muktibodh's Brahmarakshas, similarly, is corrupted by an unexpungible sense of *pāpa*, which I have chosen to translate here as "offense." But there is no mention of a specific caste violation in the poem; rather, the Brahmarakshas is eventually revealed to be a kind of pure scientist, or laboratory researcher, who turned towards expertise and profit. But this is not the only Brahmarakshas figure in Muktibodh's work.

Published in 1957, the same year as the poem "Brahmarakshas," "Brahmarākṣas kā śiṣya" is a very different treatment of this figure. An outlier among Muktibodh's fiction, the story presents a fable of a young student who is taught Sanskrit by a teacher who reveals himself, at the close of the student's study, to be a ghost, fated to immortality because he had failed to pass on his knowledge. Whereas the Brahmarakshas of the poem is a terrifying, self-torturing figure, the Brahmarakshas of the short story is a stern but kindly teacher, an ideal guru. There are other echoes between the short story and the poem, making it worthwhile to consider "Brahmarākṣas kā śiṣya" further.

Set in an atemporal Banaras, it tells the story of a wandering student "from the south" in search of a teacher. In another autobiographical echo, the student's migration references the large-scale movement of Brahmins from Maratha regions to Banaras in the eighteenth century.[32] Less well-known, however, was the migration at the same time of Maharashtrian Brahmins into the other states of the Maratha confederacy, where they primarily served in administrative roles. These communities eventually became sizable enough that they formed near linguistic majorities in places such as Indore and Nagpur, with the latter becoming a part of Maharashtra following independence.[33]

One of these families was that of Muktibodh's, which immigrated from the city of Jalgaon. Information on this migration is sparse, largely collected in the oral history of *Lakṣit Muktibodh*, but the migration probably took place in the nineteenth century. By the time Muktibodh was born, his family had for several generations been associated with the princely states of Gwalior and Indore, with his father acting as a superintendent of police.[34] In setting

"Brahmarākṣas kā ṣiṣya" in an abandoned mansion in Banaras, and naming its hero as a young boy from the south, Muktibodh's short story, despite its otherwise fantastic atmosphere, is rooted in a historical context that may have had personal resonance.

The student wanders into an abandoned mansion that is the home of a Brahmarakshas, who teaches him Sanskrit in order to be released from his curse. In that story, the effect is created as much by its description of a desolate, abandoned mansion in which the Brahmarakshas lives as by the Brahmarakshas itself. The story begins by describing eight stories of steps before flashing back to the moments when the young Brahmin is led into the mansion, describing a vast, desolate space:

> Bright red wasps buzzed around, trying to sting him from every side; but as soon as he crossed the threshold he found himself inside a massive courtyard, empty and overgrown with brown grass shining in the sunlight, with a balcony—a vast, splendid, empty balcony, covered with a fabric shade. It looked as if someone had just cleaned the space, but there was no one to be seen. A cat carefully stepped across an overhang on the third floor. He saw a staircase, too, clean and wide.[35]

Just as in the poem, the short story sets the Brahmarakshas in a vast, empty space—in both this passage and the first stanzas of the poem, the word *sūnā*, "desolate" is used repeatedly. But the contrasts are also telling. In the story, the haunted mansion is empty, but well-appointed; the young Brahmin's education takes place in a room magically well-appointed with carpets and fine foods. In the poem, however, the space itself is desolate, but surrounded by both flowers, from multiple plants, as well as "a wild raw green smell" of past greatness.

The demonic Brahmin of "Brahmarakshas" echoes the instances of the Brahmarakshas in Muktibodh's work, but deepens and expands upon them. Similarly to "Brahmarakshas kā śiṣya," the poem evokes a fable through situating the Brahmarakshas in a timeless space at the bottom of a well. The Brahmarakshas can function as a vehicle of legend, even as it evokes very real concerns over lost status and knowledge production. But in "Brahmarakshas," the figure of the Brahmarakshas draws not only from the kindly teacher of "Brahmarakshas kā śiṣya," but also from the presence of the Brahmarakshas in Muktibodh's diaries. Here, because it is written as a diary entry, the piece explicitly connects the Brahhmarakshas to Muktibodh's own life, and is presented as a symbol of Muktibodh's degraded, cursed state. The bitterness and recrimination of the diary entry is fused with the Brahmarakshas of the fable to create, ultimately, the startling figure we encounter here. The Brahmarakshas also stands out as the obverse of the Brahmarakshas in "Brahmarakshas ka Shishya."

The first thing we learn about the Brahmarakshas, perhaps in the absence of visual information, is the sound he makes. But as the second of these two stanzas makes clear, these are the sounds that are specifically associated with a Brahmin. As I stated earlier, the Brahmarakshas, up until Muktibodh's work, was presented as doomed to his demonic state by some ritual infelicity, which took various forms in different legends. Here, the reader is reminded of these rituals: the ancient virtues are not transformed into sin, and the expected recitations of the Brahmin, in his role as priest, are transformed into a stream of obscenity.

In this poem, the Brahmarakshas bears little resemblance to the Brahmarakshas of the story. The story portrays the Brahmarakshas as an ideal *guru*, and the young man as an ideal student. The story is bookended with loving, reverential descriptions of the pedagogical relationship between the two. In the beginning of the story, which is set after the student's education is complete, the student leaves reciting verses from the *Bhagavad gītā*; in the closing lines of the story, when the Brahmarakshas reveals his hidden nature (incidentally a magically lengthened arm far across a room to retrieve a piece of fruit), his curse is lifted, and the student is overjoyed that he has met such a knowledgeable and dedicated guru.

The tone of the story is almost the opposite of what we have in the poem, with a lacerating, tortured monster trapped in the bottom of a well. But the story and the poem seem to echo each other, with the story a kind of resolution of the narrative of the poem. Whereas in the poem the speaker looks down the steps of the stepwell, in the story the student ascends eight floors to find the room of the guru. And whereas the poem ends with the Brahmarakshas guru tragically unfulfilled, the story ends with the disappearance and salvation of the Brahmarakshas, he having successfully passed on his knowledge to the student.

What might account for these differences? I would propose two major differences. The first, which I will discuss further in the third chapter, is that "Brahmarākṣas kā śiṣya" is unique among Muktibodh's prose or poetry in that it is explicitly presented as a supernatural tale. The revelation that the Brahmin teacher is a ghost is made through the guru magically reaching from one room to another, to bring a sweet to the student. Unlike any other of Muktibodh's works, this story explicitly presents what is happening as an unreal, magical fantasy, without any framing narrative or other device that undermines unreality.

The second, related, difference is that this story stages, in its fable, a premodern ideal of Brahmin identity. It is crucial that the story take place in Benares, and that the learning that is imparted is knowledge of Sanskrit. Reading the poem through the light of the short story makes clear that, for Muktibodh, what was at stake in the fate of the Brahmarakshas was caste status, and that he viewed modernity in terms of the undermining of that caste status. The Brahmarakshas of the short story succeeds when he fulfills the traditional expectations of a Brahmin in terms of teaching. And the Brahmarakshas of the poem continues on because, for all of his brilliance, he fails to do so.

The sense of the Brahmarakshas as a failed, broken Brahmin in modernity is reinforced by one more set of writings that has, to my knowledge, not been discussed in Hindi literary discourse. In his posthumously collected diaries, several entries feature a Brahmarakshas. Among them was a brief meditation on work, criticism, and middle-class life, written around the same time. In this piece, the author shifts from thinking about criticism to thinking about his life as a kind of "spectral reality," in which his own, personal subjectivity is the only persistent reality. He imagines himself to be older than Raja Bhartrihari—a king who appears in a series of popular legends. He *himself* is the Brahmarakshas, older than the oldest stories:

> I'm beating my head drafting a broadcast for some minister or other when suddenly that girl was sitting and smirking in front of me. I know why she's laughing.

> She's laughing at me—only me. Fair, with a round, egg-shaped face, educated, doing this job simply as a pastime (really, just a hobby?) and laughing at me. But she doesn't know who I am. I am a *Brahmarakshas*. A *Brahmarakshas* from ages beyond counting, who always tried to do the right thing, but did the wrong thing again and again.[36]

This brief appearance opens up possibilities for thinking about the figure in other places. The most obvious point is that it establishes an autobiographical element for thinking about the Brahmarakshas, insofar as Muktibodh constructs a personal identity in his work. The brief diary is meant to give the impression of verisimilitude, with a description of Muktibodh's actual work place at Akashvani. So, as readers, even if we were to ignore the many autobiographical elements of the Brahmarakshas, such as the family history echoed in "Brahmarakshas ka Shishya," this brief mention forces us to consider the issue.

The less obvious but perhaps more destabilizing element is the context in which the Brahmarakshas appears. The lower-middle-class-ness of Muktibodh, with its frustrations, domestic instability, and workplace humiliation, is tied indelibly to caste. Even the way in which the Brahmarakshas is introduced, being preceded by a description of the ghostly reality, of *bhūtahā vāstav*, in which the author feels a vast distance from those around him, not only in the individuality of his thinking, but in his refusal to participate in the life of work. The humiliation of work is further framed as gendered through his disgust at the woman, who does not need to work, laughing at the speaker, who is imagining himself as a sallow-faced, poverty-stricken clerk. The Brahmarakshas, then, appears, at the moment of greatest middle-class humiliation, and the curse of the Brahmin demon is to live out this underworld life, even as it revels in its antiquity.

To return to the Brahmarakshas of poem and story, then, we now need to read these figures in light not only of the parody of traditional Brahminical practices of recitation, but also in terms of their relationship with the speaker outside of the well, and with Muktibodh's own construction of his self. The smell of the flowers at the edge of the opening tempts the speaker towards the dark hole of the well, but the speaker is also tempted by "the smell of past glories" that have settled about the space. In the diary the Brahmarakshas extends backwards in time. Thus, in one possible reading, the Brahmarakshas is explicitly not merely a middle-class intellectual, but the vitality of a past tradition which draws the speaker in.

The presence of the past is common among the three iterations of the Brahmarakshas. He has existed for centuries before taking up his post in All-India radio, and the place in which he finds himself now is so permeated with his achievements that it has settled as an odor, hovering above around the plants and empty owl's nests. This presence of the past helps explain, as well, some of the resonance of "Brahmarakshas kā śiṣya," which otherwise seems so simplistic and guilelessly positive. Recall that this fable, in which the Brahmarakshas is a kindly teacher, is one in which a young student, about whom the reader knows only that he comes "from the south," has found himself in Banaras, where he is led into the abandoned mansion by some insouciant and misleading locals. Beneath the surface of this simple story is a history that, again, has biographical echoes.

The Brahmarakshas, reaching perhaps the final waystation of his depiction in Muktibodh's work, is now babbling nonsense. The pure sounds of religious chants have become an enraged recitation, a *kruddha mantroccār.* The Sanskrit language, the ultimate mark of Brahminical learning and privilege—and, of course, the subject of the student's education in "Brahmarakshas kā śiṣya"—have collapsed into *shuddh saṃskṛt gāliyoṃ kā jvār*—what I have translated as "a flood of pure Sanskrit obscenity." But at the same time, the brows of the Brahmarakshas have "knitted together into / glittering strands of criticism." The use of the word *ālocnā,* "criticism," is significant, because it departs from the traditionalized language used to describe the Brahmarakshas up to this point. Instead, it broadens the scope of Brahmarakshas from traditional, religious linguistic use—stotra, mantra, *śuddh saṃskṛt*—to a distinctly modern set of intellectual references.

The Brahmarakshas

kintu, gahrī bāvṛī
kī bhītarī dīvār par

tirchī girī ravi-raśmi
ke uṛte hue parmāṇu, jab
tal tak pahuṃcte haiṃ kabhī
tab brahmarākṣas samajhtā hai, sūrya ne
jhukkar namaste kar diyā.
path bhūlkar jab cāṃdnī
kī kiran ṭakrāye
kahīṃ dīvār par,
tab brahmarākṣas samajhtā hai
vandanā kī cāṃdnī ne
jñān-gurū mānā use.

atipraphullit kaṇṭakit tan-man vahī
kartā rahā anubhav ki nabh ne bhī
vinat ho mān lī hai śreṣṭhatā uskī!!

aur tab dugune bhayānak oj se
pahcān vālā man
sumerī bebilonī jan-kathāoṃ se
madhur vaidik ṛcāoṃ tak
va tab se āj tak ke sutra chandas, mantra, thiyoram,
sab prameyoṃ tak
ki mārks, eṅgals, rasel, ṭāenbī
ki hīḍeggar va speṅglar, sārtra, gāṃdhī bhī
sabhī ke siddh-antoṃ kā
nayā vyākhyān kartā vah
nahātā brahmarākṣas, śyām
prāktan bāvṛī kī
un ghanī gahrāīyoṃ meṃ śūnya.

ye garajtī, gūṃjtī, āndolit
gahrāiyoṃ se uṭh rahī dhvaniyāṃ, ataha
udbhrānt śabdoṃ ke naye āvart meṃ
har śabd nij prati śabd ko bhī kāṭtā,
vah rūp apne bimb se bhī jūjh
vikṛtākār-kṛti
hai ban rahā
dhvani laṛ rahī apnī pratidhvani se yahāṃ
bāvṛī kī in muṇḍeroṃ par
Manohar harī kuhnī ṭek sunte haiṃ

ṭagar ke puṣpa-tāre śvet
ve dhvaniyāṃ!
sunte haiṃ unheṃ prācīn audumbar
sun rahā hūṃ maiṃ vahī
pāgal pratīkoṃ meṃ kahīṃ jātī huī
vah ṭrejiḍī
jo bāvṛī meṃ aṛ gayī.

when, however, on occasion
the flying particles
of crooked sun-rays
bounce across the walls of the *bāvṛī*
and happen to reach the water,
the *Brahmarakshas* believes that the sun
has bowed to him in namaste.
if rays of moonlight,
somehow forgetting their proper path,
should collide against the walls,
the *Brahmarakshas* assumes
that the moon,
head lowered in reverence,
has accepted him as a *guru* of wisdom.
covered with thorns as his body and mind is,
he blossoms with the experience
that even the heavens
have humbly accepted his excellence!!
and then, with a brilliance doubly terrifying
this discerning mind
takes in everything—
from the Sumero-Babylonian myths
to the sweet and noble Vedic hymns
and of all the *sūtras* from that time to today
vedic verse, *mantras, theorems*
and all of the propositions,
including marx, engels, russell, toynbee,
heidegger and spengler; sartre—and even gandhi—
from all these prince-i-ples
he composes an entirely new exposition
and as he does so, the *brahmarakshas* bathes
in the vacant, thickened depths

of the ancient stepwell.
. . . rumbling, ringing careening
these echoes rise up from the depths, and so
in the new turning of these rising sounds
each word collides with its response
in struggling with its image, form
becomes perverse action
and a sound battles against its echo.
on the lip of the well
held up on elegant green elbows
the *ṭagar*, with its white starflowers, listens
to the echoes!!
the tender flowers of the *karaundī* listen
that ancient *audumbar* fig listens as well
and I'm right there, listening
to the *tragedy*,
recited in insane symbols,
bound within the *bāvṛī*.[37]

Translation of Muktibodh's poetry can be difficult, because it is necessary to reproduce the abrupt parataxis and enjambment of the lines in the different syntax of English; among other significant differences, in Hindi, the standard position of the verb is at the end of the sentence, so that these long lines, with their precise rhythms and building of meaning, often have to be reversed in translation. For instance, were the first sentence of the first stanza to be translated without altering the syntax, the lines would approximately read:

but, deep well's
across the walls
crooked sun-rays'
flying particles, when
arrive at the bottom ever
then the Brahmarakshas believes, the sun has
bowed and made *namaste*.

The first clause of the Hindi ends with the word *parmāṇu*, which can mean "atom" but which I have here translated as particle. The word order, which I have only partially been able to bring into

English, emphasizes a parallel between the word *parmāṇu* and the word *sūrya*. *Sūrya* means "sun," as does the word *ravi*, which is used as part of the compound *ravi-raśmi*, which I have translated as "sun-rays." But the Brahmarakshas mistakes the physical properties of sun-rays, acting as both a wave and a particle and refracting downwards into the well, for the obeisance of the sun itself.

Recently, there has been increasing concern for the appropriation of scientific discourse, and a spread of pseudoscience more generally, by the Hindu right. Even prior to the general and ongoing crisis in public health caused by COVID-19, the epistemology of the Hindu right included a range of positions that claimed the authority of both scientific knowledge and ancient wisdom. Famous examples, such as current prime minister Narendra Modi's claim that plastic surgery had been invented with the transplantation of Ganesha's head, are often presented as comical, but recent scholarship has shown the long genealogy behind these claims.[38] Remarks such as Modi's indicate the ways in which Hindu nationalism adopts the hallmarks of science and technology as a mark not of a Western modernity, but of a utopian, thriving past. What Banu Subramaniam has referred to as the "archaic modernity" of Hindu nationalism has deep roots in colonial and postcolonial processes of knowledge production, and in a larger genealogy of Indian intellectual responses to Western hegemony in the nineteenth and early twentieth centuries.[39]

Hindutva approaches to science, therefore, can be seen as part of a larger problem of the fate of knowledge systems in modernity. Such problems include not only current-day claims but also the role of science in post-independence India, referred to as "Nehruvian science" by David Arnold.[40] Nehruvian Science, in Arnold's formulation, encompassed not only Jawaharhal Nehru's discussion of science, but the entire postcolonial approach to science, technology, and development, in which science was meant to take up a key role in "the autobiography of the Indian nation," becoming a cornerstone in the idea of an Indian civilization and its place in the world.[41] Although Nehruvian science, with its emphasis on state-led development, practical applications, and investment in higher education, would seem to be utterly distinct from the destructive tendencies of the Hindu right, Arnold points out that it was also deeply invested in reassessing a seemingly distinct, Indian approach to science, often summed by the career of the botanist

Jagdish Chandra Bose (1858–1937).[42] Scientists such as Bose, who seemed to excel within the intellectual frameworks of modern science even as they claimed a distinct intellectual heritage, seemed to demonstrate a possible fusion.[43] In this way, Nehruvian science, often seen as the opposite of Hindutva's archaic modernity, shares with it a claim on the role of science in an Indian civilization taking up its place in the world.

Scholarship on the problem of science and knowledge in postcolonial India has also pointed out the crucial role of caste in this formulation. Ashis Nandy, in his pioneering study of the subject, argued that Hindutva formulations of science often, either explicitly or implicitly, enshrined Brahminical intellectual traditions, within their idea of a "Hindu" science, emphasizing, for instance, pseudoscientific arguments for vegetarianism.[44] Similarly, recent scholarship has pointed out the pervasive casteism within modern institutions of science, and has argued that an emphasis on abstract sciences such as physics and mathematics privileges Brahminical knowledge systems.[45] Brahminical systems of knowledge, education, and privilege thus loom large over this discourse of science in the twentieth century.

This is undoubtedly the most famous section of "Brahmarakshas," the source of its popularity and the object of the majority of its analyses. As discussed earlier, the knowledge of the Brahmarakshas and its wide-reaching scope of the classics of world literature and philosophy are at the core of the idea that the Brahmarakshas is a tragedy of the intellectual who fails to emerge beyond his learning.

But what this interpretation does not include is the biting irony of this description. That the Brahmarakshas, in his delusions of grandeur, takes all of creation to be his student should serve as a warning. The list of authors included—Marx, the major British historians of the mid-twentieth century, the philosopher of existence and that of decline—add up to a caricature of the middlebrow intellectual landscape. The inclusion of Gandhi, with just a hint of condescension, rounds out the sense that the learning of the Brahmarakshas should not be taken entirely seriously.

Nor, on the other hand, do I want to read this passage as indicating the madness and self-laceration of Muktibodh's own self, or even of his family history. If, on one level, this can be read as a satire of the intellectual, who is bound to his prejudices and arrogances, literally a frog in a well, then it extends past the Brahmarakshas himself to the entire intellectual landscape of 1950s India. The disjuncture between the body, wounded and bleeding, and the belief that the heavens have recognized his brilliance, defines the Brahmarakshas. The next stanza returns to the speaker and reminds the reader of his existence at the top of the well, where he watches what he now explicitly refers to, using the English word, as a *tragedy*.

Why, then, is this a tragedy? Is it because the Brahmarakshas is so delusional, driven to madness by his arrogance? Has he brought himself into this condition? If we return to "Brahmarakshas kā śiṣya," the Brahmarakshas there was doomed to live on until he had passed on his teaching. In that case, is what happened here a case of mistaken identity—that the Brahmarakshas fails to recognize his true student? Or is it, rather, that the knowledge that he positions—the grand synthesis—is not in any way activated? Or, finally, is the possession of the Brahmarakshas not just this set of books but the entire Brahminical knowledge tradition of which he is a part? The latter interpretation is buttressed by the prior stanzas, so redolent with Brahminical signification.

These reasons—the explicit invocation of caste expectations, combined with the parallel of "Brahmarākṣas kā ṣiṣya"; the twisting of the "curse" of the Brahmarakshas towards the failure to live up to one's traditional occupation; and the linking of this caste status to questions of scientific rationality—lead me to argue that we cannot read this poem solely as a satire of the postindependence intellectual. To the extent that we do read it as such a satire, it is as a satire that puts caste and the status of Brahminical privilege at the center of its understanding of politics and knowledge.

The structure of the poem implies that the Brahminical reading of the first half must also apply to the second half, in which the satire is repeated as tragedy. When we read of the scientist who has vaguely given up a search for knowledge in favor of worldly power, and, more significantly for Muktibodh's work, when we see the conclusion of the poem in which the speaker expresses a longing to become the student of the Brahmarakshas, we must also read that through caste. That is to say, the relationship between student and teacher that is common to Muktibodh's long poems must be read as an explicitly Brahminical trope.

Up to now, I have discussed "Brahmarakshas" in terms that could be easily read as satire: the Brahmarakshas can be read as a parody of Brahminical learning or as a sly analysis of Brahminical privilege and resentment. But the key to this poem, and perhaps the key to the work it attempts to do, can be found in its second half. That half consists of the near-total redemption of the Brahmarakshas and the statement of the *guru-śiṣya* relationship, a theme that lies at the core of Muktibodh's work, as at the core of the revolutionary potential of the Brahmarakshas. The concept of the researcher is crucial to understanding this transformation.

The second half of the poem, in fact, can be seen as an inverse of the first half, with each element repeated and transformed. The stepwell transforms from a negative space, defined by its procession into darkness and the earth, into an inverted tower, with a shining, crystalline staircase ascending into the light. The Brahmarakshas is transformed from a deluded, insane priest into the most idealized figure of Nehruvian India, a researcher into the basic sciences. His "insane symbols" are revealed as the perfected language of mathematics and philosophy. His delusional, Casaubonian imagination of a shallow "synthesis" is transformed into a noble, philosophical question of the ideal. And his sad imagination of pupils as he sits, abandoned at the bottom of a stagnant well, is transformed into the speaker's desire to become the student of the Brahmarakshas. So, any reading must answer the question, In what way does the redemption of the Brahmarakshas reflect on our understanding of the Brahmarakshas himself? Put another way, attention to the tropes of Muktibodh's work forces us into a more complicated reading of the poem as a whole, because it forces attention to the thematic connections that play out across his narrative lyrics.

The first stanza of this second half returns to the original space of the stepwell. However, what in the first half of the poem is a place that is rooted directionally to the cityis here abstracted, presented solely as isolated, Platonic elements:

khūb ūṃcā ek zīnā sāṃvlā
uskī aṃdherī sīṛhiyāṃ . . .
ve ek ābhyantar nirāle lok kī.
ek caṛhnā au' utarnā,
punaha caṛhnā au' luṛhaknā,

moc pairoṃ meṃ
va chātī par anekoṃ ghāv.
bure-acche-bīc ke saṅgharṣ
se bhī ugratar
acche va use adhik acche bīc kā saṅgar
gahan kiñcit saphaltā,
ati bhavya asaphaltā
. . . atirekvādī pūrṇatā
kī ye vyathāeṃ bahut pyārī haiṃ . . .
jyāmitik saṅgati-gaṇit
kī dṛṣṭi se kṛt
bhavya naitik mān
ātmacetan sūkṣam naitik mān . . .
. . . atirekvādī pūrṇatā kī tuṣṭi karnā
kab rahā āsān
mānavī antarkathāeṃ bahut pyārī haiṃ!!

. . . atirekvādī pūrṇatā
kī ye vyathāeṃ bahut pyārī haiṃ . . .
jyāmitik saṅgati-gaṇit
kī dṛṣṭi se kṛt
bhavya naitik mān
ātmacetan sūkṣma naitik bhān . . .
atirekvāvī pūrṇatā kī tuṣṭi karnā
kab rahā āsān
mānavī antarkathāeṃ bahut pyārī haiṃ!!

a tall, tall staircase disappearing in darkness
its steps . . .
towards a peculiar inner space.
ascending descending
again, up and down, a stumble
sprained ankles
lashes across the chest.
the struggle between good and evil—
more terrible
is the war between the good and the better
a narrow, obscure success
a grand and noble failure!!

. . . these agonies
of liberal plenitude
are so very precious . . .
noble, ethical esteem
formed through a vision
of geometric mathematical balance
the appearance of a subtle, ethical self-consciousness . . .
. . . since when has it been easy
to satisfy such liberal plenitude
these secret tales, so humane, so precious!![46]

What was earlier a ruin now bears more than a passing resemblance to an element of popular fiction going back to the nineteenth century: the sorcerer's talisman. In the *qissā-dāstān* tradition, a magician creates a magical space within a spell, potentially infinite in scope, in which he might imprison his enemies. What is defined in the opening of the poem through its attention to a stagnant, abandoned space, is now a "tall, tall staircase," neatly flipping the identity of the stepwell, so to speak, from the well to the steps.[47] Rather than a hole in the ground, defined by its horizontal division from the everyday, here the verticality of the steps is emphasized—"ascending descending / and again up and down." This begins the transformation of the Brahmarakshas; instead of scrubbing himself in the stagnant water of the well, he attempts to rise up a staircase, a movement immediately linked to a kind of ethical self-improvement. The unnamed filth of the Brahmarakshas is now transformed into marks of progress: rather than scrubbing himself endlessly, the Brahmarakshas now features a sprained ankle as he struggles up the stairs.

The second half of this stanza is difficult to translate, because, in the original Hindi, its language is dominated by Sanskrit neologisms and tangled, unclear syntax. But the knotty prolixity here indicates a concern not just with obscurity, but with the language of science.

This language jumps out to a Hindi reader because of the density of its use of Sanskrit terms, beginning with the phrase "atirekvādī pūrṇatā," which I have translated as "liberal plentitude." In the process of translation, I placed it following the enjambed "these agonies," lessening the impact of the complicated terms. The political history of Hindi intersects with its linguistic history in the choice of vocabulary. As part of an effort both to build up Hindi as a prospective national language and to differentiate it from Urdu, technical, scientific, and philosophical language is drawn mostly from Sanskrit, with many terms calqued from English.[48] This modern Hindi is often derided as incomprehensibly complicated, bureaucratic language, especially when it is used to replace more widely known English terms. Muktibodh himself once fell afoul of this problem: when his poem "cambal kī ghāṭī" was published in the journal *Kalpanā*, a range of terms for minerals, such as "quartz" or "magnesium," were replaced with supposedly more "Indian" equivalents, most of which are still not widely used today.[49] However, in this passage Muktibodh uses this language to create a contrast with the language used in the first half of the poem. Although that language was just as "Sanskritic" as the language used here, in the first section that language is drawn from myth, folktale, and religious discourse, whereas here the language is distinctly philosophical. The shift in language from the mythical to the scientific demonstrates the connections across these two understandings of science and knowledge, reflecting a key theme of the poem, even as it demonstrates the tensions inherent in the Hindi language itself.

This tendency is carried through and made more explicit in the following stanzas, which continue to describe the Brahmarakshas in the valorized terminology established here. And whereas the Brahmarakshas is described in terms of his ritual impurity, and his "intellect" is a lightly-veiled satire of the generalizing tendencies of a middle-class intellectual (he creates a "new analysis" of all philosophy), now the Brahmarakshas is described as somehow wounded, and struggling against "the agonies of perfectionistic plenitude." The following stanzas make clear that the Brahmarakshas, presented first as a comic figure, is meant to be seen completely differently:

ravi nikaltā
lāl cintā kī rudhir-saritā
pravāhit kar dīvāroṃ par,
udit hotā candra
vraṇ par bāṃdh detā
        śvet-dhaulī paṭṭiyāṃ
udvigna bhāloṃ par

sitāre āsmānī chor par phaile hue
angin daśamlav se
daśamlav-binduoṃ ke sarvataha
pasre hue uljhe gaṇit maidān meṃ
mārā gayā, vah kām āyā,
aur vah pasrā paṛā hai . . .
vakṣ-bāṃheṃ khulī phailīṃ
ek śodhak kī.

vyaktitva vah komal sphaṭik prāsād-sā
prāsād meṃ zīnā
va zīne kī akelī sīṛhiyāṃ
caḍhnā bahut muṣkil rahā
ve bhāv-saṅgat tark-saṅgat
kārya sāmañjasya-yojit
samīkaraṇoṃ ke gaṇit kī sīṛhiyāṃ
ham choṛ deṃ uske lie.
us bhāv-tark va kārya-sāmañjasya-yojan-
shodh meṃ
sab paṇḍitoṃ, sab cintakoṃ ke pās
vah guru prāpt karne ke lie
bhaṭkā!!

the sun emerges
a blood-red river of thought
spreads across the walls;
the moon rises
his wounds now oozing,
he ties clean white bandages
on that agitated forehead.
the stars are spread out across the shores of the sky
all the points
of countless decimals
spread out across the twisted battleground of math
murdered, he finds his purpose
sprawled out . . .
the chest and limbs, splayed out,
of a scientist.
the self is a kind of delicate crystal palace,
with a staircase

and lonely steps
difficult to climb.
let's leave him
to his equations
completely resolved
balanced in feeling, balanced in action.
In the search
for an action equally balanced
and logical in feeling
addressing every priest and thinker
in his search for a *guru*
he's stumbled away!![50]

This turn in the poem is often interpreted as cementing the "tragedy" of the Brahmarakshas, through depicting his seeming fall from grace. The sudden irruption of "blood-red river of thought," of course, can be read symbolically as a reference to communism, with the idea that Brahmarakshas is tragically led astray from the right course of action. But I would argue, rather, that these lines are meant to repeat the action of the first section of the poem. Whereas earlier the sun and the moon were received by the delusional Brahmarakshas as pupils, now they illuminate the wounded figure. And by that logic, at the moment in the first half of the poem in which we discover the "new synthesis," instead the Brahmarakshas (or perhaps another figure) is revealed, perhaps dead, as a researcher, or *śodhak*.

As I stated in the introduction, Muktibodh frequently used the trope of a scientist in two major senses. At times, as in his long, unpublished poem "Bhaviśyadhārā," the scientist resembled a character drawn from nineteenth- and twentieth-century science and detective fiction: the scientist as inventor. In a South Asian context, the most well-known example is Professor Shanku, created by filmmaker and author Satyajit Ray and discussed in Pablo Mukherjee's recent work.[51] This professor, descended from the *ayyār* of the *qissā-dāstān*, used his scientific knowledge to create an array of new technological tools, and, by evoking this figure, Muktibodh could make use of the generic expectations of popular fiction to create his narrative poems. Another sense, however, is that of the Nehruvian expert. The "expert" of the Nehruvian era is further evoked through the line's emphases on the mathematical work of the researcher, bringing to mind the specific emphasis in the 1950s on the basic sciences. Thus, the sun and the moon, and the field of decimal points, return to the imagery of the first half of the poem, but are now transformed into the Nehruvian ideal of the scientific expert.

This passage raises another important aspect of the long poems: the question of the allegorical. Muktibodh's idea of allegory, and its relation to realism, will be discussed more in the following chapter. Here, as the story of the Brahmarakshas becomes more complex, it creates a narrative that is often understood, by both Muktibodh and his critics, as an allegory of the postindependence intellectual. This passage, indeed, contains multiple layers of meaning, not only taking part in popular genres but also evoking religious texts—the idea of a multilevel palace of realization is common to both Sufi allegorical tales and the *Rāmcaritmānas*.[52] Accordingly, as I have mentioned, criticism has tended to read this poem as an allegory of the postindependence intellectual.

However, in this passage, an allegorical reading must take into account not only the satire of the postindependence intellectual, but the explicit framing of this tragic outcome in terms that are deeply inflected by caste. As the passage makes clear in the larger context of the poem, if at first the scientist can be understood as a victim of his own hubris, the end of the stanza reminds the reader that the Brahmarakshas is bound up, in his search for a guru, in the Brahminical codes of pedagogical practice that have operated throughout the poem. This work, therefore, participates not only in an allegory of class but also of caste.

The establishment of the Brahmarakshas as a scientist prepares the way in the poem for its final resolution, in which the speaker declares a wish to become the student of the Brahmarakshas. In this way, the poem echoes the endings of most of Muktibodh's long poems, and a focus running through his work on the relationship between the guru and student. In "Aṃdhere meṃ" (In the Dark) (the subject of the final chapter), the search for the guru runs through the entire poem, which begins with a visitation by this figure and ends with the speaker declaring a permanent search. Other poems describe the *mitra*, or friend, who has made a revolutionary of the speaker.[53] All of this means that, by evoking the brahmarakshas as a guru figure, Muktibodh is turning towards the trope of revolutionary education that runs through his entire work.

kintu yug badlā va āyā kīrti-vyavasāyī
. . . lābhkārī kārya meṃ se dhan,
va dhan meṃ se hṛday-man,
aur, dhan-abhibhūt antahakaraṇ meṃ se
satya kī jhāīṃ
nirantar cilcilātī thī.
ātmacetas kintu us
vyaktitva meṃ bhī prāṇmay anban . . .
viṣvacetas be-banāv!!
mahattā ke caraṇ meṃ thā
viṣādākul man!
merā usī se un dinoṃ hotā milan yadi
to vyathā uskī svayaṃ jīkar
batātā maiṃ use uskā svayaṃ kā mūlya
uskī mahattā!
va us mahattā kā
ham sarīkhoṃ ke lie upyog,
us āntariktā kā batātā maiṃ mahattva!!

pis gayā vah bhītarī
au' bāharī do kaṭhin pāṭoṃ bīc,
aisī ṭrejaḍī hai nīc!!

bāvṛī meṃ vah svayaṃ
pāgal pratīkoṃ meṃ nirantar kah rahā
vah koṭharī meṃ kis tarah
apnā gaṇit kartā rahā
au' mar gayā . . .
vah saghan jhāṛī ke kaṃṭīle
tam-vivar meṃ
mare pakṣī-sā
bidā hī ho gayā
vah jyoti anjānī sadā ko so gaī
yah kyoṃ huā!
kyoṃ yah huā!
maiṃ brahmarākṣas kā sajal-ur śiṣya

honā cāhtā
jisse ki uskā vah adhūrā kārya,
uskī vednā kā srot
saṅgam pūrṇ niṣkarṣoṃ talak
pahuṃcā sakūṃ.

but times change and now he traded in fame
. . . wealth from good, profitable work,
while from within that wealth his heart and mind
and, from within that self overcome by wealth,
the shadow of truth
continued to burn.
but the consciousness
within the self
was inherently out of sync . . .
a despairing mind
tracing out the footsteps of greatness!!
if only i have met him then
i would have felt his pain
told him his value
his greatness!!
crushed between
two hard stones,
inside and out,
such a sad, pathetic *tragedy*!
in the *bāvṛī*
still he recites
in mad symbols
how in the palace
he wrote out his math
and died . . .
like a dead bird
in a thorny bush
gone forever
that gem, unknown and now gone for ever
why!!
what has happened!!
i would like to become
the tear-stained student of the *brahmarakṣas,*

so that i could deliver that unfinished labor,
the source of all his pain,
to some collected, whole conclusion.[54]

The tragedy of the Brahmarakshas is that he is crushed between the stones of internality and externality; these lines are almost always read as referring to the ethical struggle between the education of the brahmarakshas and his failure to take political action. And in many ways, I would not disagree with this interpretation. Everything about the Brahmarakshas supports the idea of his unfinished task of education, the contrast between his present-day state of abject ghosthood and his former role as a scientist, and the importance of philosophical language to his role as a researcher. I have no reason to doubt the intention of the poem.

However, the way in which the poem links together the figure of the revolutionary scientist with the demonic Brahmin demands that we pay attention to the content of this poem. And that content indicates a disturbing connection between the Brahmarakshas and the scientist that relates to caste privilege, not to revolutionary intent. The poem insists that we understand postcolonial tragedy of the scientist, the intellectual, as inseparable from the language of Brahminical privilege. And that means, of course, that the poem reveals the underground fissures that run through the entire Nehruvian project. These fissures are that the ideal of education and of Western scientific knowledge were shot through with Brahminical ideals of educational attainment, ideals that are visible in such seemingly unrelated points as mathematics.

Ultimately, my aim in this reading of "Brahmarakshas" is not to claim that Muktibodh was not genuinely invested in the political, and indeed revolutionary, potential of his imagery—that is, I do not intend to excise the politics of this poem from my interpretation. Rather, attention to the imagery and sources of this poem, and its connection with the larger complex web of Muktibodh's oeuvre, including, perhaps especially, the role of the autobiographical, forces us to see a dimension to this work that would otherwise go unnoticed. The imaginative world of Muktibodh's work, so often described by critics as creating a single, unfinished poem, can be read as an entire ecology, one incorporating the elements I have described in the case of "Brahmarakshas." Attention to this ecology allows us to see how the Brahmarakshas links together the cursed and cursing demon with the noble, abstract scientist who is frequently presented as the hero of postindependence life.

This connection is formed not only through the narrative of this poem but also in its poetic structure, in which two halves echo and comment upon each other in their form, diction, and tropic content. This structure makes inescapable the connection between the researcher and the Brahmarakshas. But this connection is not only that intended by the narrative of the text, in which the researcher, in his abstract life of the mind, died without passing on his vast knowledge and was reborn as the Brahmarakshas. Rather, the other ways in which these two figures are connected imply the influence of casteized ideals of being a Brahmin, through ritualized superiority, access to knowledge, and the corresponding danger of sin as impurity, on the ideals of scientific research implied by the researcher.

This conclusion, with regard to "Brahmarakshas," prompts us to ask questions about the larger influence of caste and Brahminical ideals of science and learning on the social, cultural and political history of postindependence India. To what extent does the idea of the researcher, and the emotional relationship of the student who wants to learn at his feet, rely upon an ideal of learning, knowledge, and science that can only be understood through a history of Brahminical practices of learning? Ultimately, Muktibodh's Brahmarakshas has the potential to reframe not only our understanding of Muktibodh's work, but also the idea of the scientist, and of a "scientific point of view," that plays out over the twentieth century.

Conclusion

My reading of "Brahmarakshas" is intended to demonstrate several crucial features of the long poem. First, it shows how the long poem uses several formal strategies, including short, paratactic lines, rhyme schemes, and complex syntax, to deploy narrative. Second, "Brahmarakshas" shows the resulting ability of the long poem to incorporate a range of mythological tropes, genre conventions, and generally fantastic aspects in ways that would be difficult within the paradigms of realism in Hindi prose literature. Finally, these two elements—the formal strategies and the ability to incorporate a range of materials—allows the long poem to confront aspects of caste, lower-middle-class status, and anxieties around education that might otherwise be difficult to incorporate into prose literature.

That "Brahmarakshas" is able to do this with such efficiency, and with such a memorable character in the Brahmarakshas itself, is what makes this poem so canonized and prominent in Muktibodh's work, and what makes it stand as an ideal example of the long poem altogether. But with these features established, the question then is, Why was this the form developed by Muktibodh, and why were these long poems able to do things that, essentially, were very difficult or rare otherwise in Hindi literature? I have made a comparison earlier to magic realism, and it is an overarching contention of this book that the long poem was able to do the work that, in other historical contexts, took place in magic realism. The question is *why*.

In order to answer that question, in the next two chapters of the book I will, paradoxically, turn to Muktibodh's prose writings. This chapter has already engaged extensively with Muktibodh's diary and fiction writings, and many of the issues that drive the formation of the long poem are articulated there. The long poem, in fact, might be read not simply as a development in the lyric poem of Hindi, but as a development within Hindi prose literature, and a response to it.

My reading of "Brahmarakshas" has also emphasized the ways in which caste is central to this poem. The Brahmarakshas conception as a Brahmin who has failed to pass on his teaching creates a powerful image of axiety around knowledge, modernity, and Brahminical status in modernity. In the next chapter, in which I will consider Muktibodh's criticism, many of these anxieties take shape in Muktibodh's definition of the lower middle class. And similarly to the ways in which left criticism tends to see "Brahmarakshas" primarily in terms of class critique, my reading will also forefront the complex ways in which caste shapes the idea of the lower middle class, and how that in turn shapes Muktibodh's critique of realism.

It should be emphasized, however, that these ideas become visible and manifest within the structural framework of the long poem "Brahmarakshas" itself. The use of the fantastic—including elements both of myth and of popular *jāsūsī* and *talismīya* literature—becomes more possible within the narrative framework, of parataxis—sudden shifts between lines—created by this form. As will be shown in the third chapter, the route that Muktibodh takes is quite different within prose, and while the insights possible in that form are extremely valuable, they are fundamentally distinct from the utopian gestures we see in "Brahmarakshas." Ultimately, the explosive conclusion of this poem is bound up in the tension over genre and lyric form that is the hallmark of the long poem. This is why, in order to understand the long poem, we must first understand the way in which criticism and prose fiction work to illuminate the problems that, for Muktibodh, could be resolved through the long poem.

Chapter Two

Realism, Romanticism, and the Lower Middle Class

The Problem of Aesthetic Process

This book argues that Muktibodh should be seen as an exemplary figure of the literary Cold War, despite the fact that he was not involved in the international circulation that is often associated with Cold War literary history. In contrast with his contemporaries, Muktibodh did not travel internationally; his work, minimally translated into English, remains little read outside of the Hindi literature. My justification therefore rests on a kind of weak Borgesian logic: rather than claim Muktibodh as an exemplary figure in Cold War literature by virtue of his participation in Cold War literary systems, this book sees his connections as local and driven by his particular circumstances and engagement with the world. Muktibodh should be considered a Cold War writer—particularly a writer of the Cold War 1950s and 1960s—because his writing was shaped by contexts and influences specific to the internationalized, Cold War context of postindependence India.

The obverse of this statement is that, through Muktibodh's life and work, the cultural, political, and aesthetic concerns of the 1950s Cold War world are reshaped and recontextualized in postindependence life in the Hindi speaking zone. As he became central to Hindi literary criticism after his death, his works became one of the most important ways through which criticism and literary history in Hindi understood key aspects of Cold War literary history, from the transformation of aesthetic debates between realism and modernism into a dominant theme of literary criticism, to transformed conceptions of the planetary.

This process can lead to many complications, not least the perception of redundancy and repetition, through which Muktibodh can be seen to be reinstantiating debates that took place earlier. If Muktibodh is taken as the central example for interpreting debates over left aesthetics that are most often associated with interwar debates in the German-speaking world, how does this shape the periodization of those debates in a Hindi literary context?

In the 1970s, literary criticism in Hindi was transformed by several factors. Political events, such as the impact of Naxalism and the Emergency, were transformative moments that retrospectively came to be seen as a dividing point from an earlier era of pre-independence literature. Parallel to English-language criticism, however, Hindi was also shaped by the increasing presence, via translation from English, of writers such as Louis Althusser, Walter Benjamin, and Theodor Adorno, themselves newly appearing in translation from French and German. From the late 1960s onwards, these thinkers, via translation from the *New Left Review*, began to appear regularly in *Ālocnā* (Criticism) and other literary journals in Hindi.[1] The long history of left debate in Hindi in the postindependence period, which was frequently reduced to the two camps of *pragativād* (progressivism) and *prayogvād* (experimentalism), was increasingly refracted through new frameworks of criticism, as part of a larger process of the translation and dissemination of the Western Marxist critical tradition.[2]

Comparisons of Muktibodh to Brecht date back at least to 1980, when, in a special issue of the left-wing journal *Kaṇk*, Muktibodh was compared to German playwright Bertolt Brecht, with the left orthodox literary critic Ram Vilas Sharma placed in the position of the Hungarian critic György Lukács.[3] Hindi critics saw in Lukács' defense of realism, as opposed to expressionism and other modernist art forms, both a deeper understanding of the larger history of aesthetic debate in the Soviet world and an echo of Ram Vilas Sharma's evaluation of Muktibodh's work as escapism and, ultimately, the triumph of existentialism in Hindi literature. Muktibodh's defense of modernist poetics, in turn, allowed him to stand out as a committed yet oppositional left figure.[4]

A closer look at Muktibodh's and Brecht's critical positions would seem to strengthen this parallel. Brecht's critique of realism indeed bears uncanny parallels to that of Muktibodh. The articles written by Brecht between 1938 and 1940, although not published in German until 1954, stand as some of the most forceful left critiques of Zhdanovist/Lukácsian theories of realism, and particularly the formal attack on expressionist and modernist formal techniques associated with that school of thought. Brecht's argument relied on the idea of a "realist perspective" (*realistische Betrachtungsweise*), which in turn depended on what he called, paraphrasing Francis Bacon, "dynamic forces" (*treibenden Kräfte*).[5] These dynamic, or even driving forces reorient the logic of realism itself, maintaining the idea of a social totality while abandoning the restriction on technique. In Brecht's example, Shelley's "The Mask of Anarchy," with its plainly allegorical procession of figures towards London, becomes more realist than Balzac.[6] Shelley's poem, in which a series of fantastical, allegorical figures depicts contemporary English society in the wake of the Peterloo massacre, is more capable of depicting real social relations that Balzac's novels, which—in Brecht's view—only present the formal appearance of realism.

Muktibodh framed his own critique in strikingly similar terms. His position is laid out both in a series of essays and in the preface to a book-length work of criticism. As was the case with Brecht, Muktibodh relies on a distinction between a "realist style," or *yathārthvādī śailī*, and a "realist perspective," or *yathārthvādī dṛṣṭikoṇ*. Just as Brecht's realist perspective could better grasp the driving forces of a total sphere of activity, Muktibodh's redefinition of realism intervenes in the problem of narrative. Drawing from the Sanskrit aesthetic theory of *rasa*, Muktibodh describes a work of art in which reality operated in the background, or *nepathya*, with the depiction of emotional situation forefronted.[7] Crucially, both Brecht and Muktibodh object to Zhdanovist approaches to realism not because of their insistence on subjective expression—both writers have a more complicated position on that problem—but on the relations between narrative, allegory, and the underlying totality.[8]

Brecht's and Muktibodh's shared critique drew its power from their reading of crucial works of allegorical poetry. Readers of "Aṃdhere meṃ," with its midnight procession of thugs, editors, and politicians, cannot miss its connections with "The Mask of

Anarchy." But Muktibodh's reading of *Kāmāyanī*, and his insistence that the importance of the poem lay not in its pseudohistoricist mythological story but in its depiction of the social conditions of early twentieth-century North India, performs a similar work to that done by Brecht's reading of Shelley. Both Brecht and Muktibodh develop their criticism through reading an allegorical work whose power is created by the relation between allegorical structure and the social context in which its narratives unfold. Muktibodh's more extensive analysis of the fundamentally conservative *Kāmāyanī* creates a new model for understanding his own literary inheritance, just as Brecht's reading of Shelley is at the core of later left reassessments of romanticism.[9]

This chapter begins with comparison in order both to demonstrate the deeply shared histories of left critical traditions and to suggest limits to this comparison. The complex and specific histories of left aesthetic debate in South Asia are often rewritten—not only by later literary historians but by contemporary participants themselves—as echoes of the literary history of the European and Soviet left. Why is it that these two writers, separated across language, came to form such a strikingly similar argument, and arguably oriented around the same exemplary work? That Brecht and Muktibodh worked with similar problems, and came to similar conclusions, is to some extent dictated by the larger history of realism in the twentieth century and its part in a Soviet-aligned world system of literature.[10] Even as Brecht's essay was suppressed and unpublished, other, similar points could have been made in journals such as *Soviet Literature*, particularly during the period of the thaw following Stalin's death.[11]

Beyond a possible direct means of influence, the echo of Muktibodh's critique of realism, emerging almost two decades after that of Brecht, indicates the ways in which debates commonly understood as between realism and modernism repeat and mutate in different contexts. Brecht, writing in the context of the realism-expressionism debates taking place in *Das Wort* in the 1930s, directed his criticism both at the increasingly restrictive atmosphere in Moscow, as well as at National Socialist attacks on "degenerate" art. His idea of realism and its relation to the *treibende Krāften* of social reality must therefore be read in the context of European literary culture in the late 1930s.[12] Muktibodh, by contrast, situates his critique of realism in his larger understanding of Hindi literature—specifically, its relation to ideas of the fantastic and the rejection of traditional narrative forms; the binding link between realist literature and the emergence of a middle class in colonial India; and the foundational status of Hindi modernist poetry as emerging from the movement for Hindi as a national language. What might be read at first as a derivation from an earlier aesthetic debate reveals itself to be a unique, parallel response—one which demands a detailed analysis of its own genealogy.

The (Lower) Middle Class in Postindependence Hindi Literature

When Muktibodh died in 1964, it would not be unreasonable to guess that he would become known more for his criticism than his poetry. He had already published a book of essays, as well as *Kāmāyanī: ek punarvicār* (Kāmāyanī: A Reconsideration); the latter was a book-length analysis of a poem considered a landmark in Hindi poetry. His criticism, published widely in major journals throughout his career, was well-received, and, since his death, this body of work has only grown, buttressed by a continually growing series of articles, many of which were written under pseudonyms.[13]

Accounts of Nehruvian India have focused on the emergent Cold War, nonaligned India's relation to the postwar powers, and the ways in which this situation shaped literary culture following independence. These issues, articulated within the framework of Hindi literary culture, are inflected by the history of the movement to make Hindi a national language, which emphasized the social utility of literature, the problem of realism, and the idea of individual experience. Muktibodh's writing broadly engaged with these themes. Many of his essays were explicitly addressed to the question of the *laghū mānav* (minor man), the concept and political content of *nayī kavitā* (new poetry), and the doctrinaire ideology of left literary politics.[14] A series of essays, eventually collected in the volume *Nayī kavitā kā ātmasaṅgharṣ* (The Struggle of New Poetry) dealt with a range of topics; despite their title, they are probably evenly split between criticism of *nayī kavitā* and that of the perceived, orthodox progressive line. He criticizes progressive critics because, as he puts it, their dismissive attitude towards *nayī kavitā* poets closes off the possibility of engaging with the new critiques of society embedded in these poets. *Nayī kavitā,* however, was criticized for disallowing certain kinds of experiences, and certain kinds of social affiliations, as disallowed within the rarefied confines of Hindi modernism.

In his discussion of the concept of the *laghu mānav,* he built on this idea of a restrictive, self-censoring *nayī kavitā* to move towards a deeper sense of disturbance. Whereas Lakshmikant Varma emphasized the need for a "new environment," and, in line with writers like Rajendra Yadav, emphasized the suitability of new ways of writing to depict a new middle-class society, Muktibodh saw the *nayī kavitā* poets—and the orthodox left as well—as equally missing a larger point, which he called a "poisoned, declining civilization":

> Until *nayī kavitā* recognizes the reality of a declining, half-fallen civilization, and connects itself to the basic questions of that civilization, until it is able to organize itself to be involved in the struggle to construct humanity, and reflects the suffering and oppressed faces within it and shows the shining light in their hearts, our work is truly incomplete. I can accept that we can't finish this job in a day. But with a discerning sensitivity, the pain of experience, and tireless labor, we can move in that direction.[15]

Muktibodh's critique of *nayī kavitā* is linked here to a larger frame: the element of a declining civilization that seems absent in Lakshmikant Varma's "new environment." Instead, he joins a "discerning sensitivity" to "the pain of experience." This pain contrasts with the idealized, restrictive "aesthetic experience" that Muktibodh attributes to *nayī kavitā.* Muktibodh links this broader sense of experience to personal expression: "Today's poet cannot perfect his own consciousness, cannot truly maintain a consciousness of self [*ātmacetas*], until he is not conscious of the universal [*viśva-cetas*]."[16] Muktibodh sees this tension between self and universal in the critical debates of his day; elsewhere he further develops this connection into his own theory of the poetic process.

Why, though, was this civilization "poisoned?" What were the ideas that he was gesturing towards? In his criticism, he repeatedly emphasizes the kinds of experiences that, he claims, are not acceptable within either of the camps of poetry. It is based on this idea that he critiques *nayī kavitā* aesthetics as not being able to include the kinds of emotions that he sees as dominating postindependence life. Similarly, he rejects the left emphasis on realism as too quickly rejecting the personalized emotions associated with *nayī kavitā*. Ultimately, this drove Muktibodh towards an examination of genre and the creation of the long poem. But in order to better understand how he viewed these emotions, aesthetic experiences, and processes, we need to understand how he actually analyzed society. And in order to understand that we need not only to look at his explicitly critical pieces, but to consider as well his "diary" writings. In these pieces, he examines society in terms of the emerging world of the small-town lower middle class, a world that would increasingly come to dominate Hindi criticism.

The lower middle class, or *nimna madhyam varg*, tends to be discussed less in literary history than the middle class as such.[17] This reflects a broader ambiguity around the idea; historical and sociological accounts have described the lower middle class in Europe as emerging in two moments, first as the shopkeepers of the petite bourgeoisie and second as the army of clerks and bureaucrats at the close of the nineteenth century.[18] Rita Felsky has described the modern lower middle class as that which never thinks of itself in a positive sense.[19] Ultimately, however, the emergence and sometime numerical dominance of this class demands deep analysis, leading to work that puts the middle class at the center of its account of modernism.[20]

In an Indian context, multiple scholars of the "middle class" have pointed out that, for all of its importance as a concept, it is at times frustratingly undefined.[21] Part of the problem is common to other historians of the middle class such, as Ehrenreich in the American context, who developed an idea of the "professional middle class" to account for departures in the United States from Marxist understandings of class development.[22] But some problems of definition are specific to the Indian middle class; its emergence in colonialism from various antecedent groups; the difference between economic, occupational, and cultural definitions; and the sociological importance of the term.[23] Research on the middle class in India has viewed it as an example of a "fractured modernity," which, in the early analysis of Sanjay Joshi, is born out of a cultural process of differentiation, rather than a specific social or economic issue.[24] Joshi argues that the expressive qualities of the middle class in the late nineteenth and early twentieth centuries, using the example of Lucknow, are key to their ability to enter into the public sphere and become the hegemonic voice of India by the late nationalist period.[25]

The idea of the middle class became especially important in the literary history of Hindi in part because the political movement to establish Hindi as a national language emerged from the same processes from which the modern Indian middle class emerged in North India. The seeming universality of Hindi, which claimed to speak on behalf of a national group, goes hand in hand with the universal claims of the middle class. The emergence of the *naī kahānī* (new story) in the 1950s, with its depictions of urban life and the tensions of new domestic arrangements, is often seen as emblematic of postindependence middle class life—even if recent scholarship has traced this literatures engagement with a longer trajectory of the middle class in Hindi literature.[26] Despite the counterexample of *āñcalik* (regional) literature, typified by the works of Phanishwarnath "Renu," the Nehruvian period is often seen in Hindi as one of a stable and hegemonic discourse of the middle class, in contrast with the diverse voices that emerged along with the "disillusionment" of the post-Nehruvian period that followed.[27]

However, even as *naī kahānī* writers, such as Rajendra Yadav and Mohan Rakesh, emphasized an ideal of universalizable, individual experience, Preetha Mani's recent work has shown how this position was itself shaped by tensions related both to the trauma of partition and the instability of the postindependence Indian middle class, riven by tensions over religion, caste, and gender.[28] In Hindi literary history, the post-Nehruvian era is frequently seen as the moment in which a modernism oriented around universalizable experience breaks down in favor of new forms of political commitment and a literature of specificity that grapples with the disillusionment of the post-Nehruvian period.[29] But if we begin to examine Muktibodh's criticism, which is seemingly directed at the dominant, globalized debates over progressivism and experimentalism, we can begin to see a different trajectory: an attention to the lower middle class of the small city. In his critical writings, this idea of the lower middle class emerges as a prime motivation in Muktibodh's critique of realism—as we shall see, the unanimity of Hindi literature was broken apart not necessarily by external political changes but by the inherent tension of its construction itself. Muktibodh's work is therefore an indication of a larger trend. It may also be seen as an early indication of a fracturing of the idea of Nehruvian middle class—one that, if we consider it in light of the discussion of the Brahmarakshas in the previous chapter, may raise the question of upper-caste anxiety and resentment.[30]

Vasudhā (The World), a monthly journal published from 1956–1960, can help to explain the emergence of the lower middle class as a specific identity in Hindi literature. The journal was edited by Harishankar Parsai, who is today better known as a satirist than editor.[31] In its format, *Vasudhā* did not depart from journals such as *Kalpanā* (Imagination) or *Dinmān* (The Measure of the Day), which were more long-lasting and are better known today. However, in its small circulation and explicit support of a local network of writers, *Vasudhā* can be seen as a precursor to the small, more intimately made journals, or *laghu patrikā* (little magazine) of the late 1960s and 1970s.[32] The majority of the writers for the Jabalpur-based journal were themselves based in the mid-sized cities of Central India, such as Nagpur, the university town of Sagar, or Bhopal, and the articles frequently referred to a local identity, separate from centers of Hindi publishing in Delhi, Allahabad, and Banaras. Vasudhā describes a form of postcolonial modernity shaped by the small towns and cities, often dismissed as backwaters, that continue to make up the bulk of the Hindi reading public.[33]

Along with this regional identity, *Vasudhā* also stands out for its emphasis on the lower middle class as a specific social category. Rather than view its natural audience as a generalizable middle class, *Vasudhā* emphasized the new body of administrative professionals in postindependence India as a specific group. In 1956, for instance, a column by the writer Pramod Varma distinguished between two classes of middle-class writers:

> The first class of writers is habituated to look at every aspect of life from high above. With a telescope if necessary. They are thoughtful, educated, civilized, aesthetically minded, and fashionable. The other class of writers are,

> we may say, those who are bornof intense class-struggle. Their resulting irritation, neurosis, and despair, their awkwardness and passion, and uncompromising spirit gives their writing a unique character. As an enlightened reader, we could never agree with the critic who denies the pain of the lower-middle-class writer and, calling this the absence of a world view, wants to pass by, as well as those critics who find an absence of such neutral qualities as beauty and mastery.[34]

Varma's comments create a new space for thinking about the lower middle class. The ironic reference to a "first class" that looks at life with a telescope makes plain a sense of contempt and distance—but one unrelated to the supposed Cold War division of experimentalism and progressivism. Instead, Varma's comment shifts the distinction to matters of cultural capital; the "other class" stands out for its departure from aesthetic norms.[35] Varma's comments contradict a range of positions on the relation between literature and history in India; whereas the critic Vijaydevnarayan Sahi would see the desperation of the Hindi modernist poet in terms of the aftermath of nationalism and a loss of purpose, and critics such as Ramvilas Sharma would see in this form of awkwardness an escapism from the problem of class, Varma sees a unique form of class struggle, outside of the grand story either of the nationalist movement or the Indian left.[36]

A Writer's Diary

In 1957, Muktibodh began contributing to *Vasudha* in a series called "Ek lekhak kī ḍāyarī" (A Writer's Diary). These pieces almost always consisted of a conversation between an unnamed narrator—implicitly, given the title, Muktibodh himself—and a given interlocutor on contemporary social life, followed by complex discussions of aesthetics.[37] Most frequently, a conversation unfolds as a duo wanders through a series of urban spaces—chai stalls, disused temples, quiet shops—and occasionally, the interior space of a home. The aesthetic discussion cannot be seen outside of these seemingly digressive frames. Discussion of professional constraints, consumer objects, and domestic tension, common features of lower middle class discourse, punctuate the narratives. The wide-ranging discussions of aesthetic questions that arise, and that make up the critical message of these pieces, are thus always embedded in the context of lower-middle-class life.

One piece, "Saṛak se lekar ek bātcīt" (A Conversation on the Street), illustrates these points, mixing together a critique of *nayī kavitā* with a sketch of rejection and frustration. The piece projects its aims with its title, indicating that it is meant to be a conversation in a new kind of public space. Indeed, the conversation plays out in a small tea stall in Indore, with an anonymous friend. Neither the friend nor the author is named explicitly. The friend, like the author, seems to be a writer; a recent poem has been rejected for publication. The publisher told the friend that his poem was too passionate. This is ironic, the author notes, because a recent, widely circulated article of the journal *Ājkal* argued for just this quality.[38] The two then go on to discuss the hypocrisy of Hindi literature, which, despite arguing for authenticity and passion, cannot accept in literature kinds of feelings that are prevalent in the contemporary Hindi poetry being written in cities like Indore. Most of the pieces proceed in this way: the pieces stress, again and again, the characters that populate the small cities of postindependence India. The interlocutors are composed of the schoolmasters, journalists, and clerks who make up the lower middle class of Pramod Varma.

As the two begin to discuss the social context of poetry, they insistently link up the idea of objective aesthetic standards with the feelings of the lower middle class. Muktibodh claims that the editor saw passion, or *āveś*, as "prose," and not "verse." This refers not only to the shift towards free verse in *nayī kavitā*, but also towards the idea that *nayī kavitā* was meant to be prosaic, "prose" thus referring to the emphasis on a restricted sense of the everyday. He goes on to note that the passion described was felt by the editor to be "something that only refers to the self [*vyakti-sambaddh*], personal, not intimate [*ātmīya*]." This is a subtle distinction—the term used, *ātmīya*, is used to describe intimacy, comfort, and closeness. Here, whereas *vyakti* refers to the concrete individual and the social circumstances that shape them, *ātmīya* gives a sense of comfort, relatability—perhaps something comparable to the Dutch word *gezellig*, or the Spanish *simpático*. The passion of the piece, then, is something too personal, and repellant, rather than something that might build a closer relationship with the reader.

What he says next, however, both emphasizes this point and pushes it in a specific direction. After underlining the idea of *nayī kavitā* repelled by the "passion" produced by the experiences of everyday life, he goes on to explicitly produce a theory of elites and literature: "The deciding factor," he tells his friend, "is not intellect, but classiness [*bhadratā*]."[39] In using *bhadratā,* Muktibodh uses a term common in Bengali—at the root of the term *bhadralok,* or educated gentry—but relatively rare in Hindi.[40] He goes on to explain that this is the *bhadratā* of the metropolis—of the rapidly growing force in Hindi literature that was gravitating towards Delhi. As he puts it, "This classiness [*bhadratā*] is not the elegance of the qasbah, it's something shared among all of the wealthy and classy civilizations of the big capitals. These large state capitals are now being gathered into a *world capital* like Delhi. The qasbah is being drawn towards the city."[41] Muktibodh displays here a keen sense of the geography of Hindi literature, and the increasing anxiety over the prominence of Delhi after independence.[42] He goes on:

> You are a half-educated poor person from a city or a qasbah. Your circumstances are filled with bloody, human reality. You are being ground up in the wheel of a system [*yantra-cakra*]. In this suspended state, you try to encounter reality. Your attraction to the scars of a painful reality, towards passion, is natural. But they will not view this impulse with a positive eye. You want to research—ethically—your own reality. For them, this action is divorced from the context of life. Don't present your ground down circumstances and activities to them in their naked, animal colors. This is not art.
>
> But do they say this openly? Absolutely not. They are not foolish enough to become the target of others' anger. But the inclinations which they adopt for *nayī kavitā,* even if they appear blameless from above, are made use of so that a critical and sharp expression cannot become respectable—it becomes something fit only for the street.[43]

Muktibodh's language echoes, almost word for word, the statement of Pramod Varma quoted above. This is no surprise; the two were close friends, and Varma himself references Muktibodh in his column. These statements were part of a growing critique of post-independence Hindi taking shape in small towns, something that would become a crucial element of Muktibodh's reception, culminating in Shamsher Bahadur Singh's description of Muktibodh as a forgotten, outsider poet.[44] But where Pramod Varma's critique is primarily sociological, discussing the life of such a writer, Muktibodh connects this idea of the lower middle class to the aesthetic outcome. Not only is the writer "ground up in the wheel of a system"; this experience is intimately connected to the way in which they "make acquaintance with reality." Tellingly, Muktibodh pitches this as the experience of a hypothetical everyman, defined by geography and education in ways that exclude from consideration any other categories of identity, such as religion, language, gender, or caste.[45] The sharp-edged depiction of the literary universe of Hindi underlines a sense of betrayal that a seeming unity has fractured into a new, institutionally superior upper middle class and a "half-educated," poor lower middle class. Like Varma, Muktibodh emphasizes the inherent value of the seemingly unappealing and unaesthetic experiences of this group.

By the late 1950s, ideas associated with *nayī kavitā* were increasingly being critiqued—particularly those associated with the journal *Nayī Kavitā*, and with critics such as Lakshmikant Varma, who emphasized the importance of individual experience and an attention to the individual moment of that experience. This idea was later critiqued by progressive critics as *kṣaṇvād*, or "momentism," and compared to the idea of a "cult of experience" as described by Philip Rahv in *Partisan Review*.[46] But as Muktibodh's essay demonstrates, critique was not coming from the stalwarts on the left like Ram Vilas Sharma. Sharma, who would consider Muktibodh's writing as escapism, would consider a great deal of *nayī kavitā* writers as "dwarves," and would advocate instead for the aesthetics associated with the 1930s emergence of progressive poetry in Hindi.[47] In that sense, Muktibodh's position can be read as an emergent literature, distinct from any supposed split between *pragativād* and *prayogvād*, which would be at the basis of more openly antagonist literature such as *akavitā* (nonpoetry), which would emerge in the 1960s.[48]

In another piece, "Vīrkar," the emphasis shifts from the sociology of literature to the nature and quality of this experience. Again, the piece begins with a discussion between two characters. The friend, Virkar, who is "an ordinary *high school teacher,*" is contrasted with Muktibodh, who ironically presents himself as a refined, enlightened, and bohemian poet; after summing up Virkar's life and qualities, he adds that "his greatest quality was his friendship with me."[49] He describes his and Muktibodh's class and circumstances as so different that their work can only appear "obscure" to mainstream literature. Muktibodh claims that "a writer of our class has an overload of experiences—but he forces them all *underground,*" using the English word.[50] But unlike the previous piece, here the conversation partner interrupts, mocking the narrator's despair and replacing the image of the underground with one of the ocean:

> Come on, get up, you fool! Let's go home, it's getting late. . . . Well sir, this poet of yours drowns in these waves that keep washing over him, his eyes fill up with water so he swims with his eyes closed! But then he cannot pull his head out of the water and see the blue expanse of the ocean! It would take a great mental effort to recreate these things in a series of examples. He doesn't have the time for that. And if he does, then only a little.[51]

By contrasting the underground with the ocean, the image replaces repression with omnipresence—a series of waves. The ocean of experience is invisible, not because the writer forces experience below the surface, but because the writer is unable to express the overwhelming, omnipresent experience of his social world. The speaker's further reflection on this idea merges the images of the underground and the ocean, creating a process of creation and sublimation:

> I was quiet. Up to a point, he was absolutely right. Now look at me! If you consider the world into which I enter every day, it's a kind of dream story [*svapna-kathā*]. A

> grand novel. A story in images [*citra-katha*], filled with so many scenes, beautiful and sensitive, full of terror and despair. A great deal is possible even if I restrict myself to the theme of my own life. But what do I do? While living my real life, I cannot simultaneously undergo sensitive experiences and present those very same experiences in an image created by the imagination. To do that I need to go home and become absorbed. For this reason I have theorized, whether anyone likes it or not, that if these sensitive matters and truths are pushed into the underground, then that's not such a bad thing.[52]

The elemental images of the sea and the underground, battling and merging together, ask the reader to consider the aesthetics of the lower middle class not as condition, but as process. The image separates an oceanic, inaccessible world of experience from a private space of the imagination. In doing so, the experiences that would otherwise be desperate, neurotic, and unappealing become the material for an aesthetics of imaginative transformation. Crucial to this aesthetics, in its construction, is narrative structure—described here as story, novel, or even *citra-kathā*, a narrative formed of images.[53] This tension between narrative structure, individual image, and expression becomes, eventually, a crucial element of Muktibodh's aesthetics.

The language of "Vīrkar" reflects this change through introducing a new vocabulary, one that describes the newly fluid aesthetic process through the language of classical Sanskrit aesthetics. Virkar now refers to the speaker as a "sympathetic medium," or *samvedanātmak mādhyam*. *Samvednā* is one of the more contentious terms in Hindi literary language. The term is at the core of discourses of realism from the 1930s—as in, for instance, Premchand's call for a sympathetic perspective.[54] In this context, as a *samvedanātmak mādhyam*, the sympathy of the speaker instead turns inwards, away from a general sense of sympathy, towards a self-conscious sensibility to his own circumstances. Sensed experiences can be seen, from this perspective, as *sthāyī bhāv*, or stable expressions. Borrowing from the conceptual framework of rasa, the reconception of the experiences of the lower middle classes as a *sthāyī bhāv* makes a specific claim on the aesthetic standards that the piece begins with by claiming that they can be integrated within the secondary emotions of rasa.[55]

The essay ends with Muktibodh once again in reverie:

> I was lost in myself. Slowly, we began to move apart. I began to repeat in my mind—truly the life-materials associated with literature are too many. Even if not exactly alongside spontaneously occurring various sense-experiences, still, step by step, in some form, the projection of experiences also proceeds upon the screen of imagination [*kalpanā-paṭal par*]. How can this fact be denied? Although, Virkar had not presented this point in such a clear manner. To truthfully present the temporal images of these experience-projections upon the screen of the imagination, there was a necessity not only for deep thought and curation, but also, much before this, a necessity for a *world-view* [*viśva-dṛṣṭi*]. In the absence of this view, we cannot see the importance of our own experiences, and for this reason we give preference to only a few specific experiences or illusion of experiences [*anubhavābhās*], and suffocate [*galā ghoṇṭ*] everything else.[56]

Muktibodh here navigates the landscape of late 1950s cultural criticism, between a modernist ideal of experience and a progressive ideal of committed literature. By claiming the importance of a world view here, Muktibodh is gesturing towards the progressives in a way that will seem, to Nirmal Varma in 1981, as if he is pulling back from the imaginative capacities with which the passage begins.[57]

The piece therefore concludes quite far from its initial depiction of the lower middle class, as a sociological group. By the end of "Vīrkar," the emphasis is not on the sociological composition of the lower middle class, but rather on the quality of that experience, its relation to reality, and the techniques through which it can be understood and expressed. The relationship to rasa-theory gives the piece a powerful framework through which the seemingly inadmissible experiences of contemporary lower-middle-class life can be expressed within the idioms of Hindi modernism. But in shifting towards the question of aesthetic process, the essay opens up the larger question of the nature of that process. The earlier discussion of the inadmissibility of experience now becomes the challenge of how to actually present that experience, the necessity of finding new ways of transferring these new experiences into literature. But "Vīrkar" and other essays do not fully address this, even as they make it the essential subject of Muktibodh's aesthetic. It is in a more extended piece that aesthetic process is more fully addressed.

The Third Moment of Expression

"Vīrkar" presents, in a condensed form, the shift away from a description of the lower middleclass and its relation to the sociology of Hindi literature towards a theory of the imagination and its role in creative process. The most complete description of this theory, however, takes place in "Tīsrā kṣaṇ" (The Third Moment), which is generally cited as Muktibodh's most important work of criticism.[58] Published in *Vasudhā* in November 1958, the piece builds on the digressive, conversational style of previous pieces, but stands apart in that it develops and presents an entire and complete theory of art that, in its comprehensiveness, acts as a capstone to Muktibodh's aesthetics and has cemented its prominent place in Muktibodh's reception. "Tīsrā kṣaṇ" is also an ideal place to examine the confrontation between the individual and the social, which was perhaps the main subject of Muktibodh's aesthetics as a left Hindi modernist. It both develops Muktibodh's theory of aesthetic experience and embeds that elaboration in the specific historical context of Hindi aesthetic and cultural history in which he worked.

"Tīsrā kṣaṇ" describes a series of conversations with a man named Keshav. Keshav is presented as an old school friend, a friendship somewhat forced by connections between the two boys' families. Muktibodh finds Keshav severe and dull, and Keshav misses few opportunities to dampen Muktibodh's romantic enthusiasm. Nevertheless, Muktibodh has memories of wandering through the forests and barren lands near their home and of long discussions of philosophy and politics, which in the context of their youth in the 1920s and 1930s includes the waxing of the Gandhian era and the first movements of criticism towards it, the news of five-year plans and economic advancements in the Soviet Union, and the rising popularity of yoga and other mystical exercises—of which Keshav in particular is quite fond—and the popularity of philosophies of *advaitā vedāntā* or nondualism, which posits the essential if unrealized unity of the individual with the divine.[59]

Just as "Vīrkar" presents the world of the lower middle class as both underground and ocean, "Tīsrā kṣaṇ" takes care to present a nuanced view of the experiential world of its two protagonists, which it frequently depicts in terms of a vast underworld. "Tīsrā kṣaṇ" takes this much further, however; the piece is as much an exploration of the social and imaginative world of the lower middle class as it is a work of aesthetics. The opening of the piece, in which Keshav and the speaker explore the landscape around Ujjain, an ancient city and pilgrimage center in Central India. The characters are frequently imagined to have an affinity with a magical, underground world: Keshav, in particular, is thought to have lived in some other life in a city of the past:

> Inside the womb of the earth is an ancient lake. Around its shores lie frightening steps, terrifying statues of the gods, mysterious old dark-chambered temples. History has suppressed and buried all of this; covered by depths upon depths of soil, layers upon layers, mountains upon mountains, the whole scene is buried under the earth and invisible. There are bungalows, and beautiful girls wander around wearing sparkling clothes. In one of those bungalows lives my friend Keshav who, maybe in his previous birth, or a birth even before that, must have drunk the water of that lake in the womb of the earth, must have walked along its shores.[60]

The scene mingles together the idea of Ujjain—which, though a small city by the 1950s, was one of the most important locations of the ancient Sanskrit world—with the modern, middle-class city.[61] The "mysterious old dark-chambered temples" mix with bungalows, the distinctly colonial and postcolonial house style that dominated the Civil Lines and modern cantonment cities that, in modern India, frequently adjoin the "older," implicitly precolonial city.[62] The passage builds on the familiar, Dostoevskian idea of the "underground" of lower middle class life to present it as a mythical present: rather than merely depict suppressed experience, it now is a repository of historical memory, and Keshav, with his combination of cold, practical careerism and mystical interest in Yoga, does more than emphasize the sociological ideas of "Vīrkar." Instead, the image of the city by the lake, and its combination of an ancient space with contemporary India, foreshadows the role of the mythical and the fantastic in Muktibodh's aesthetics of imagination:

> I'll tell you something. Whenever I express an opinion or feeling I become very excited. There is darkness in it, and there are stairs in the darkness. The stairs are wet. The lowest stair is underwater. Deep black water. And I, I myself, am scared of that dark water. Someone is sitting in that deep black water. Maybe it's me. A strip of moonlight is spread across that deep and utterly dark black water, in which my own eyes are sparkling as if two blue pearls were lit up from within.[63]

The image of steps leading into a pool of underground water also appear in "Brahamakshas," which was discussed in the first chapter. Here, however, the image is deployed to illustrate the imagination as something buried underground, separate, and only partially accessible. This idea of the imagination precedes an aesthetic experience that would seem to defy the obscurity of an underground well:

> We got up and left and ended up standing below a far-off peepal tree. Suddenly I was startled. I don't know why, but I was terrified of some strange feeling. In the darkness beneath that peepal, I told him in a weird and excited voice, "Evening, colorful evening, has pooled together inside me, settled there. It has a strange, colorful power. I'm scared of that tender, burning, magical power—as if I'm scared of myself." And I was really trembling.
>
> As I was speaking the evening had grown dark. The tree took on the personality of a stupa. The birds went quiet. At once, a stillness spread everywhere. And

> then, campai flower flew up from inside this stillness on the heights of yellow waves. The moonlight that hung on the dome of the college and the tops of the trees shimmered like a white dhoti.
>
> At once Keshav, placing his still, loose hand on my shoulder, said, "Do you remember how you once asked me the definition of beauty?"
>
> Not paying attention, I said in a voice full of disinterest, "Of course."
>
> "Now you're experiencing beauty on your own."
>
> I don't know what I was experiencing. I can only say that some sweet indescribable force had jolted me from the inside. I can only say that inside me was a cavern and a personality. That's what I felt. I had felt it a few times before. But now it had truly grabbed me from the inside. "What I am myself I have become in itself. I've become 'expanded' from myself, unique, non-self!"[64]

The aestheticized experience of landscape, with its nature imagery, would appear, at first, to be far from the idea of the imagination as an underground source. But the passage turns at once towards a sense of alienation between the subject of aesthetic experience, the object, and the experience itself. That experience has a "tender, burning, magical power," and will, by the end of this passage, be described as a "cavern," echoing the earlier language.[65]

Gradually, the essay turns towards a dialogue between Keshav and Muktibodh on aesthetic process. The dialogue depicts a gradual transformation from the aesthetic process presented by Keshav's more conservative aesthetics to Muktibodh's idea of "three moments." The latter, which presents the work of art as a process of experience, imagination, and expression, is similar to a range of romantic theories of the imagination.[66] Muktibodh presents art as the result of three moments: the first being experience; the second, the transformation of experience, by the imagination, into fantasy (for which Muktibodh almost invariably uses the English word); and the third, the transformation of the fantasy into an artistic object. Muktibodh's theory, at least in "Tīsrā kṣaṇ," focuses mostly on the fantasy, including the ways in which it becomes something autonomous from the mental process. Paralleling the frequent discussion of the imagination as a magnetic force, Muktibodh draws from the language of a nuclear chain reaction.[67] Once experience takes the form of a fantasy, that fantasy then begins to autonomously transform itself as it takes on more and more materials in the process of expression within language: "That which passes through this process is the flow of all of personality and life. The *fantasy* flows through this ceaselessly, developing and changing the whole time. In this way the *fantasy*, shedding its original form, takes on an entirely new one. The *fantasy* will move so far from that original *fantasy* which is being contained in words that it becomes difficult to say whether the *fantasy* is a reaction of its original form."[68]

Muktibodh goes on to describe the fantasy as possessing a "fundamental form," which means that it cannot, by its nature, align with any specific social fact. In this sense, then, the fantasy can—and frequently is in Hindi criticism—read as a defense of the autonomy of art, and the relationship between the autonomous fantasy and social reality. But I would also like to draw our attention to the insistence, in Muktibodh's discussion of this process, on what he here calls the "flow of all of personality and life." Again, whereas in earlier pieces this material was depicted as suppressed, here, in the description of a romantic aesthetic process, that material now exists in abundance and acts as a kind of nuclear fuel, transforming and sustaining the atomic process of artistic creation.

The prominent use of the term fantasy, written in English in the original Hindi, points towards a range of intellectual influences, including both the original theories of romanticism in Germany and England and twentieth-century interpretations on the left. The most important of these is possibly the work of Christopher Caudwell, a British Communist who, along with Ralph Fox, exerted an outsize influence on the Indian left before their deaths in the Spanish Civil War.[69] Caudwell's *Illusion and Reality*, prominently makes the argument for a left engagement with theories of the imagination and psychoanalysis.[70] However, there does not seem to be any direct analysis of Caudwell's writings in Muktibodh's work. Similarly, discussions of left approaches to the imagination in Soviet journals in English frequently echo the terminology of the imagination, and the fantasy, that appears in essays such as "Tīsrā kṣaṇ."[71] None of these sources, however, can definitively be said to shape Muktibodh's idea of three moments, especially not when we consider the depth of aesthetic process explored in this essay.

"Tīsrā kṣaṇ," in its synthesis of Romantic theories of the imagination, modern revisions of rasa, and left debates over the relation of art to the social, can be read in terms of the intellectual history of the Nehruvian 1950s as a key response to the problems posed by Hindi modernist poetics and, in particular, the debates over political commitment and personal expression that are discussed through Hindi criticism of this time. But the seemingly irrelevant conversation is crucial to its underlying message and importance to Hindi literary history. As in "Vīrkar," the interplay between experience and imagination is the most important element of artistic process. The reason for this—and what sets this theory apart from contemporary debates on literature—is that it elevates the experiences of lower-middle-class life, and places them at the center of its analysis.

In addition to the pieces that were published in *Vasudhā*, Muktibodh's collected works today include a wide range of unpublished pieces that were often more scattered and intimate and blur the line between criticism and fiction. In these pieces, Muktibodh indicates, repeatedly, that he felt that after independence the life of the educated lower middle class was stagnating in ways that could not find a place in contemporary discourse. I will discuss in further chapters more about how that found articulation in his fiction and poetry, but in this chapter, I am concerned with how he viewed his aesthetics as inseparable from that problem. At the same time, Muktibodh was deeply committed to a political system and philosophy. So while all the evidence indicates that Muktibodh saw the ultimate goal of his literature as contributing towards a horizon of political revolution, he saw that his own position, and the position of those around him, was the basis from which he had to work. As he puts it in these writings, these experiences, of frustration, underemployment, shame, and guilt, and the emotions produced by these experiences, seemed to fit neither in progressive literature—which, by the 1950s, was increasingly beset by acrimonious debate—nor in Hindi modernism, which at the time was rigidly focused on the universalization of individual experience, with an implicit emphasis on the more educated and connected middle class.

But as "Tīsrā kṣaṇ" shows, the possibilities of the romantic theory of the imagination, and especially of the autonomous process of the fantasy, allowed Muktibodh to newly consider the entire imaginative world of the lower middle class as part of his canvas. The dialogue between Keshav and Muktibodh becomes a crucial moment in postindependence Hindi literature not only because it depicts the hopeless world of the postindependence lower middle class, but because it showed the ways in which the boundless ocean of that imaginative world could be tapped, explored, and expressed.

Realism as Underground

If the fantasy emerges at the center of Muktibodh's thought, it is because it enabled him to center the imaginative world of the lower middle class. In doing so, it evoked not only the growing self-awareness of the lower middle class after independence and emerging world of life in the small cities and towns of the Hindi speaking world, but also a growing frustration with both *nayī kavitā* and left literary aesthetics. In the years following his death, a series of prominent writers, such as Vinod Kumar Shukla, Rajesh Joshi, and Uday Prakash, took up different aspects of this legacy, so that Muktibodh's work is often thought of as a precursor of a literature of fantasy in Hindi.[72]

For that reason, I would like to close this chapter by returning to Muktibodh's critique of realism, and his distinction between perspective and style, that has such a strong parallel to the work of Bertolt Brecht. Muktibodh's *Kāmāyanī: ek punarvicār* (Kāmāyanī: A Reconsideration; hereafter referred to as the *Punarvicār*) is a monograph-length critique of Jayshankar Prasad's epic late *chāyāvād* poem *Kāmāyanī*. Written around 1960, the monograph, and especially its preface, is the location of one of Muktibodh's most famous definitions of fantasy and critique of realism, one that appears uncannily similar at times to prominent Western Marxist critiques.

Kāmāyanī itself, a long, mythological poem that was widely received as an attempt to recreate the epic form of Sanskrit *kāvya*, was an object of continuous critical discussion after its publication in 1936. *Kāmāyanī* has a prominent place in Hindi literary history, widely considered one of the most important products of pre-independence *chāyāvād* poetry. The poem was composed of several mythological stories, but primarily that of Manu, the survivor of a great primordial flood; this story was then presented as an allegory for modern life, as interpreted through Prasad's monist philosophy. The poem, written in a quantitative, thirty-one-measure meter, begins with Manu looking out over a flooded, destroyed world, before describing his relationship with two women, Shraddha and Ira. Shraddha, whose name means faith, is presented as an ideal of womanhood, whereas Iṛā represents rationalism and the idea of progress. Eventually, after a series of events with both women, the poem ends with Manu's realization of the unity of all creation at Mount Kailasha, through a vision of the dance of Shiva.[73]

As one of the most influential works of long narrative poetry prior to Muktibodh's own long poems, *Kāmāyanī* is a natural place to debate the questions of genre, realism, and the fantastic that animate Muktibodh's criticism. Prior debate over this poem had focused on the relation of *Kāmāyanī* to the aesthetic ideals of Sanskrit *kāvya,* and Muktibodh's *Punarvicār* was, to an extent, criticized for the way in which it dealt with these qualities.[74] The *Punarvicār* dismissed *Kāmāyanī*'s claims to mythological truth, and analyzed the poem instead as a conservative, feudal reaction to modernity, driven by Prasad's own anxieties over the loss of status he perceived in the early twentieth century. Because *kāvya* maintained such tremendous prestige, this aspect of the *Punarvicār* drew a great deal of criticism and was seen as disrespectful to the legacy of Prasad's work. Ultimately, however, it is *Kāmāyanī*'s role as a vehicle for Muktibodh's critique of realism and defense of his own long poems that is the most important critical contribution of the *Punarvicār*.

As in "Tīsrā kṣaṇ," the *Punarvicār* presents a theory of artistic production focused on the individual imagination, in which a complex interplay between social experience and individual reaction produces an autonomous work of art. "Tīsrā kṣaṇ," however, focuses on the social context of experience and its transformation through the imagination. The *Punarvicār* is more concerned with defining the final work of art, and although it presents the same process, it does so in a way that emphasizes a complex sense of stasis. The first paragraph of the preface, for instance, instead of presenting art in terms of three consecutive moments of time, presents it in terms of its triangularity, with the sides of a triangle representing the individual, the social, and the transformative imagination. The shift from the temporal to the spatial focuses on a stable system, presenting a cohesive work of art—reflecting not only the emphasis in the *Punarvicār* on practical criticism, but also its argument in that the work of art can be understood as inherently socially engaged, even as it seemingly departs from realistic aesthetics.

As opposed to the imaginative but sometimes opaque discussions of pieces such as "Vīrkar" and "Tīsrā kṣaṇ," the preface of the *Punarvicār* directly takes up the problem of realism. In this it is comparable to other pieces written late in Muktibodh's life that directly criticize the proscriptivism of the left, and that eventually led to an anonymous letter written to Amrit Dange, then the chairman of the Communist Party of India.[75] In that letter, written in English, Muktibodh explicitly defended the progressive possibilities of Hindi modernist poetry. The *Punarvicār*, however, stands out not necessarily for presenting a critique of restricted definitions of realism, but for presenting a new, positive definition of realism, which builds on ideas of imaginative process and rasa aesthetics:

> The work of art recreates lived experience through the imagination. Embedded within the Realist style, the work of art presents images of the Real, according to an order arranged by the internal rules of the Real itself. However, within the Romantic, emotionalist [*bhāvavādī*] style, the imagination has more freedom, and for that reason presents the particulars of experience through compound images [*samaṣṭi-citroṃ*], through symbolic images. Within the fantasy, the imagination of the poet, while presenting the essential particularities of life, presents a kind of image poem [*citrāvalī*] that causes the objective [*tathyātmak*] life, which has made experienced particularities explicit, to become greatly implicit, subsidiary, behind the stage [*nepathyavāsī*]. In essence, in the fantasy the aspect of emotion is predominant, and the causes of the emotion becomes implicit and subsidiary, while at the same time that emotional element, exciting the imagination, creating more and more images, presents such an embodied form [*mūrt-vidhān*], which is true only to its own form. In this tangible form the causes of emotion

> are only indicated, only echoed. However, without that backstage foundation, that underground—deep within the earth—without the cause of emotions, that tangible form cannot articulate its relevance to life.[76]

In this dense passage, Muktibodh indeed parallels Brecht's distinction between a realism as form and as perspective, but whereas Brecht frames his critique in terms of *treibenden Kräften,* Muktibodh emphasizes relationship between reality and the work of art, defined as a compound of multiple images, both combined together and maintaining a symbolic charge. Rather than present a narrative structure that mimics experienced reality, what Muktibodh describes as an emotionalist style presents an image in which the real maintains a subsidiary, underground position. Much of this passage draws from the language of rasa theory, in which there is a complex relationship between the emotion, or *bhāva,* which is expressed within a piece of theater or literature, sentiment, and *rasa,* which results from their enactment. Here, similarly, Muktibodh insists on the manifestation of *bhāva* through an embodied, concrete image, or *mūrt-vidhān.*

The passage ends by referring to the backstage, underground formation of reality, without which the emotion cannot take a tangible form. In this, the *Punarvicār* echoes the language of the earlier "Vīrkar" and "Tīsrā kṣaṇ," which emphasized the necessary transformation of experience in the "underground" of the imagination. In the *Punarvicār,* likewise, Muktibodh insists on the "cause of emotions" and the interrelationship between the image and its background. But whereas those earlier pieces were shot through with lower-middle-class life, and made clear that there was a constitutive relationship between the two, the *Punarvicār* is programmatic in its presentation of a model of art. This tendency culminates in this manifesto-like statement: "In a realist style are presented the images of the real, bound according to the rules of reality's nature and pace [*svarūp aur gati*]. In other words, the Realist style is a depiction of the objective-emotional aspect [*vastu-pakṣ*], and on the basis of that affinity articulates the emotional aspect."[77] The passage, once again, seems to recapitulate debates over realism and expressionism. The realist style is bound, by its narrative and generic objective, the *vastu-pakṣ.* Through framing aesthetic process in the language of rasa, realism becomes a relation between *vastu*, or object, and *bhāv*, or expression. The realist style, in which *vastu* dominates, becomes one that is organized around a narrative framework determined by that objective style. The contrast, then, is not between solipsism and social engagement, but between two methods of determining the same ultimate artistic objective.

Having distinguished between a realist style and a realist perspective, the piece goes on to reframe this distinction as one between craft and spirit:

> There is a difference [*antar*] between the craft [*śilp*] and soul [*ātmā*] of art. This is all too possible that a so-called realist artist looks at reality with colored glasses, and through an impure perception of that reality, makes an impure analysis, and in this way he perverts that reality, all the while believing that reality is according to his understanding, and that may be the form of his reality—he has deformed the images of reality through his imagination.[78]

Here, Muktibodh again makes an argument that can be seen as a direct critique of orthodox realism, which might be seen in many different locations. The distinction between *śilp* and *ātmā,* offers further evidence of the way in which Muktibodh frames his intervention in a classical aesthetic vocabulary. The problem of realism, which elsewhere in Muktibodh's work is seen in terms of the lower middle class, is here reframed in terms of the relation between form and content. The question of the *ātma* of art is counterposed to the craft, or *śilpa*. Through his differentiation of object, feeling, and image, he has created a space where "realism" can suddenly be redefined.

If realism can be rethought—in ways that clearly echo Brecht and other critiques of realism—as a distinction of craft, rather than social commitment alone, then how can the new product of the imagination—the distorted, deformed images—relate to an aesthetic system? Muktibodh's understanding of Prasad's own approach in *Kāmāyanī* becomes the basis for defining this new relationship between the imagination, social reality, and aesthetic process. Rather than accept *Kāmāyanī* as a depiction of myth,

Muktibodh views it as a response to the painful, contradictory relationship between Prasad and the world: "He began to oppose this nationalism—and the capitalism which was at its base—just as the idealist philosophers of the west had always done. The influence of these thinkers reached India via Bengal. And these thinkers began to tell nationalist India that it should not repeat the mistakes of the West. Ravindra's [Rabindranath Tagore] book *Nationalism* is worth reading in this context."[79]

For Muktibodh, Prasad's position, and his critique of modern life, is unacceptable. But the fantasy of his poem is crucial; to this end, the *Punarvicār* separates the fantasy from the ideological content of the poem. The necessity, therefore, of focusing on the claims to ancient pedigree becomes clearer. The claims to ancient pedigree would serve to validate the cultural nationalism of *Kāmāyanī*, which grounds its critique of modernity not in any analysis of contemporary society, but rather in contrast to an ideal past. This in particular is something Muktibodh found intolerable, not least because it would be the basis for the traumatic banning of his history textbook due to a court case brought by the Hindu Mahasabha in 1962. Muktibodh's insistence on the invalidity of Prasad's version of the past is therefore connected to a Marxist critique of Prasad's class position.

Muktibodh's positive critique of the work, however, requires a defense of its allegorical and fantastic framework. This is why Muktibodh argues that a text can maintain a fundamentally "realist point of view" even if the style is "emotionalist." *Kāmāyanī* is therefore the example of an emotionalist work, and, despite many problems with the poem, Muktibodh views it as a crucial model. The reason for this is that it succeeds in representing at a deeper level the social position of its author through a symbolic frame, rather than a realist depiction. This is then a secondary reason to critique so thoroughly the work's claims to the representation of history.

Kāmāyanī was often viewed in critical literature as a mythological epic: Muktibodh, however, saw *Kāmāyanī* as an allegorical poem not of modern life as understood through history, but rather as a depiction of the emotions and reactions of the author himself. Its importance lay in its success in using a wide range of materials to depict the imagined fantasy of Prasad, based upon his own reality and in its success in creating a poetic language and form that was successful in evoking these realities. By arguing that *Kāmāyanī* possesses a "realist point of view" through the indirect relation between feeling, or *bhāv*, and the objective, or *vibhāv*, Muktibodh reframes his theory of organic form as one in which the sensation of the first moment becomes the *vibhāv*, and the fantasy is depicted as the *bhāv*. *Kāmāyanī*, in presenting an image that "is true only to its own form," is an example of precisely the kind of poem that is possible under Muktibodh's own aesthetic theory, and it thus becomes a poetic model.

At stake in this chapter has been the history of aesthetic thought in Hindi. How can this aesthetic thought be understood in ways that are attentive to its originality, as well as its complex genealogy across multiple scales of literary criticism? In this case, Muktibodh's criticism was profoundly global in its engagement with discourses of realism and modernism, so that it seems to be occurring simultaneously with the critique of realism made by Brecht. However, this chapter also demonstrates the ways in which Muktibodh's engagement with these concepts must be read through the many strands of Hindi criticism and literary history with which he worked.

The emphasis in the *Punarvicār* on the interrelation between social reality, narrative, and image reflects a development of ideas that, even as they draw from a range of debates taking place both within Hindi and in international modernist and left aesthetics, trace a direct line that begins with the depiction of the lower middle class. The tension of his thought lies in the concept of a social reality that must be transformed through the imagination in order to take aesthetic form. Within the *Punarvicar*, this concept reaches a clarity tdriven by an extended analysis of another work of art. But these ideas also draw their clarity from their relation to Muktibodh's own aesthetic practice, in the shape of the long poems that were increasingly his primary artistic output. Ultimately, the object of the *Punarvicār* is as much these long poems as it is Jayshankar Prasad's work. The creation of these long poems draws from the complex relationship between Muktibodh's critical thought, his prose fiction, and his poetics. But as his criticism demonstrates, they also reflect the particular social circumstances of lower-middle-class life in the Nehruvian era.

Chapter Three

Muktibodh's Prose Fiction and the Question of the Real

A central theme of South Asian literary history is the complicated reception of realism, and the survival within realist modes such as the novel and the short story of nonrealist tropes, narrative structures, and the genres themselves.[1] A key text in this history is Premchand's 1936 speech to the All-India Progressive Writer's Association, eventually published as "The Aim of Literature," and that remains a key statement on realism and progressive literature in South Asia.[2] Premchand's rejection of nonrealist genres was framed as a move away from, as Ulka Anjaria writes, "elite aesthetic traditions":[3]

> Tales of sorcery [*tilasmātī kahāniyāṃ*], ghost stories [*bhūt-pret kī katha*] and tales of love and separation [*prem-vi-yog ke ākhyān*] may well have influenced us in another age, but today hold very little interest for us. Without doubt, the writer who is sensitive to human nature can describe the truths of life in the love stories of princes and in tales of sorcery, and create a work of beauty; but even these works will prove that in order to create an effect in literature, it is crucial that there is a mirror to the truths of life.[4]

Premchand mentions three distinct genres: *tilasmātī kahāniyāṃ*, *bhūt-pret kī kathā*, and *prem-viyog ke ākhyān*. The first includes both the

Persianate *dāstān* tradition that formed some of the most widely read popular literature of the nineteenth century and examples of the early novel such as Devkinandan Khatri's *Candrakāntā*. The second category, translatable as "ghost stories," gestures towards Sanskrit story cycles, including popular and frequently retold cycles such as *Baitāl pacchīsī* (Twenty-Five Tales of the Vampire Baital), and the deeper story tradition, most prominently drawn from the Sanskrit *Kathāsaritsāgar*. The third refers, in its use of the term *ākhyān*, to the genre of stories frequently associated with Sufi orders, and discussed extensively in the work of Aditya Behl. His seemingly offhand dismissal of them, therefore, betrays in fact a deep familiarity and historical typology of nonrealist genres.

Premchand's statement indicates not only that these genres would survive in some form—both in the work of Premchand and in that of the many writers who would reference him in postindependence literature—but that the rejection of nonrealist genres was rooted in intimate, lifelong familiarity with them. Even as popular fiction is subject to extensive reassessment, recent scholarship has reinforced a history of rejection in favor of realism, and contemporary popular revivals of the *dāstān* are often constituted in the light of that rejection.[5] But this polarity flattens the ambivalence of writers, such as Premchand, who continued to engage in various forms with these popular genres, and it obscures not only the survival of nonrealist genres, but their memory within realism itself.[6]

Further complicating this picture, the intersection between realist literatures and nonrealist elements is today seen almost exclusively through the rubric of magical realism. As Mariano Siskind has shown, the idea of magical realism, despite its purported origins in interwar German art prior to *Neue Sachlichkeit*, took distinct form with the work of Alejo Carpentier.[7] Even prior to the coordinated international success of *Cien Años de Soledad*, however, it was frequently defined in universalistic terms, rather than Carpentier's insistence on the political possibilities of magical realism to depict the realities of marginalized groups.[8] In the case of South Asian literature, magical realism is perceived through, and bound up in, the larger "boom" of South Asian literature in the late twentieth century. As Roanne Kantor has argued in her recent work, there are strong parallels between the relation of South Asian literature on the global market and the success of Latin

American literature prior to this. Magical realism, most crucially through the success of *Midnight's Children* in 1981, became so associated with South Asian fiction that, as Kantor notes, texts such as Sa'adat Hasan Manto's "Toba Tek Singh," which bore neither a historical connection to magical realism nor any of the formal qualities associated with it—except for a certain vagueness of its setting—came to be depicted as magical realism, solely because they departed from and critiqued the realist mode of the progressives.[9] Similarly, in Muktibodh's prose fiction, although there are strong parallels between some of the goals and tropes of magical realism, ultimately these short stories take up their own, specific approach to the fantastic.

Building on the reconceptualization of realism implied by magical realism, recent work posits various forms of "peripheral" arealisms as part of a larger configuration of responses to global capitalism. Although in the introduction to this book I discussed how this discourse relates to the position of the lyric in world literature, it also shapes the ways in which we read prose literatures. Nonrealist elements in prose fiction, both through the discourse of magical realism and the more recent scholarship of peripheral realism, sees these literatures primarily in terms of the novel, and primarily in terms of the hybridity and global cosmopolitan associated with postcolonial literature. It is telling, for instance, that language as a category is almost completely absent for Pheng Cheah's account of postcolonial literary worlding.[10] Thus, the fantastic in prose literatures exists in an irresolvable tension with multiple discourses of modern literature, unable to be seen outside of these lenses even as it frequently does not fit within it.

A consideration of nonrealist elements of narrative literatures, therefore, has to navigate between assimilating them to possibly inappropriate global models such as magical realism and taking into account the tense discursive space in which they are deployed in specific literary cultures. The task, therefore, is to disentangle the multiple genealogies of the fantastic in South Asian prose literatures, both in order to see their purpose and to understand how they are brought about to specifically respond to certain pressures. In the case of this study, as I have discussed in the second chapter, Muktibodh's critique of realism had as much to do with his idea of the lower middle class in postindependence India as it did with a more global series of debates over realism that are more familiar. Similarly, as we will see, Muktibodh experiments with realism in prose fiction in ways that, at first glance, could easily be read as a form of magical realism. Such a reading would even have the benefit of drawing upon a similar political mode of critique that was essential to magical realism in the work of Alejandro Carpentier and others. To read it in this way, however, would both force Muktibodh into speaking on behalf of spaces of marginalization to which his work would be alien and also miss the specific genealogy of his own experimentation with the fantastic. This separate genealogy, through Muktibodh, creates its own lineage in Hindi literature that sets it apart from the direct influence of magical realism in the works of Rushdie and others, and constitutes a specific tradition of engagement with the fantastic, even if at times it draws from a similar politics towards literature.

Scholarship on magical realism—and realism in general—has focused overwhelmingly on the novel, taking it to be the primary genre of narrative theorization and social totality. As multiple scholars have pointed out, however, the most prominent narrative genre in Hindi and other South Asian literatures has been not the novel but the short story.[11] Recent work in English has begun to complicate the model of the short story as existing in a minor relationship to the novel in a South Asian context. Preetha Mani, for instance, argues that the short story in South Asia was developed not necessarily with reference to the novel, but in a contentious relationship to the lyric poem. Citing the criticism of figures such as Rajendra Yadav, Mani argues that postindependence short story writers often counterposed their idea of the short story not to the novel, but to the poem.[12]

Preetha Mani's recent work on *nayī kahānī* argues for a "modernist realism" as the aesthetic category of Rajendra Yadav (1929–2013) and other short story writers associated with the group.[13] In Mani's argument, *nayī kahānī* authors such as Rajendra Yadav defined the short story against both a modernism that they associated with Agyeya's individualist short stories and a sense of social responsibility they associated with Premchand and his idea of *ādarśonmukh yathārthvād*.[14] In the preface to his 1966 anthology *Ek duniyā, samānantar* (One World, Parallel), Yadav discusses *nayī kahānī* in terms that were drawn as much from aesthetic debates around Hindi modernist poetry—*nayī kavitā*—as they were from the problems of realism and narrative that a reader might expect. He contrasts the ideal short story with the "vertical" of *nayī kavitā* and the "horizontal": "the story is neither the personal story of the 'I,' nor the impersonal reporting of circumstances."[15] As genre, then, the short story was made to exist on an axis in which *nayī kavitā* played an essential part. This definition underlines both the inherent instability of genre and the crucial role of the *nayī kavitā* poem in defining a literature of subjectivity. The result is that genre takes on a normative role in expressing questions not only of literary form, but of political subjectivity and social identification.

Poetry and Prose

Nirmal Verma was one of the most prominent writers who were frequently associated with *nayī kahānī*—it was, in fact, Namvar Singh's analysis of Verma's "Parinde," in his book *Kahānī, nayī kahānī*, that set many of parameters of the new story.[16] Verma's work, which frequently featured anonymized characters in strange, unnamed cities, departed from the generic parameters associated with the short stories—especially the fine-grained studies of middle-class life associated with writers such as Rajendra Yadav.[17] Verma, in approaching Muktibodh, sees him both through the prism of political debate at the time and through the critical discourse of genre and the short story.

His 1981 essay "Muktibodh kī gadya kathā" (Muktibodh's Prose Fiction), published in the Bhopal journal *Pūrvagraha* at the height of Muktibodh's reception and coinciding with the release of most of his short fiction, forms a crucial document for understanding how Muktibodh's prose fiction is understood. It can therefore be seen as one of the first, inaugural moments in the new understanding of Muktibodh that was central to *Pūrvagraha*: one that was dependent not only on Muktibodh as an alienated, postcolonial subject, but also on Muktibodh as equally a poet and a short story writer. For this reason, in his essay, the politics of understanding Muktibodh and his legacy intersect directly with the politics of genre and literary form.

Verma frames Muktibodh's fiction as a crisis of postindependence life:

> Several Hindi writers have written on the boredom, meaninglessness, and desperation of the small city, but Muktibodh was the only writer who captured, in all its weakness, self-delusion, and scrubby [*bīhaṛ*] nightmares, the spiritual crisis of the qasbah-dwelling Indian—which is a story not only of external reality, but is in itself a document of their souls. This is one reason why we cannot draw a line between his stories, his essays, and his diary—all his prose writing, piercing through traditional disciplines, becomes a single sharp, pained thought.[18]

For Verma, all of Muktibodh's prose literature centers on this same, dominating issue of what he calls the "qasbah-dwelling Indian," which Muktibodh would have likely called the "lower middle class." The qasbah is defined here not in terms of a networked sociality, as it is often thought of in recent scholarship, but relationally, in contrast to the village and the city.[19] If the city and the country present two poles of modern Indian experience, then the qasbah is that which offers neither of these possibilities—presenting instead, it seems, an endless void.

Verma's definition of Muktibodh's lower-middle-class or qasbah identity, however, is predicated entirely on his prose works, and by extension on a distinction between prose and poetry. Verma's essay therefore becomes at the same time a critique of the Hindi short story via Muktibodh's prose fiction and an interpretation of Muktibodh's work, dependent upon a theory of genre in which poetry, with its explicit moments of fantasy and revolution, is posed against prose, with its depiction of lower-middle-class paralysis.[20] As a critique of the short story, Verma poses this work against an American "cult of experience";[21] whereas American fiction emphasizes the validity of individual perception and experience, Muktibodh, from both a political and aesthetic perspective, insisted on an evaluation of experience—even if, in Verma's analysis, he was never able to articulate this standard: "Muktibodh could never respond to this question of what was valuable in our experience, and what was meaningless—is this knowledge of discernment also buried in experience? When he was pressured by this question then he searched for shelter in the rather vague and unclear thing which is a writers *viśva dṛṣṭi* [worldview]."[22] Poetry becomes the place where Muktibodh's vision bursts free from what Verma sees as the ambivalence of his prose:

> He [Muktibodh] accepts that [faith in literature means] to believe in the independent, autonomous experience of man, which rejects any worldview [*viśva dṛṣṭi*], any central truth, and instead is brave enough to fix the *vision* of their inner world [*sansār*]. Muktibodh himself, in the most creative moments of his poetry, does just this—or rather, in the most impacted moments of this internal contradiction he goes from prose into poetry, when on the pages of his stories and his diaries there is a continuous struggle taking place between Muktibodh's faith and doubt.[23]

This passage contrasts a central truth with the criterion of one's inner perception, but he makes clear that, for Muktibodh, it is only at certain moments he is able to ignore his "faith" in favor of what Verma calls the "inner world." It would be not be unreasonable to view Verma's entire interpretation of Muktibodh around the politics, shared by *Pūrvagraha,* of opposition to the left in Hindi literary criticism.[24] Throughout his essay, Verma insists seeing Muktibodh as torn between his left politics and, as he puts it here, "the independent, autonomous experience of man," arguing that Muktibodh, even if he was unable to articulate a worldview in opposition to his Marxism—and instead "searched for shelter," in a worldview he was unable to explain or articulate—in both his prose and poetry created a structure that was ultimately independent of it. But what is the role of genre in this construction?

Verma's essay, and Verma's ideas about Muktibodh's work, ends abruptly at the distinction between his short stories—which, for Verma, is the entirety of his prose writing—and his poetry. If the social material of Muktibodh's is present in his stories in a "frozen" form, then the poetry is the location of that frozen form thawing into life, even as it is beyond the horizon of analysis:

> This imminent event is poetry; the possibility of poetry is found within the story. This event does not occur in the stories, the poet of Muktibodh, through a remarkable artistic balance [*sanyam*] is continually postponed within the story, but the explosive idea of it is always present in it as if the *timebomb* of the story is buried somewhere in the narrative space [*kathyasthal*], and all the trees, shrubs, mountain peaks, lakes, ponds, dark alleyways, waiting for this explosion, are encased in ice, still and frozen in fear.[25]

Verma defines the poetic here not in formal terms, but as an event, or *ghaṭnā*, that is held in stasis in the story. The word that I have translated as narrative, *kathyasthal*, appears to be Verma's own neologism, a combination of *kathya*, "discourse," and *sthal*, "place or location." It forefronts not necessarily the formal structure of plot, but rather all of the elements present within narrative—but in Verma's categorization of Muktibodh, explicitly not moving. For Verma, it is essential that the narrative of Muktibodh's work, in his short stories, is frozen and unmoving.

The narrative structure of the short stories and their middle-class paralysis implies what Verma calls the "explosion" of the poem. But the idea that the poem presents an explosive, narrative force, whereas the short story presents a frozen narrative, is predicated upon a distinction between prose and poetry that is defined by ideas of narrative realism:

> What are these things, that even as they are, are not? Upon examining them a bit closer it seems, that they are nothing other than the buried symbols of Muktibodh—the still theoretical material [*upādān*] of the story—which enter into their second life in the dark caves and mysterious lakes of the imminent poems—and which then they are not still and silent and neutral—they are the entire web, in which Muktibodh's poem takes shivering life. That which appears to be encased in ice in the story—in the poem they become electrified with an electric current and illuminate Muktibodh's entire inward journey.

> But beyond this begins another journey; a doorway into poetry, where, in this essay, I do not have the courage to enter.[26]

For Verma, the structure of social paralysis, of a world frozen in ice, of the "desperation and self-loathing" of the qasbah, is what makes possible the wild, fantastic moments of Muktibodh's poetry—moments with which his audience, in 1981, would have been far more familiar than the world of his short story and essay. He demurs, however, from investigating this world. This demurral, which Verma poses as a question of bravery [*dussāhas*], has the effect of both foreclosing poetry from analysis and of cementing a distinction between poetry and prose that has little to do with formal attributes such as meter, address, and narrative. It has to do instead with the social, political, and thematic content of Muktibodh's work. Poetry is the place for "dark caves and mysterious lakes," content associated, ultimately, with the "tales of mystery, ghost stories, and tales of love and separation," that Premchand had so profoundly rejected. His idea of Muktibodh's work therefore, in presenting a profound gulf, renders *gadya*, prose, as the place where realism lives, a realism that cannot give life to the social world of the lower middle class, but that cannot not present it to the reader either. Poetry is the place of fantastic, otherwise impossible transcendence of such boundaries.

Verma's essay is important not only because it underlines a shifting interpretation of Muktibodh from his poetry to the larger scope of his work, but also because it makes clear the inextricability of genre from the politics of literature in the twentieth century. It crystallizes a problem of genre that, I have argued, is crucial to understanding Muktibodh's long poems. Verma sees Muktibodh as torn between his political beliefs and an inner world—but, crucially, he sees that playing out at the level of genre. In the world of his prose writing, Muktibodh is unable to transcend the limitations of his worldview.

And yet, to what extent is its distinction between poetry and prose borne out by the literary material? How did Muktibodh's own short stories engage in the antinomies of genre argued here? And in what ways might they have proposed alternate solutions, even if ultimately, Muktibodh, too, saw poetry as a realm alternate and separate from prose? To investigate these questions, I will examine a series of Muktibodh's stories that seem to contradict Verma's narrative of a frozen world—one that has more to do with the critical, diary pieces I discussed in the previous chapter. In the stories I will discuss here, parables, fables, and leaps of fantasy intrude upon realist narratives, are subdued, and yet linger in the memory as a possibility.

Verma ended his analysis of Muktibodh's work by referring to poem as the place where "dark caves and mysterious lakes" burst into life. However, there is no shortage of mysterious, subterranean spaces in his prose writing. As I discussed in the previous chapter, Muktibodh's most developed piece of aesthetic criticism, "Tīsrā kṣaṇ," features a long imagination of the speakers friend, wandering around a lake at the center of a buried ancient city. But, at each moment in Muktibodh's fiction and criticism, these moments of the fantastic are segregated into the space of the imagination and brought into explicit limits. As Verma might argue, the ancient lake of "Tīsrā kṣaṇ" is a still, unliving thing, something "is not even as it is," to use his phrasing. These fleeting images, memories of dreams, and sudden reveries appear throughout his prose literature. Yet, as Verma argues, they are silent, frozen moments, siloed away from the narrative of the story—in his neologism, an underlying substance of what is said, or something in the *nepathya* (behind the curtain), as Muktibodh would put it.

Distorted Fable

The majority of Muktibodh's short stories fit Verma's model in their realist depiction of a paralyzed, frustrated middle class, living in the unglamorous, peripheral cities and towns of Central India.[27] These stories, which blend with Muktibodh's journal-like "diary" pieces, depict a lower middle class living lives of frustration, anxiety, and resentment. In a small number of late short stories, however, the imaginative space of the fantasy expands beyond the paradigm of a still, frozen image, to take on narrative shape. Embedded within a realist depiction of the social world of the lower middle class, in these stories a sudden interrupting narrative, in the form of a parable or anecdote, takes over the story.

"Pakṣī aur Dīmak" (Bird and Weevil), from its title, seems to be an animal fable—a *Pancatantra* story, perhaps, the reader imagines, with a modern, cynical twist.[28] But the story itself seems at first to contradict this. It is set in a resolutely drab, lower-middle-class milieu, a loosely fictionalized version of the Rajnandgaon where Muktibodh taught at the end of his life. In a perhaps sly bit of misdirection, the opening of the story evokes the natural world of its title only in an extended description of a python that has wrapped itself around a bicycle and fallen asleep, only to be beaten to death: "We managed somehow to identify its head. Then quickly, with a '*finial*,' we attacked it and knocked it unconscious. How thrilling was our wild attack! With a sensation of deep terror that alerted us to our cowardice, we mercilessly beat its writhing body with sticks."[29] The opening of the story does two things. First, it introduces the theme of animals and violence, which will appear again later. Second, it reproduces the eventual logic of the story: any hope of enchantment from the natural world is immediately crushed and destroyed. The snake is never mentioned in the story again.

The story follows this young, disaffected professor as he walks with his wife across the college campus and considers the frustrations of his life. The atmosphere, a kind of horror scenario of domestic life, is almost a picture-perfect depiction of Verma's idea of Muktibodh's short stories: centered in a masculine, lower-middle-class world, threatened both by the emerging hierarchies of Nehruvian India and the threatening new world of companionate marriage. Significantly, and not for the first time, Muktibodh's domestic world is bereft of any characters except the husband and wife, seemingly locked here into irresolvable conflict.

Throughout the story, the narrator is seized by digressive moments that pull him (and the reader) away from the narrative. As he passes the college principal's Chevrolet, for instance, he suddenly finds himself entranced by the curving, chrome surface of the vehicle. The scene is one of horror:

> Next to the steps, standing on the shining road of red earth mixed with mica, stood a beautiful "Chevrolet."
>
> It was the "Chevrolet" of that man in the homespun saffron kurta; I stood behind him, and looked at—and just so—the car's number—when it's black, smooth

> surface, which was shining like a mirror, began to display my face to me.
>
> The face was terrifying! All the proportions were ruined. My nose was half a yard long and just as wide. My face became long and pinched. My eyes, pockmarked. My ears practically disappeared. Fascinated and perplexed, I stared at my face, unable to look away.
>
> And then I stepped back two steps; and I found that in that black shining mirror of the motor, my cheek, chin, nose, and ear became wide, absolutely wide. The length practically disappeared. I couldn't look away, I kept on looking until in some corner of my heart some dark gutter broke open. It was the gutter of self-perception, sorrow and hate.
>
> Suddenly a cry broke out of my mouth. When will I be free of this man in the saffron kurta, when!
>
> And it suddenly seemed to me that I was trapped in a net, since some unknown time I had been trapped in this terrible machine with all its gears. My legs were broken, my ribs ground to powder, I couldn't scream, my voice was caught in my throat.[30]

The details in this passage precisely delineate a range of class anxieties: the Chevrolet, a symbol of Western modern, stands on the red earth; it's shining paint becomes a literal black mirror, in the impossible, scientific, and mechanical curves of which the distorted image seems to reveal the true soul of the narrator: "the gutter of self-perception, sorrow, and hate." The narrator finds himself trapped within his position as a teacher, a prototypical member of the lower middle class, finding himself distorted and ground by his superior's automobile.[31] The terrifying distortions of the narrator, however, is bound up in the aesthetic processes of his thoughts. The vision of "self-perception, sorrow, and hate" is a "gutter," but also a fantasy, something contained within aesthetic process as Muktibodh understands it, and safely contained within the grim, paralyzed realist story that he is telling us.

Thus far, as I have argued, the story exemplifies Nirmal Verma's model of prose fiction—and his argument that it is a unique document of the frustrations of the lower middle class in Nehru's

India. What then follows, and in fact gives its title to the story, however, is something different. The narrator feels caught in a machine, because he feels indebted to, and controlled by, loyalty to the principal: "I would remain faithful to him, because I was his man. He might be bad, he might be corrupt, but he alone was the means by which I drew my salary! Personal devotion still mattered, and it was the only reason that I could be considered dependable. Indeed, it was the reason I found myself a member of several important committees."[32] This tension affects the narrator's relationship with his wife, who recognizes his frustration, but pushes him to engage with the university, to build the kind of social relationships that would ensure success.[33] The resentment that the narrator feels towards domestic life percolates through the text and seems to be presented to the reader as a self-evident sign of the lower-middle-class frustrations of the protagonist.[34] The narrator, at this point, decides to tell a story, noting that, if he transforms his own reaction into some kind of expression, its value would be transformed: "The essential truth of my life was like a kind of hidden wealth. It contained its own hidden struggle, its own hidden drama. It was not formed through expression. But still, perhaps in expressing it, its value might be increased, it might have some remaining use."[35] The narrator here discusses the basic material of allegory: expressing something hidden through some alternate, narrative means. It is telling, in fact, that here the "essential truth" is a hidden struggle or drama: both forms imply, on the one hand, narrative tension and release, and, on the other, explicit expression. The narrator has, up to this point, been drawing the action of the story almost entirely into his own, inner space; his reverie in consideration of nature or his feelings of suffocation in his interactions with his boss. But here he turns explicitly towards both the narrative—the telling out of some story—and the expressive. And the story that follows, explicitly designed to comment on his life, can be read as an attempt to join the inner contemplative world with the outer one.

The story that the narrator tells would easily fit within the generic constraints of the *Pancatantra* animal parables. The narrator tells the story in the manner of a fable, with repetition and with the beginning phrase "Ek thā pakṣī" (there was a bird) as opposed to the syntactically standard "ek pakṣī thā." And the plot of the story fits neatly within the neat moral reasoning of a parable: a protagonist makes a series of bad decisions that reveal his moral character, and lead eventually to some unpleasant outcome. But the story is punctured several times by parenthetical asides in which the narrator tracks his wife Shyamla's reaction to what he is saying; while these asides might mimic the oral aspect of the parable, they also serve to recenter us in the original story, with its dynamic of the marriage.

This is the story: a young bird comes across a man with a cart selling weevils out of a sack. The price: two weevils for one feather. For the birds, who usually live from what they find in the trees, ground-dwelling weevils are a delicacy, and the bird happily trades its one feather for weevils. Gradually, the bird becomes addicted to weevils: other food begins to taste bland, and he gradually, against the advice of his family, trades away most of his feathers. By then, the bird can no longer fly and must hop along the ground. When, one day, the cart disappears, the bird begins to collect weevils on his own, until he has amassed a large collection. When the cart returns, the bird attempts to trade his surplus of weevils for the feathers that he had earlier traded away. But the trader scoffs at the bird: "I trade feathers for weevils!" he says, "not weevils for feathers!" The now-flightless bird is eventually picked up by a black cat, "his drip-dripping blood making a line of spots along the ground."[36]

How is the moral of the parable connected to the social antinomies presented in the story that surrounds it? The bird, rather than take part in a kind of natural economy in the trees, relies instead on a fixed value of exchange to trade his own feathers for weevils. The problem with this is twofold: first, for every feather the bird sells, he is less able to fly. Secondly, as he later finds out, the exchange value between feathers and weevils is fixed by the trader and nonnegotiable. This basic aspect of exchange, and of trading away a part of yourself, is meant to resonate throughout the story. The narrator's life bound to the machinations of the educational bureaucracy of which he is a part and his helplessness in the face of the pressures of society are all meant to be symbolized by the story.

The narrator explicitly deploys the story as a way to reveal his hidden truth. As he tells the parable, Shyamla's reactions and engagement with the story are conveyed in parenthetical asides. And as he finishes the story, he exclaims: "No, there's something left in me, much remains! I won't die like that bird. I can still climb out of all this. The disease is not incurable. This cycle of ills that come from being bound to a fashionable life [*ṭhaṭh se rahne ke cakkar se burāī ke cakkar*] I still have an energy for life [*prāṇśakti*]!"[37] The narrator is telling this story to reveal a truth about himself, but he also attempting, rhetorically, to convince others of this truth. The reaction of the characters around him, however, does not support such an attempt: his wife, Shyamla, immediately asks him where he read the story, failing to give the narrator the reaction that he was hoping for, before moving on. The plot then loops back to the question of predatory animals; a local farmer comes carrying a dead snake, which, he reveals, is a poisonous krait. The story thus closes with the return of the narrator to the position at the beginning of the story of a contrast between a predatory nature and an enervating social reality. In what way, then, did the parable serve to illuminate this reality?

The question of the effectiveness of the parable, either in causing social action—in which case it is a failure—or in illuminating something about the character—in which case, from the point of view of the reader, it was unnecessary—raises the question of what the parable is doing in the story in the first place. Why insert an ineffective parable in the midst of a short story? Posing this question prompts to ask how Muktibodh himself may have understood this story, and its possible "effectiveness." The protagonist's seeming disappointment at his wife's reaction, in the framing of the narrative, is meant to present to the reader his disappointment, and the impossibility of him expressing himself in his context.

And yet, the story remains. It interrupts the narrative and presents its own, radically different form of narrative and expectations. It is a complete departure from Verma's idea of a frozen social state, even if the lively, narrative-driven parable seems only to reinforce the paralysis of the story. If it does convince either us or the characters in the story (and perhaps it does), then it does do something else—it tells us of the possibility of different modes of narration and different epistemologies of truth that might be operational within them. Elsewhere, such parables are woven into stories in more complex ways.

Anecdotes of Imprisonment

"Pakṣī aur dīmak" forefronts a frustration and self-loathing that, at the moment of its greatest tension, lapses into a sudden, utterly different narrative space of the parable. It's birds and weevils operated in a generic mode that is hermetically sealed off from the realist narrative of the lower middle class in which they are deployed. The role of the story is seemingly to demonstrate its ineffectiveness as a solution—it can be read, in fact, not necessarily as a critique of realism, but as a satire of attempts to escape it through allegorical tales.

In other places, however, the role of the fantastic is far more ambiguous. "Samjhautā" (The Compromise) was, like "Pakṣī aur dīmak," written in the last years of Muktibodh's life, and like "Pakṣī aur dīmak" features a long tale buried within a framing story of lower-middle-class frustration. "Samjhauta," however, is a story far more indebted to Kafka and the surrealist, aphoristic tale than the fairy tale–like "Pakṣī aur dīmak," and the internal story, rather than a clear parable, is an almost—but not quite—unbelievable tall tale. Furthermore, the setting of "Samjhauta," in an unnamed, labyrinthine bureaucratic office building, in which the tale is told *to* the speaker by his work superior, intermingles the surreal atmosphere of the story itself with that of the tale within it.

"Samjhautā" takes up the modern, bureaucratic space by depicting it not in terms of the social movements within it, but in terms of its spatial infrastructure, as a massive office:

> It was filled with darkness, hazy, narrow, an endless *corridor* and stone walls. High up in a cornice a pigeon's nest, and from to time a soft cooing that makes the silence of six o'clock deeper still. The empty corridors, after some twists and turns, arrive at a staircase. The staircase climbs upwards, stops and turns before ending at another long *corridor*.
>
> All the doors are closed. Locks hang on the hinges. A strange, sad, lonely silence spreads across this second floor. I walk quickly. My sandals are silent. Outside, someone is busy making sackcloth.

> In the distance, only one door is open. A hint of light reaches the corridor from within. Not light, really, because a green sheet hangs over the doorway. When I arrive at the room, in the hazy darkness outside, I can make out the figure of a seated man. I pay him no heed and enter the doorway.[38]

By opening the story with this description of an office hallway, empty after the end of the work day, "Samjhautā" foregrounds the centrality and power of space. The dark, abandoned office, with its strange geometry, locked rooms, and guarded entrances, hints at the ways in which the bureaucratic world is composed of a series of hierarchies, but also bounded spaces and ways of understanding often exclusive to a given member of the system. Opacity is the defining feature of this space.

Within this space, the narrator meets a man, a supervisor. The precise relationship of this man to his supervisor is unclear, but the narrator appears to be meeting him for some kind of disciplinary action. The disciplinary action, too, is left unstated, but both the narrator and the supervisor agree that the narrator is being made to be a "scapegoat" for the unnamed infraction. The supervisor is kind, sympathetic; he even, by referring to the narrator as "Comrade," hints at his own leftist political affiliations. But the supervisor is also a contradictory figure who has wrenched himself up the bureaucratic ladder: he wears fine clothing, such as a black wool coat, but like the boss of "Pakṣī aur Dimak," he is short, squat, and dark, and known to be a canny operator of the signifiers of caste and class in order to get ahead. By dispensing with hierarchical formality and presenting himself to the narrator as an understanding interlocutor, the supervisor aims to step outside of the complex, hierarchical system of the bureaucracy in which the story takes place.[39]

The story the supervisor tells is part of this effort: when the narrator is distraught by his situation at the office, the supervisor tells him a story that, he hints strongly, belonged to his own youth. A young man from a poor family is educated, but finds himself unable either to fit into the patronage system of his own caste or to ascend the ranks and break into the upper caste world of educated jobs. One day, while contemplating suicide, the man comes across a circus and, enchanted by the cosmopolitan composition of the circus workers and the freedom of the traveling life, begs to join. He is rejected several times, but after enduring the abuse of the strongman guards of the circus, he is accepted by the manager, whom he never sees.

To the young man's surprise, when he is accepted to the circus, he is immediately taken and locked in a small room. After several days of confused isolation, he is moved to a new room with the thick smell of a bear; this is where his training begins. After days of constant whipping, beating, and starvation, he is given a diet of raw meat, which in his hunger he learns to eat without retching. After weeks of further isolation and torture, the young man's transformation from human to animal is nearly complete. He is then led into a ring and confronted with a lion. The ferocious lion attacks at once, and the young man, despite his transformation, is immediately pinned down. But at the moment at which he expects his throat to be bitten into, he hears a voice in his ear: the lion, like the young man, is also a man in an animal skin. He tells the young man that there's no need to die, and the two of them can help each other: "Come, let's be friends," the lion says. "If we have to live the life of animals, let's live properly at least, and make an agreement with each other."[40]

The supervisor tells the young man this story, he explains, to underline the importance of compromise. When the young man, probing the comradeship of this supervisor, asks if he is now to sign the paper, the supervisor tells him: "No doubt, I'm giving you the warning, and you're receiving it: I'm the lion, and you're the bear."[41] When the young man protests, arguing that he will be accepting a "warning" for something he didn't do, and that he furthermore sees no point in writing an endless series of "explanations," the supervisor underlines the logic of the system that he has tried to explain: "If you don't know how to write explanations, then what are you doing in service? I've written three hundred and eight explanations. I've never received a single warning, though, because I know how to write them, and maybe too because I'm a lion, not a bear. I've been an animal long before you. So then I've got *seniority* on my side. Maybe someday you'll be a lion too."[42] The manager speaks in the byzantine jargon of bureaucratic life; it is never explained, for instance, what is contained in an "explanation," or why the manager would have had to write three hundred and eight of them. There is no explanation for why the narrator is expecting a warning, or even what the relationship is between the narrator and the supervisor that is prompting the meeting in the first place. The world of bureaucracy has an isolating feeling that produces instances of servitude and humiliation even as it promises a measure of financial stability: when advising the narrator, the supervisor tells him, "There are a thousand hats in the world, but only if your head is on your shoulders!"[43]

The tale of the man who, as part of a circus, transforms into a bear brings strongly to mind Kafka's short story "A Report to the Academy."[44] In that story, a man reports to a scientific academy the story of how he transformed from an ape to a European man. After being captured by a ship off the African coast, the ape learns, slowly and painfully, to imitate human behaviors, such as speaking and drinking. Eventually, as the ape reports, it becomes as difficult for him to imagine becoming an ape again as for a human to reverse its evolution; describing the space between himself and his past being as a hole through which wind comes, he says, "The opening in the distance, through which it comes and through which I once came myself, has grown so small that, even if my strength and my will power sufficed to get me back to it, I should have to scrape the very skin from my body to crawl through."[45] The Kafka story is the obverse of the tale within "Samjhautā": a transformation between animal and man, bringing up themes of atavism, acculturation, and subjugation. But whereas in "A Report to the Academy," the focus is on the palpable anger and frustration of the ape, which brings up again and again the question of finding "a way out" of the cage in which he is placed, and the different value of freedom implied by such an imperative, in "Samjhautā" the focus is on the shared imperative of the lion and the bear to live together, to find an arrangement to mitigate and survive their mutual obligation. Rather than end the focus on the fractured, impossible internality of the ape as living in modernity, barely suppressing a sense of outrage and desire for freedom, "Samjhautā" presents the fable of two prisoners very much still within the prison and finding a way to live within it.

The anecdote has to be considered in the context of the larger story, in terms of who is telling it and why. As the story makes absolutely clear, the tale is told by a supervisor to his subordinate, the narrator. He tells it, claiming for himself the role of the former subordinate, in order to explain to the narrator how to survive in a bureaucratic world, claiming for himself the present position of lion. The transformations, then, are multiple: from supervisor to helpless, unemployed young man, from human to bear, and from bear to lion. This latter transformation has taken place offstage, over the course of time—a time delineated also in obscure, bureaucratic terms, as "three hundred and eight explanations." This final transformation, too, is one that occurs within the system: first the supervisor, in telling the story, transforms himself into the position of the subordinate; then, he describes the transformation from outside to inside. The transformation from bear to lion is described as being the ultimate success, but only within the closed, hierarchical world of the bureaucracy.

"Samjhautā," then, uses the story of the young man and the circus on several levels: as a way of explaining one's own personal history of accommodation to a larger system, as an allegory for that system and its capacity to transform and debase its members, and, finally, as a kind of gift, an attempt by the supervisor to help the narrator by convincing him to find a way to survive within this larger system. Tellingly, the manager refuses to answer the question of the identity of the unseen "manager" who had controlled the circus within the story, saying instead, "Why don't you ask instead who that manager is who's turned me and you, and everybody else, into a bear or a lion, or an elephant or a cheetah?"[46] The manager, asked for this detail, instead interprets the story and points out the final level at which it signifies something outside of itself: the point of consideration of the larger "manager" or managerial force, which subjugates everyone involved in it into a position within a hierarchy of either predator or prey.

In "Samjhautā," as in "Pakṣī aur Dimak," a smaller, nonrealist story is embedded within a larger one, and in each case, a character in the story uses the substory as a means of explaining an aspect of the real that feels excessive and incomprehensible: in "Pakṣī aur Dimak," the narrator of the story tries to employ an animal parable to explain how he feels like he has given up an essential autonomy in order to take part in an inherently unfair and predetermined economy; in "Samjhautā," the supervisor tells a Kafkaesque story in order to explain the hierarchy of the bureaucracy and the relations possible between two members at different points of that hierarchy. In both cases, the substory reveals a crucial truth about the social world of the story while also coming up against the limits of the substory to explain or effect the world of the story. In "Pakṣī aur dīmak," the parable fails to interest the narrator's wife, perhaps not least because it flattens out the complex social world through which she is trying to guide the narrator. In "Samjhautā," the tale comes up against a ragged edge in the form of the unseen, unknowable "manager": the allegory can only extend to the bureaucratic system itself, and not to the overarching power that prompts the creation of that system in the first place. In both cases, the substory can explain something essential, but only at the cost of excluding larger, but still crucial factors.

If "Pakṣī aur Dimak" engages with the potential of the parable to explain modern life, and ultimately suggests its insufficiency, then "Samjhautā" hints at the possibilities of a fable based not on the characteristics of nature, but rather on the new world of the office. Again, "Samjhautā" displays an awareness not only of the social reality of the newly emerging hierarchical world of the postindependence bureaucratic universe, but of the capacity of the story and the different narrative capabilities inherent within it to depict that new social reality. In so doing, the story succeeds in confronting the new hierarchies of work with an aspect of social life that would elude the story if it only depicted a frozen, changeless social reality.

The Nehruvian Paranoid Mood

"Clauḍ Ītharlī" (Claude Eatherly; written hereafter as Claude Eatherly) is both typical of Muktibodh's prose literature and one of the most enigmatic of his short stories. Published posthumously and possibly unfinished, it describes an enigmatic, recursive conversation between two men, one of whom claims to be a member of India's Central Investigation Division, or CID, and who tells a story of an American tied to a chair in a warehouse.[47] The CID agent claims that the manis in fact Claude Eatherly, incorrectly described as the pilot of the *Enola Gay* (he was actually a weather observer in an accompanying plane, although he did witness the explosion over Hiroshima), and in actuality a prominent protestor against atomic warfare.[48] As this story is interrogated, and eventually revealed to be a kind of recruitment tool on behalf of the agent, "Claude Eatherly" functions as both a critique and satire of India's role in the new Cold War, as well as an interrogation of subjectivity and narrative in the short story.

In its use of pulp fiction language and exclamations, mysterious abandoned city, and story of a spy, "Claude Eatherly" draws heavily from popular fiction, and the language of the detective story, or *jāsūsī upanyās*.[49] Muktibodh's literature frequently references both the detective story and *dāstān*-based narratives such as *Candrakāntā*, one of the most popular early novels in Hindi.[50] Here, the narrative is driven by a particular form of curiosity towards the modern city:

> I crossed the street, and paused for a moment beneath some foreign flowers, wild and beautiful but odorless, that had spread over the wall of the compound.
>
> I don't know what came over me, but nearby was a tall electric pole—which sent straight lines of wire in six directions across silent streets—and I suddenly noticed that a ladder, tall enough to climb on top of these two-story buildings, leaned against it. Perhaps the construction of these long, sturdy walls is still done in the old style.
>
> Motivated by natural curiosity to see what might be there, and what angle might provide the best view, I climbed on the ladder, and my vision extended through the transom window set in its blue frame in the tall, yellow wall across the street.
>
> And, I was transfixed.[51]

The first three paragraphs present a precise, almost clinical description of urban space. The story begins with a description of an abandoned industrial space, eerily empty of people and defined by isolated physical details. The odorless foreign flowers have taken root, an invasive species growing wild over the walls of the factory compound. The space is formed by a series angles and straight lines: the wire that stretches from the electric pole, the blue frame of the transom window.

The alien and artificial details of these opening paragraphs draw attention to the "natural" curiosity of the speaker, who enters into this environment through climbing on the ladder and triangulating his own vision. This action transforms the narrative, bringing it to life and bringing in a new, bolder language. The speaker *stabdh rah gayā,* "remained transfixed." As the proper story kicks into gear, the speaker's discovery of the mysterious man tied to a chair is suddenly vivid and pulpy, with sudden interjections of *aścarya!* (Surprise!) and "ab yah kyā?!" (And what is this now?!). The internal monologue, which begins with a clinical detachment, becomes filled with exclamation marks as the speaker registers his surprise at the increasingly strange and unsettling events that are unfolding in the story.

The framing of the story as a detective story becomes increasingly dominant in the story, as it increasingly revolves around the conversation between the speaker and the mysterious, CID-affiliated man. The movement through urban space, as the duo wander from the industrial city-center to the wealthy, bungalow-strewn Civil Lines area that begins to the west of the factories, and enter into a cheap, *pān* shop wallpapered with pinups of foreign women torn from newspapers, is inseparable from the paranoid imagined world of their conversation. The streets are, the speaker notes repeatedly, eerily empty, and at the *pān* shop, he becomes sure that the men at the table next to him are paid informers, listening to their conversation.[52] Ultimately, the status of urban space shifts becomes explicit when the man in the warehouse is revealed to be the American war hero and nuclear protestor Claude Eatherly, doing penance for his role in the bombing of Hiroshima. When the speaker asks, incredulously, what Claude Eatherly is doing in an Indian city, the spy wonders why he would be so surprised:

> As if scoffing at my ignorance, he said, "There's an America inside the center of every big Indian city. Haven't you seen the women with their sparkling red lips and golden pale skin, haven't you seen their expensive clothes? Haven't you seen all those well-educated people driving

> around in their wonderful cars? Haven't you seen the exquisite new variety of prostitution? Haven't you seen *Seminar*? Once we went to London and called ourselves "England-returned." And now we go to Washington. If we had our way, and we could really be that rich, and have all those atom and hydrogen bombs and rockets, then who knows! Don't you read the news?[53]

"Claude Eatherly" can be read primarily as a satire on American foreign policy, no doubt through the interpretation of passages such as this one. But beneath the stinging critique of India's position in the late 1950s, as it was increasingly drawn into the orbit of American foreign policy, before being forced to rely on American military aid in the Sino-Indian war of 1962, lies a pitch-black view of the contemporary Indian city.[54] The recreation of the American city—a vision, not coincidentally, directly shared by concepts of development—echoes, in this depiction, an early division of Indian cities into British-colonial zones and the older city. The influence of America echoes both a postcolonial anxiety about neocolonialism and Gandhian statements on the inherent foreignness of the Indian city.[55] But the anger is directed just as much at the new, wealthy technocrats of Nehruvian India, as hinted by *Seminar*, the long-running English-language magazine of policy, social science, and economics that had only just been founded in 1959.[56] And the locus for that anger, significantly, is the modern Indian city.

That leads us to a key element of the story: the spying. That the interlocutor of "Claude Eatherly" was a spy has a fine pedigree, both in Hindi in general, with its long history of popular "jāsūsī" novels, and in Muktibodh's work. Particularly at this time, Muktibodh was conscious of the existence of spies, and indeed as an underground Marxist he felt frequently that he was the subject of surveillance for his political beliefs.[57] At one point in the story, a point that probably reflects his life, he notes that in various small *hotels* (small cheap restaurants) and tea rooms, among the people having conversations would be "dark eyes that could look into the black depths."[58] Elsewhere in his work, the actions in his stories would mimic the language and plots of early twentieth century *jāsūsī* novels. "Bhaviśyadhārā" (The River of Future Time), for instance, opens with a scientist knocked unconscious with sleeping powder, a staple of *jāsūsī* novels, finding its origins in the *dastān* narratives of the nineteenth century; the story further unfolds utilizing the melodramatic language of a mysterious crime.[59]

Here, the presence of the spy deepens, hinted at by the description of the city throughout the story. If the changing city that the narrator moves through has hints of an internalized but shifting and changing idea of the global, then the spy presents himself as a kind of intermediary between these different planes of existence. The spy reveals the identity of the prisoner as the American Claude Eatherly and the spy who underlines the presence of America within this Indian city. This, in fact, may explain what is otherwise an anomalous element in the story: the narrator's frequently stated discomfort with what he calls this "womanish character," bolstered by the spy's stated personal history: he claims to have been the illegitimate child of a wealthy merchant and one of his servants, and to have been supported financially throughout his life and career by this merchant even as he was raised by his mother, who continued to work in the merchant's house.[60] The narrator is frequently disturbed by the spy's gender ambiguity, by his youthful body, in a manner that might otherwise seem out of place. But it may serve to emphasize the nature of the spy in the story as someone who exists uncomfortable in the interstices of society, between the public and the private, and has the capacity to make visible not only the seams between various orders and spheres of society but also the different connections between the local and the global. The spy pretends to be something he is not, and pretends at intimacy, in the service of a larger, often abstract, purpose. In this way the spy always makes the political local.

Ultimately, the elements of the story that might at first glance seem the most internationally and globally engaged reveal themselves as internal anxieties: the spy makes it clear that the narrator, with his guilty conscience and inability to effect political change, is no different in his guilty conscience than Claude Eatherly, who has been driven mad by his sense of helpless responsibility. The moments of the story in which the narrator imagines an international, global perspective are in many ways the moments in which he is most terrified by the situation at hand. As I mentioned above, this can be seen in the spy's description of the "ultramodern neighborhoods" of an Indian city, which each contain a small America within them. This occurs throughout the story to the narrator, as a kind of central, impossible point that prompts an unfolding series of disturbing imaginaries. Ultimately, through considering the possibility that the prisoner in the asylum is Claude Eatherly, the narrator imagines the international itself:

> Who is this person who talks to me like this? I felt, truly, like I had left the world, and arrived some two hundred miles above it, where the sky, the moon and the stars, the sun, were all at once visible. Rockets were flying. They came and went, and the earth appeared like a big blue ball, where we weren't from any one country, but from all of them. My mind filled with a terrifying, disconcerting feeling of weightless restlessness. All this lasted maybe for a single instant. But that single instant was terrifying. Terrifying and full of doubt.[61]

This passage inverts the imagined logic of science fiction familiar to contemporary American pop culture, especially in late-1960s variants such as *Star Trek* and *2001*, in which an internationalized world, in which boundaries between nations have disappeared, is presented as a positive utopia; here, the literal weightlessness of space is transformed into the mental weightlessness of collapsing boundaries. In contrast, too, to the frequent appearance of interplanetary travel in the musings of Muktibodh's characters, here the moment of departing the earth, and most importantly its sociopolitical structures, is an occasion not of freedom but of dislocation and terror.[62]

It is in this sense—as an internalized, mediated sense of a globalizing capitalism, represented by America—that the question of atomic war, and the guilt of Claude Eatherly, is presented. Claude Eatherly is described by the spy as a "war hero," using the English phrase, and is, in journalistic fashion, rendered deeply specific. The places in Texas where he commits his guilty crimes are all named, along with the time he spent in mental institutions, and even an accomplice in one of his robberies is given the particularly American-sounding name of "Roy L. Mantooth."[63] But this overwhelming guilt is framed in terms of the mental contradiction that the spy claims to have discerned in the narrator himself: "The point is," he says, "that the ones who feel this massive injustice but don't stand up to it feel, inside, like they're some kind of sinners, and they should keep on feeling this way. Between Eatherly and these people this is the fundamental unity and similarity."[64] The guilt of Claude Eatherly is given emotional weight in the story by the repeatedly established guilt of the narrator, who feels unable to engage in the social or in politics, and even the supposedly villainous—and distant—imperialist politics of America is framed as entirely internalized by the Indian intellectual class. When the spy compares every city to America, he asks, "Are we inspired by the literature of Indonesia or China or Africa, or the poetry of Lumumba? *Chi-chi!* That's the literature of animals, of beasts!"[65] The guilt of Claude Eatherly and the question of the international, here, is only possible in a framework of contempt for any kind of solidarity in the postcolonial world.

The ending of the story, however, abruptly cancels the core element of Claude Eatherly. In the final paragraphs, the narrator learns that the CID agent has invented the entire story of Claude Eatherly's present as a means of screening the narrator, who, as a debt-ridden writer, is seemingly an ideal candidate to become a spy:

> I made my face stern. Becoming grave, I said, "But, why are you telling me all this?"
>
> "Because I am a C.I.D. man, and I am screening you. I want you to join my division. Why would you refuse? Can you really tell me that this goes against your conscience?"
>
> "So you told me all this to feel me out? And, everything you've said is made up? To discern my heart? You villain!"
>
> "I only used those references appropriate to you, so far as was possible—I was only making the kinds of points that you would understand."[66]

Perhaps because of the sudden, bizarre denouement of the story, which ends without any real resolution of what has suddenly been revealed as its true narrative, "Claude Eatherly" is often considered incomplete. And yet, if we read the story in light of the previous two stories discussed, "Claude Eatherly" is arguably as complete, both in its framing narrative and in its overarching narrative, as these other two. The reveal of fictiveness tears apart the possibilities of international engagement—seen not only through the anxious restaging of Western epistemologies, but also through engagement with futuristic technologies—to place the narrator, instead, in a web of the forced informant. It is worth noting that, in the space of the story, the *jāsūs* is not that of international espionage, but rather of a group of men overhearing the narrator in a tea shop. That is to say, the possibility of glamour, excitement, and international critique that are raised by the spy's tale are replaced instead with a grim, everyday paranoia that, by the late 1960s, had begun to dominate Muktibodh's actual life.

I propose that we read "Claude Eatherly," then, both as a fractured depiction of paranoia in Nehru's India—one that arguably, in its paranoia and fragmentation, parallels and foresees developments in science fiction that would be classified as New Wave—and as a comment on its own creation and on the realist short story form in which it is entangled.[67] The unwriting of its central, impossible fable seems to foreclose the possibility of a science fiction in Muktibodh's work. It also seems to point towards the irresolvable aporia of Hindi literature more generally: Muktibodh seems unable to find a way to depict his own lower-middle-class experiences without resort to the fantastic or unreal, and yet, in these three stories, that unreal is ultimately contained within the realist framework of the short story. That it does so in such a way as to foreclose the utopian gestures inherent in the fantastic indicates, as well, Muktibodh's approach to prose fiction.

Through the Window

Verma, in his essay on Muktibodh's short fiction, compares Muktibodh's "plotless" short stories with *nayī kahani*, claiming that Muktibodh's stories are more attentive to the lived reality of the middle class that was supposedly the goal of *nayī kahānī* writers: the "space of experience that was attacked with such clamoring by '*nayī kahānī*'—poverty, employment, the shrinking of the joint family, suicide."[68] He writes: "What are they waiting for? We won't find the answer in the content [*kathya*], but rather in the location of that content [*kathya-sthal*]. Muktibodh was fundamentally a poet, but his prose—whether it was his stories or the *Diary*—are very different from what we might call poetic or lyrical prose. Rather, it has such hardness and stoniness that no one could imagine that they are reading the prose of one whose fundamental sensitivity is expressed in poetry."[69] Verma indicates that the importance of these stories is not the substance but the location, or background, of that substance. By this, he refers to the atmosphere that he has described and that I have shown in my discussion of these stories: the still and frozen small cities, the paralyzed social situations of the characters, the meandering conversations that dissect these situations and, as Verma puts it, "peels back layer after layer" of "the frozen situation of life."

In these stories it is precisely the possibility of narrative momentum that is at stake. These stories seem to unwrite themselves, drawing a sharp contrast precisely between the narrative space of the parable, anecdote, tall tale, and so on, and the "frozen" narrative that enfolds it. That is to say, the "failure" of these embedded stories could be the point. Each of these stories embeds within itself a nonrealistic narrative—a fable, an anecdote, a science fiction thriller—only to explicitly undercut that nonrealistic narrative within the framing of the story.

And yet, these stories, in their surrealism, use of the fantastic, and hesitant engagement with the possibility of the allegorical, indicate a path forward for Hindi fiction that is perhaps more recognizable than any of Muktibodh's other legacies. As his fiction and autobiographical writing gradually become more available, his prose work has increasingly gained in influence; Verma's essay, published in 1981, reflects this growing trend. Muktibodh's prose, with its indelible depiction of the small city, resonated with generations of writers in Hindi.

One of the most prominent writers influenced by Muktibodh has carried forward this complicated engagement with narrative, genre, and the fantastic. Vinod Kumar Shukla, today one of the most prominent fiction writers in Hindi, is directly influenced by Muktibodh's depiction of the lower middle class and the frozen life of the small Indian city. His *Divār meṃ ek khiṛkī rahtī thī* features such a mode of foreclosed fantasy, in which the passage reveals a utopian rural idyll, but one that is available only when passing through a window. When a visitor attempts to enter this space on his own, by walking behind the house, he finds that bypassing through a door reveals only a barren patch of land:

> He was so disappointed. He should never have told his children and wife about the beauty of that backyard. As soon as he got home his children would ask, "Did you see the banyan tree? The river? The monkey? Did you drink old grandma's tea? Did you walk on the path smooth and clean? Did you see the children dancing? . . . He'd answer that he'd looked and looked but couldn't find it. . . . He'd looked at the district office, at the bus stand, and couldn't find it. It was filthy. And even filthier behind the house.[70]

The foreclosed dreams of the visitor in *Dīvār meṃ ek khiṛkī rahtī thī*, dreaming of a pure, fresh stream, receive only filth and disappointment. While Shukla's works tend towards the possibility of enchantment, they still exist in the tense space of the small city and the lower middle class, where any hope of enchantment and discovery is crushed. And yet despite this seeming pessimism, *Dīvār meṃ ek khiṛkī rahtī thī* is a light, cheerful novel, holding out the utopian possibility of enchantment in a way that is distinctly missing from Muktibodh's work.

As we will discuss in the following chapter, it was indeed through the long poem that Muktibodh felt he was able to engage with the allegorical in ways that, for him, were intensely productive. And yet, his short stories present us with ultimate forms of narrative and critiques of genre that are themselves a crucial legacy within Hindi literature. So, the division between prose and poetry, for both Verma and Muktibodh, was very real—even if his work, through these experiments with nonrealist narrative genres, strained against it.

Chapter Four

The Long Poem between Genre and Form

Muktibodh's long poems, with their phantasmagoric depictions of contemporary society, were immediately seized on as prophetic and revealing the growing tensions beneath what contemporary poet Rajesh Joshi has called the "heavy curtains" of Nehruvian India.[1] These heavy curtains, which Joshi categorizes as a soft, heavy cloak of optimism, concealed a world of dread, anxiety, and corruption that would seem to break open in the following decades, but was visible in retrospect in the dark fantasies of Muktibodh's poetry. Central to the appeal of the long poems, therefore, was their ability to access aspects of the fantastic and the allegorical that otherwise seemed inaccessible.

As I discussed in the first chapter, the long poem troubles generic distinctions, and in the case of Muktibodh's long poems, it engages directly and repeatedly with discourses around narrative genres through its frequent references to the novel and its insistence on a lyric engagement with realism. An emerging body of scholarship has argued that the idea of the lyric, despite frequent attempts to read it as a classical or even natural form, in fact is created through practices of reading and criticism.[2] The question of definitions troubles any theory of the lyric, and especially of the lyric's relation to the social rather than the individual expression.[3] Muktibodh's long poem, or *lambī kavitā* in Hindi, engages directly with the theory of the lyric, even as it insists on its importance to ideas of realism, which would seem to be opposed to ideas of the lyric as a form of address. Muktibodh always referred to his works as *kavitā*, a term that, across most South Asian languages, came to be used to refer to the short, lyrical poems that became dominant in the late nineteenth and the twentieth centuries. The complex history of the emergence of the modern *kavitā* in Hindi and other South Asian languages, and the processes of differentiation from other forms of short poetry, such as the Urdu *ghazal* or the short poetry of Braj, is outside the scope of this chapter.[4] But attention to the form of Muktibodh's long poem shows the ways in which his work can be read across genre, and how his work extends the possibilities of the Hindi and Marathi poem, even as it insists on the formal capacities of these lyric genres.

In the chapter that follows, I will first consider the ways in which Muktibodh's long poem has been understood within Hindi literary history before turning to Muktibodh's own understanding of his work. I will then analyze the formal state of free verse and the lyric with which Muktibodh interacted, especially the influence of the *muktachanda*, or free verse, of Marathi modernist literature, arguing that it should be seen as a crucial element in Muktibodh's long poem. This is important not only because it reshapes our understanding of the literary landscape of North India, but also because it points towards the ways in which detailed formal analysis, in this case of meter, can help us to think through problems of genre, world literature, and modernism at different historical scales. I will then finish with a reading of "Aṃdhere meṃ." The twisting, phantasmagoric narrative of "Aṃdhere meṃ" cannot be separated from its use of the long poem form developed and shaped over fifteen years by the time it was written. As I will show, it draws upon the resources of this form in order to twist and reshape the narrative potentialities of the long poem, and, upon this base, to attempt an allegorical representation of contemporary society. That this allegorical representation was possible in the long poem and not, for Muktibodh, in prose fiction, indicates the role this form plays in illustrating tensions over genre, narrative, and realism that extend beyond Muktibodh's personal career into the larger history of Hindi literature. Ultimately, I will argue, the long poem serves as a unique case study of modern Hindi literature, as well as a path forward towards our understanding of generic experimentation within twentieth-century modernisms.

The Magical World of an Extended Poem

From the beginning of Muktibodh's reception, critics in Hindi have struggled with defining the long poems. On one level, comparisons were obvious: as early as 1960, Ashok Vajpeyi, in a letter written to Muktibodh, compared "Aṃdhere meṃ" to *The Wasteland*, writing in a letter that "if *Wasteland* is the greatest work of art produced by modern Europe, then without a doubt this extended poem [*pradīrgh kavitā*] is for Hindi a work which is just as weighted and important."[5] Vajpeyi, then only nineteen years old, was praising a poet for whom he had great respect, and the letter does not elaborate on the comparison with Eliot's famous poem. But the terms used are significant—the poem is not simply long but *pradīrgh*, lengthened or extended; and like *The Wasteland* it is literally heavy, *guru*. At the moment of its emergence in Hindi literary history, Muktibodh's long poems are viewed not only as a momentous achievement, but as something massive and unwieldy.

Other early critics of Muktibodh, who like Ashok Vajpeyi knew him personally and were responsible for establishing his reputation, compared his work not to poetry but to painting. The poet Shamsher Bahadur Singh (1911–1993), four years before writing a preface to *Chāṃd kā muṃh ṭeṛhā hai*, published a far less well-known essay that is one of the first substantial works of criticism of Muktibodh's late poetry. Titled "Mere priya kavi" (My Favorite Poets), the 1960 piece discusses several writers, all of whom Shamsher had been working with for multiple decades. As I discussed in the first chapter, Shamsher saw Muktibodh as representative of the "educated lower middle class individual [who] is hung on a bizarre hook."[6] For Shamsher, the "fantastic world" of Muktibodh's long poems—typified by works such as "Brahmarakshas," discussed in the first chapter—expressed this terrifying reality. He compared Muktibodh's works not to the modernist long poems of the Anglo-American tradition, but to mural painting: "The long poems of Muktibodh possess an expansive pattern. A massive *mural painting*—modern experimentalist; hyper-modern. In which each object is solid and firm; bound together in the net of a *tragic* relation."[7] Shamsher's conception of the long poem as mural depends, looking forward to Benjamin's concept of the dialectical image on seeing the extension of the lyric image into a space of narrative and allegory; in this way, like modern scholars of the Anglo-American modernist long poem, this criticism confronts the problem of narrative in poetry.[8] Each individual object or image is bound up, using the English word, in a "*tragic* relation"; Shamsher, himself a painter as well as a poet, calls these poems "a *grim*, terrifying museum of still images."[9] Muktibodh "prepares every one of these images with great effort, before sealing them in amber and moving on."[10]

The comparison to painting culminates in the remark that "his style, so filled with power and energy [*śaktiśālī*], reminds me of certain Mexican muralists."[11] Shamsher, a painter, compares these poems to paintings throughout his essay, and his comment here can be read in a range of ways, including both the political position of the Mexican murals in history, as well as their approach to creating mythic, popular narratives.[12] The comparison serves as a reminder of how Muktibodh, from the beginning of his reception, was read into international aesthetic debate. It also indicates that Muktibodh's long poems, even as they just barely were becoming visible and available to criticism, were viewed as a problem of image, narrative, and allegory.

Shamsher also presents these long poems, and what he calls their "fantastic world" (*bhūtahā lok*) as a problem. The images of Muktibodh's fantastic world at times seemed to overwhelm the narrative allegory. But Shamsher's presentation of this betrays an anxiety about Muktibodh's work that echoes through his reception. Emphasizing the dramatic, horrifying imagery used in the long poems, Shamsher writes:

> My problem with Muktibodh (it happens often to readers; I'm also nothing more than an ordinary reader), the very first problem, is reading them! (To be honest) the gigantic expansiveness [*dīrghakāy virāṭatā*] of the work makes you despair. *A great reality*; in all directions, inside and out. Object and style and inner sense, creative process and the reader's initial reaction—in all a bizarre *grimness*. How would I escape it. I am surrounded and tangled, the reader must remember the fate of the "*guest*" of Coleridge's *Ancient Mariner*. There is no release from it, until the moment of freedom—the consciousness of freedom.[13]

In contrast with the declarations elsewhere in the essay, this passage stands out for its quavering tone and sudden entry of the first person. Shamsher suddenly speaks in parentheses, as if adding an apologetic aside. The emphasis in his evaluation on grim, terrifying images seems to overwhelm and despair the reader. He turns to the guest in Coleridge's poem, who is gradually overwhelmed by the story he is told. Appropriately, Shamsher's citation both raises a point of comparison and undermines it; Muktibodh's long poem implicates their readers just as, within Coleridge's poem, the guest is implicated and drawn in. The uncertain tone of this passage is appropriate to the seemingly direct implication and involvement of the reader.[14]

But despite this success, Shamsher returns to the awkwardness, difficulty, and strangeness of Muktibodh's work, and especially his long poems. Shamsher, who was already known for his delicate, surrealist lyric poems, presented himself as the opposite of Muktibodh: "Not abstract, but solid. Lyrical like a breeze, gentle meaningless—none of these things: instead in every line he stares at every image in its fullness, and brings it into a violent clarity."[15] Here, too, he portrays Muktibodh as a lonely, haunted figure, standing like a jagged peak as he examines the world. But even more than in the previous essay, he sees Muktibodh's writing as excessive and overwhelming:

> His symbols continually lay the foundation for "story" (or "saga," *myth*). The lightning of the marvelous and unique sparkles in his creative process. Casting aside custom and tradition, the forceful demand for rebellion and a new humanism fills his vocabulary with excitement and *rhetoric*, and the image moves almost into ugliness; but he never causes difficulty on the basis of object or idea. It is true that from time to time Muktibodh, in the stream of his own created "*myth*," flows further away than is necessary.[16]

This quote reveals a tension between image and narrative through which images—or, here, symbols—are continually creating the potential for story. The image is drawn into near-ugliness by that drive, rather than the objective idea of the work itself. The danger with Muktibodh's work, the engine driving its difficulty and awkwardness, is the flow, or *pravāh,* of this embryonic narrative structure.

Shamsher's idea of Muktibodh's poetry as at once vital and excessive was repeated over the next decades of Muktibodh's reception. This was the case, intriguingly, even as the materials available for criticism continued to expand. For instance, the poet and essayist Kedarnath Singh (1934–2018), writing in 1980, framed Muktibodh's writing in terms of alienation, what he called "a fistfight with the imagination of the present."[17] Singh drew from a much larger canvas of Muktibodh's work than the long poems collected in *Cāṃd kā muṃh ṭeṛhā hai,* including the short stories and criticism that have been so prominent in this study, and the essay was written as a review of *Bhūrī bhūrī khāk dhūl* (The Brown and Dusty Earth).[18] Whereas Shamsher viewed Muktibodh's work entirely in terms of the lower middle class and its oppression in Nehruvian India, Kedarnath Singh drew from this new posthumous collection of Muktibodh's work, which contained what Singh saw as more localized poems.

Singh noted that at times the awkwardness and repetition of Muktibodh's poems made them difficult to read; this awkwardness stemmed, he argued, from Muktibodh's attempt to overcome his own alienation from himself. Crucially, for Singh, this alienation included not only a left interpretation of the middle class alienated from its historical purpose, a point that had recently been made by the critic Namwar Singh.[19] Rather, for Singh, this alienation included the personal, such as Muktibodh's background as a Marathi-speaker, leading him to "twist" the syntax of Hindi and producing an essential strangeness.[20] But, ultimately, Singh echoes Shamsher's idea of the long poem as bearing an inherent allegorical relation to contemporary history, and producing an inherent difficulty through its attempt to fuse together a range of disparate images.

Muktibodh's long poems, for these critics, present persistent problems of difficulty—caused, in various ways, by the tension between poetic image and the narrative structure of the poem. What is it about these works that strikes Hindi literature as both so essential and as so indigestibly strange? This chapter takes up the formation and structure of these long poems to answer this question and to better understand how these long poems can be seen as a response to questions of realism, image, and narrative that occupied Muktibodh's own critical thinking.

The World of Beauty and the World of the Novel

> I think I might give this endless poem of mine the shape of a short story. Possibly, some monthly will give me at least fifteen or twenty rupees for it. I'll prove to my friends that I'm not useless, that I can earn some money! And in four days I'll start writing an exam guide [*kuñjī*]. That would work, wouldn't it?
>
> —Muktibodh, "Ek lambī kavitā kā ant"[21]

One of the challenges presented by a study of Muktibodh's long poems is that they are inseparable from his own self-presentation as a representative member of the lower middle class. Just as his critique of realism and literature, as discussed in the second chapter, reads the international debate over realism into the context of an emergent class and caste critique in Nehruvian India, his own consideration of the long poem is refracted through economic anxiety, resentment, and questions of genre. As this quote indicates, Muktibodh was aware that his long poems would be difficult to publish, and that in the 1950s economy of weekly and monthly magazines, the benefits of publishing short stories outweighed those of writing often unpublishable—for length, if not for content—long poems. How, then, did Muktibodh frame and explain these poems as a compulsive—and yet vitally necessary—form?

Long before he wrote his long poems, Muktibodh was concerned with these problems. *Tār Saptak*, the seminal 1944 anthology of which he was one of seven members, included for each a brief autobiographical and poetic statement. Muktibodh, who described the "shadows of the multifarious forests blood-tinged twilights of the winding Kshipra river" as his first poetic inspirations, gives in his autobiography a crucial account of his early education. It also includes the first indication of his later poetic concerns:

> Those were also days of spiritual struggle. On the one hand was the new Hindi poetry of beauty [*saundarya-kāvya*], and

> on the other was the more humanist world of the novel [*upanyās-lok*] in Marathi literature, which had a subtle but powerful influence on my childhood mind. The novels of Tolstoy, with their connections to the great problems of mankind, or Mahadevi Varma? Call it the influence of the time or the desires of my age, or both together, I chose for my domain the world of beauty in Hindi; and that second desire still kept after me, like your conscience stays just behind your mind as it follows you along the road.[22]

Muktibodh goes on to describe this as a tension between beauty and "the sorrows and joys of all mankind," but the comparison between the novel and the poem prefigures the themes and ideas that would eventually become dominant in his work. Here, he is opposed to the work of the poet Mahadevi Varma (1907–1987), typically understood to be one of the four major poets of the *chāyāvād* period. But unlike the other three major poets—Jayshankar Prasad, Sumitranandan Pant, and Nirala—Varma stands out for her investment in Brajbhasha lyric poetry traditions, and Muktibodh's reference to the "world of beauty" in the Hindi poetry of the early 1930s can be read as emphasizing this particular aspect of the *chāyāvād* tradition.[23] The novel—and, intriguingly, Muktibodh emphasizes here Marathi novel tradition that he grew up with and elsewhere associates with Hari Narayan Apte (1864–1919), rather than the realist novels of Premchand in Hindi—presents, in contrast, a humanistic tradition that here, as in the quote that begins the introduction to this book, he associates with the novels of Tolstoy.[24]

After noting the variety of themes in his early work, which he describes as a "migratory instinct," he writes of the necessity to expand the scope of art beyond the individual, and the need to disprove the idea that "this age produces not artists, but volunteers," he writes:

> This very inner curiosity is the reason for the different locations and frequent movement of my poems. But I still have not been able to grasp in my art the *objective* form of these states of curiosity [*jijñāsā-vṛtti*]. My experience tells that this will only be obtained through the

> novel. However, in poetry there can be a poem which is an image of life—or rather a scientific "*type*"—of its emergence, or a poem of an intense idea, or a pure poem of word-images. This is exactly what I wish to practice [*prayog*]. The old tradition certainly cannot be dispensed with, but it is my own tradition and it should, certainly, be transmitted.[25]

The voice of Muktibodh in 1944, newly converted to Marxism, still influenced by Bergson—both of whom he mentions in this essay—at the cusp of a shift towards modernism in Hindi poetry that would soon become permanent, and devoid of the dark, bitter critique that would become central to his later criticism, nevertheless focuses on an essential dualism between poetry and prose. The novel, he claims here, is inherently capable of producing an objective form of the world. Poetry, by contrast has the capacity to generate what he describes variously as an image, type, or idea. His description of the poem seems to draw from both modernist traditions of imagism and from what he calls the "old tradition" of the Hindi and Brajbhasha lyric.[26]

Whereas the description of the novel, in its rhetorically unfraught relation to the real, is concise and confident, the description of poetry and its abilities is prolix and contorted. Muktibodh seems to be grasping at something here: the poem, which seemingly fails at the only important task of art, can nevertheless do something different, and essential—but the description of this evades the grasp of the artist. The succession of terms describing the artistic capabilities of the poem, even at this very early stage, describes a problem that Mutkibodh would continue to work through for the next twenty years.

The end of Muktibodh's life was, by most accounts, a difficult time. Although he achieved some financial stability with a position as college instructor in Rajnandgaon, that stability was undermined when, upon the publication of a history textbook intended for high school syllabi in 1962, he became the subject of a statewide court case launched by the Hindu Mahasabha. The case ultimately led to the book being pulled from publication, and the trial saw several public processions that, according to some accounts, included chants of *Muktibodh murdābād*, or "death to Muktibodh." According to his younger brother Sharachchandra, after this event he "broke from the inside" (*andar se ṭūṭ gayā*).[27]

In this context, which also saw the creation of some of his most enduring writing, his criticism and personal writing took on a more and more despairing tone, but they also shed light on some of the most crucial aspects of his writing process that concern us. As the twentieth anniversary of *Tār saptak*'s publication approached, Muktibodh was invited to update his personal statement, and include a selection of his newer poems.

Revisiting his younger self must have been difficult; his collected works include four attempts to write the statement, only one of which was published while he was alive. The statements, to varying degrees, describe postindependence life as a torment, filled with harsh experiences that cast a dark shadow over his works. They also demonstrate that the problem of poetic form, which can be seen in an initial stage in his first *Tār saptak* statement, has shifted to the center of his thinking. In a longer draft statement, for instance, he writes:

> Even though in later years, slowly, the black color of my poetry has begun to melt a bit, the *imagery* has grown without pause. The themes, too, have continuously become more and more varied and expansive, to the point where, after 1952 or 1953, my poems have expanded their form and shape. Although the earlier poems were not particularly short, now they were truly extended [*pradīrgh*].
>
> How did all this happen? Why did the *imagery* grow like this? Why did the topics become so expansive? Why did the poems become extended? Answering all this is outside my abilities. It is, truly, a question for me as well.[28]

The word Muktibodh uses to describe the length of his poems is *pradīrgh,* which I have translated as "extended." Although the term is somewhat uncommon in Hindi compared to Marathi, it is used by Ashok Vajpeyi as well in his letter to Muktibodh. In contrast, Shamsher often describes Muktibodh's works as *viśāl,* a word I translate as "massive" or "expansive," and which carries with it a sense of grandiosity, even beauty; the dominant Hindi magazine of the 1940s, for instance, was titled *Viśāl bhārat,* "Great India," and expressed an expansive, internationally connected India at the verge of independence.[29] In calling his poems *pradīrgh* rather than the more quotidian *lambī*, "long," Muktibodh emphasizes what seems to him to be a length that is overwhelming and unmanageable, a compulsion of his work that he seems unable to explain even to himself. These long poems are not simply long, narrative projects but something, at least in this account, grotesque and excessive. In the statement that was eventually published, describing the relatively short new poems he includes, he writes, "Perhaps I can no longer write poems shorter than these."[30]

An anxiety over length, a concern with the boundaries of poetry, and a connection between this and his growing pessimism and idea of the lower middle class: by the end of his life, these had become abiding concerns of Muktibodh's criticism. One of the most illuminating examples of this is found in one of the personal essays collected in *Ek sāhityak kī ḍāyarī* (A Writer's Diary), "Ek lambī kavitā kā ant" (The End of a Long Poem). Like his other considerations of the long poem, it mixes a personal discussion of anxiety—the essay begins with a grimly humorous discussion of just how unappealing and unpublishable Muktibodh imagines his endless poems might be—with one of the most perceptive and in-depth analyses of how he views the purpose and structure of his work.

Whereas in his early *Tār saptak* statement, Muktibodh framed the issue as one between an "objective reality" of the novel and the imagistic intensity of the lyric, it is clear in "Ek lambī kavitā kā ant" that a more sophisticated theory of realism and narrative informs his thinking about the long poem:

> The facts of reality are knotted together, and all of reality is dynamic [gatiśīl]. The reality that becomes the subject of expression is equally dynamic, and its material is equally interconnected. This is why I can never write a short poem; a short poem is, in fact, simply unfinished. (I'm speaking for myself.) And I can't count how many poems I've left incomplete in this way. I lack the art of an ending, and this is my tragedy.[31]

This passage brings narrative to the fore in the form through claiming that reality is dynamic and interconnected. The passage arguably reflects the twenty years of development not only of Muktibodh's poetry, but of his criticism, and his involvement in some of the international debates on aesthetics with which he was familiar. As was discussed in the second chapter, Mutkibodh was familiar with the question of realism and its relation to social totality, even as he refracted the problem through the idea of the emergent lower middle class. Whereas in the 1940s, he was concerned with the poetic image and its relation to an objective reality, and the question how poetry could create a comprehensible language of modernism, here he is more concerned with the stakes of narrative in poetry and poetry's relation to an inherently narrativized idea of realism. But, at least according to this passage, lyric narrative, even as it combines and incorporates the isolated elements of reality, does not allow for any narrative closure as might prose literature.

Why not simply transform these pieces into infinitely more rewarding prose stories? Muktibodh answers this question at the close of the essay, in an extended description of an allegory that—in a far milder echo of Brecht than that which was discussed in the second chapter—he uses as the base to construct an alternative model of realism. After a long discussion of corruption of postindependence society, he writes:

> So, I used these sooty colors in one of my poems. The difference is only that in that same place, the actions and causes, the relations of this darkness are also presented. Now, poetry is not an essay in which someone might learn about the state of the world today; nor is it a play, in which a character might appear and present this life-reality [*jīvan-yathārth*] in an abstract form. Besides music, poetry is the most abstract of the arts. In it reality is presented only as a feeling [*bhāva*], or as an image, or as an idea. The theatricality of a poem is in fact the dynamism of feeling. In this, the narrative [*kathā-tattva*] contained within a poem is also a history of feeling [*bhāva kā itihās*].[32]

As elsewhere, Muktibodh's aesthetic theory works through *rasa* theory. The narrative within a poem is a "history of feeling" because this feeling is the visible, or present, emotion, which, in traditional theories of rasa, would indicate an underlying "savor" defined as *rasa*. In this formulation, however, the dynamic feeling presents the dynamic and interconnected nature of reality itself.

The idea that a dynamic, interconnected reality can be presented through a suggested narrative implies the allegorical, which is precisely how Muktibodh views his work: "There is only the appearance of plot, a mirage of theatricality. It is a purely subjective poem and the color of that poem is dark, absolutely dark. Fear, terror, uncertainty, curiosity, curiosity and its resolution, worry and anxiety glimmer out from it. It is actually an *allegory*."[33] The allegory—Muktibodh uses here both the English word and *rūpak*, a term that in modern Hindi is usually differentiated from *pratīk*, or symbol—serves in this criticism to indicate the ways in which the poem, from its subjective basis and through its use of what Muktibodh calls "imagery" to depict a dynamic, interconnected reality. He then goes on to describe the allegory itself:

> There is an individual, who feels they have entered into a kind of forbidden compound. Inside that compound is a bungalow—old and falling apart. A mysterious bungalow. There the individual meets a secretive man. They meet a second man as well who is completely mad. In the end of the poem it is stated that the steps inside this house go deep into the earth. The two enter into several countries, they quietly enter into the city clocktower as well as into the utmost locations of the forehead of men. Everyone in this house has made their peace with it and found their balance. As a result, they have all broken from the inside, their hearts have cracked into pieces. It is clear from this that this place is ruled by a kind of parliament of apes. Or nihilism. In brief, a mansion, a symbol of a selfish logician and the people, who have compromised with this and lied to themselves. The soul, within this mansion, has already been murdered. And even as all are aware of this conspiracy they remain silent, because they have compromised with the power of this house.[34]

This story, with its mysterious mansion, uncertain geography, and atmosphere of paranoia, could fit any of the works that have been thus far discussed in the book, from the shifting staircase of

"Brahmarākṣas" to the short stories of compromise and fear discussed in the previous chapter. In Muktibodh's own understanding of his work, this is possible only in the poem, as long and unwieldy as it might be, because only the poem can present the allegory of society that he has sketched in the essay: "In prose this allegory appears in a chained sequence; but in a poem the chain breaks, just as dreams appear within a dream—breaking and apart and overturning each other. In my poem, I have tried to be true to this chaos."[35] I believe this essay serves as the most important and illuminating document of Muktibodh's understanding of his own poems, because it presents what he views as the essential quality of poetry: the ability to present an allegorical narrative. Prose, in his account, cannot but be syntactic in its structure, and there presents the allegory "in a chain." Curiously, however, this statement follows immediately from the readable and effective allegorical story that was outlined in the previous quotation, and is followed by the bitter, sarcastic declaration of intent to write short stories with which I began my consideration of Muktibodh's writing. Why is it that that it is only the poem that can present a narrative that is like a dream, so that prose can lead only to participation in the economic system that Muktibodh critiques?

To answer that question, I think we need to understand the formal structure of these poems—the ways in which they create the broken, uncertain structures of narrative that Muktibodh believes are uniquely capable in accessing the real. This consideration will include not only the imagery and content of the long poems but also their syntax, grammar, and their poetics. The poetics of the long poem are far from the rough, excessive qualities described by Shamsher or Kedarnath Singh, nor would I attribute them to a struggle with the Marathi language. Marathi literature, and the approach in Marathi to modernist long poems, may however turn out to play a crucial role.

The Multiple Pasts of Free Verse

Prayogvād and *Nayī kavitā* are historicized as the moment in which free verse became dominant in Hindi poetics, in contrast with the *chāyāvād* and post-*Chāvāvād* poetry that dominated through the

1930s. Essays like "Arth kī lay" (The Rhythm of Meaning), published in the journal *Nayī kavitā* (New Poetry) in 1956, cited I. A. Richards and T. S. Eliot to argue for a poetics in which rhythm and meter would be linked to the meaning of a poem.[36] But even as *nayī kavitā* would seem to mark its global postwar canonization, this essay shows how Anglo-American modernist aesthetics was reinterpreted in Hindi through the critical vocabulary of the *chāyāvād* period that preceded it. After framing *nayī kavitā* as a wholesale critique of the entire rasa system of Sanskrit poetics in favor of a new era of objectivity, the essay concludes with a quotation from the poetry of Sumitranandan Pant:

> *chand bandh khul gaye*
> *gadya kyā banīṃ svaroṃ kī pāṃteṃ?*
> *sonā pighal kabhī kyā*
> *pānī bantā? kaisī bāteṃ!*
>
> The dam of verse has broken
> Have lines of song become prose?
> Does gold ever melt
> Into water? What nonsense![37]

These lines indicate the revolutionary advent of free verse, even as they modulate and undercut its impact. They were written, however, by a poet who, thirty years previously, had announced his own poetic revolution in the preface to *Pallav*, his first collection of poems. Pant's *Chāyāvād* claimed a sharp break not from verse itself, but from the metrical forms of an earlier generation of poets such as Maithilisharan Gupt.[38] These poets attempted to establish a modern Hindi poetry that would be distinguished from the earlier Brajbhasha verse of the nineteenth century through its adoption of complicated—and prestigious—Sanskrit meters associated with the great *kāvya* poems. In their place, Pant and the other *chāyāvād* poets favored a range of verse forms taken from registers outside of the Brajbhasha tradition, which often were closer in their sound system to the still-new language in which these poets were writing. But as Pant's later poetic quote indicates, the *chāyāvād* poets did not consider this to be an abandonment of verse itself; even if the lines of poetry loosened and softened, they would not dissolve into water.

For *chāyāvād* poets, their language was not "new" in the sense of a Poundian modernist aesthetics of newness; quite literally, the Hindi in which they wrote was seen as an entirely new language. Modern Hindi, taking its shape from the same dialect used to write Urdu, known as *Khaṛī bolī* and centered in and near Delhi, departed dramatically from the Brajbhasha that had been a dominant language form of poetry for the previous three hundred years, and would be canonized in literary history as the predecessor to modern Hindi poetry.[39] Pant's preface to *Pallav* was a manifesto of a new poetics for a new language, explicitly tied to the political project of modern Hindi and claiming poetic experimentation as a nationalist imperative.[40] The poetics which resulted did not discard meter but, if anything, emphasized its importance through experimentation, adopting new verse forms drawn from folk songs and materials outside the Brajbhasha canon.

Thus, when Jagdish Gupt cited Pant, he recalled a tumultuous history in which, within living memory, poets had attempted to adopt classic Sanskrit meters, discarded that in favor of new and experimental metrical forms, and now were discarding those new meters in favor of a "dam breaking" of free verse. A comparable shift had taken place across other literary cultures of South Asia—although in Hindi this was accompanied by the complication of an entirely new register. But poets such as Muktibodh and his contemporaries, even as they adopted free verse forms for the vast majority of their work, continued to operate under a "ghost of meter," not least through their childhood poetic educations in *chāyāvād*. But where in the case of Eliot this expressed itself in the recurring use iambic pentameter, for writers in Hindi the situation was more complicated. In particular, in contrast with the dominance of stress-timed meters in English, writers in Hindi dealt with a wide range of metrical traditions, some of which drew from a distinction that was shared by literary cultures across South Asia, between moraic and syllabic meters.

Classical Sanskrit featured a moraic system of meter, comparable to that used in ancient Greek and Latin, which relied upon a conception of syllables as short, *laghu*, or long, *guru*, based on the distinction between long and short vowel sounds in Sanskrit. With the important exception of the syllabic meters of an earlier Vedic Sanskrit, both the *gaṇa* meters, associated with *kāvya* poems such as the *mandākrāntā* meter, and *āryā* meters, which used a complex system of the numerical counts of individual mora, assumed a binary length of syllables between long and short. This system was also the basis of the most prominent meters used in Brajbhasha and Avadhi poetry, such as the *dohā* and *chaupāī* meters used in the *Ramacaritamānas*. Moraic meters continued to naturally fit in the poetics of these languages that maintain a distinction between length in vowels.[41]

Other modern languages, however, did not always maintain the same distinction between vowel length, so that gradually the moraic system of Sanskrit became less and less practical, even as it often continued to be used. In languages that had lost some or all systems of vowel length, meters based upon a syllabic count came to predominate in popular culture, eventually becoming the basis for new metrical systems as they were adopted in written language. In Bangla, for instance, the dominant meter used before free verse is the *payār*, which features a syllabic count rather than the use of mora. Even in Hindi, moraic meters often existed alongside folk meters, even as the moraic meters were largely dominant.[42] In all of these languages, though, poets in the *chāyāvād* and comparable poetic movements debated whether their metrical experiments would be based on moraic systems, which were often coded as "classical," or syllabic systems, which were seen as more popular and rooted in living linguistic traditions.[43] At stake in all these debates was not only a formal poetics, that is, the metrical shape that might become a standard basis for a "modern" poetry; but rather, the position of a given poetics vis-à-vis the range of literary cultures and traditions available. Would Hindi be influenced by the rhythms of Braj or Urdu, still perceived as ineffably melodious? Or instead, would it find its inspiration from a range of folk traditions, with looser meters that came closer to the shape of *kharī bolī* speech that was the new poetic idiom? In short, through debating meter, writers at this time debated the position of their poetics to an entire literary history, as well as a politics of language.

Although Muktibodh's earliest poems used meters common to *chāyāvād* poetry, and even some of his *Tār saptak* poems used a range of blank verse forms, his later poetry is written in free verse. As discussed in the first chapter of this book, long poems such as "Brahmarakshas" and "Aṃdhere meṃ" do not make use of any structures associated with *kāvya* narrative poetry, despite Muktibodh's deep familiarity with them. But they do feature a regular rhythmic structure common across the long poems, and criticism in Hindi has analyzed Muktibodh's free verse as drawing from a range of predecessors. Although one recent work has argued that Muktibodh's free verse should be seen as an extension of the use of the syllabic *ghanākṣarī* meter used by Nirala, I would like to suggest, however, that the poetic structure of the long poem draws significantly from an underresearched aspect of Muktibodh's background—Marathi literature.[44]

The influence of Marathi on Mutkibodh's work was, in his initial reception and afterwards, seen as primarily negative, and refracted through the politics of Hindi after independence. A special issue published after his death in the Maharashtra-based Hindi journal *Vīṇā*—one of the first volumes dedicated to his work—framed his decision to write in Hindi as a matter of national integration, noting with pride that he did this despite growing up in a Marathi-speaking household.[45] Other critics, seizing on a casual comment that Muktibodh "was relearning Hindi literature," framed his difficulty and awkward language as a linguistic defect of "incorrect Hindi." Even sophisticated and crucial accounts of his work, such as those of Shamsher Bahadur Singh and Kedarnath Singh, saw his Marathi bilingualism as a sign of roughness, with Kedarnath Singh describing it as a source of his "linguistic alienation."[46]

I would argue, however, that the influence of Marathi on Muktibodh's work, far from evidence for his writing as that of a rough outsider to Hindi, demonstrates the richness of the multilingual milieu of Central India, and especially that of the cities of Indore, Ujjain, and Nagpur, in which Muktibodh lived and worked for most of his life. That his brother Sharachchandra became a major poet and critic in Marathi—the only instance of which I am aware in which two brothers became major literary figures in two different languages—points towards the vitality of this world. Writers in both these languages were linked in networks created by family and friendship, in addition to reading across language and translation. For Muktibodh, therefore, access to Marathi poetics was not a source of awkwardness but of inspiration.[47]

Muktachanda between Marathi and Hindi

As is the case in Bangla, modern Marathi similarly lost most distinctions between long and short vowel sounds, creating a tension in its modern poetics between Sanskritized moraic meters and more popular syllabic meters. Quantitative *ovī-abhaṅga* meters, which featured extremely short line lengths measured in four, six, or eight syllables, featured prominently in the religious *santa* literature of figures such as Dnyandev (1275–1296), Eknath (1533–1599), and Tukaram (1568–1650), as well as long, narrative works, such as the *bhaktivijaya,* all of which provided a strong counterbalance to the moraic meters used in early twentieth century verse.[48] The *abhaṇga* in particular was capable of a great deal of compression, with its short lines and minimalist rhyme scheme, as in this example from Tukaram:

Āmhāṃ gharī dhana
Śabdāṃcīca ratneṃ
Śabdāṃcīca śastreṃ
Yatna karūṃ

The wealth of my home
These jewels of words
With words in my hands
I struggle.[49]

Here, the first three lines have six syllables, and the final line has four. The meaning here hinges on a play of repetition and difference, with *śabda,* word, changing its reference from *ratneṃ,* jewels, to *śāstreṃ,* arms, tools, or weapons. The poem strips the Marathi language of as much information as possible, using the shortest possible means of indicating syntactic relationships and avoiding any verbs until the final *yatna karūṃ.*

For the first generation of Marathi modernist poets, metrical experimentation was a common concern.[50] Bāl Sitaram Mardhekar (1909–1956), whose 1947 *Kāhī kavitā* is considered a watershed moment in Marathi modernist poetry, caused a sensation—that later led to an obscenity charge—by using these forms to describe modern life.[51] The first lines of "ovī 16" not only underline the sexual connotation of the *śivaliṅga*—an abstract representation of the penis of Shiva that is used as a religious object—but also compare it to the speaker's own sexual drive:

> *Śivaliṅga mājheṃ liṅga; heṃca aśāntīceṃ biṃga,*
> *Jyāñcyā jhujeṃ sañjñāriṅga; vyāpileṃ gā.*
>
> Shiva's lingam and mine,
> Right here is the crack of unrest;
> As they wrestle
> In the ring of the mind,
> It spreads open and wide.[52]

Here, the *ovī* is divided into two lines, split into four feet or sections. The first three sections are composed of eight syllables, and the final, four. These lines still have the power to shock in their comparison of the speaker's body with the divine form of Shiva; they are also striking because, while perfectly fulfilling all the technical requirements of the *ovī*, they use the traditional form to describe a psychoanalytic struggle of the mind, including a very rare use of an English word compounded with Marathi to form *sañjñāriṅga*, "the ring of the mind."

Roughly contemporary with the more well-known Mardhekar, Atmaram Ravaji Deshpande "Anil" (1901–1982), also experimented with *ovī-abhaṅga* meters; but whereas Mardhekar played on the ironic distance between form and content, Anil used them as the basis for *muktachanda*, literally "free verse." Despite its name, *muktachanda* was not precisely free so much as it was modular. Anil's *muktachanda* was composed of sets of feet that can be combined to make a line of multiple lengths. These feet were themselves composed of syllable counts of four, five, or six that were neither long nor short, and distinguished by a light stress at the beginning of the line. The stress—which has no place in any traditional South Asian prosodic systems—could be used to serve to differentiate syllabic feet without the use of a caesura, rhyme, or line break.

Anil created his *muktachanda* system specifically for the purposes of creating long narrative poems. The first and most prominent of these was titled *Bhagnamūrti* (The Broken Statue), first published in 1940. The poem included a long afterword in which Anil explains the *muktachanda* in detail, describing it as a modernist interpretation of the *ovī-abhaṅga,* with its linked syllabic units providing a metrical structure that would be able to address the modern world, even as it was rooted in what he saw as the natural and popular rhythms of the Marathi language, through its concision and brevity.[53]

The opening lines of *Bhagnamūrti* demonstrate this system:

Bhagnamūrti — ! āṇi / bhagnamandira
Samoraca āhe / ticeṃ paḍakeṃ
Avaghe cāraca/ pāṣāṇastambha

The broken statue—! And a broken temple
Its ruins lying all around
Pieces of rubble in all directions[54]

Here, the first line contains two feet, one of six syllables and one of five. The first foot, "*bhagnamūrti — ! āṇi*" (Broken statue—! and) contains the beginning of a second phrase, creating a tension between the flow of the line and the syntax of the poem, one emphasized by the stress placed on the first syllable of the foot. In this case, that stress falls twice on the prefix *bhagna,* "broken," to draw out both the breathiness of the opening *bha* and the sharpness of the consonant cluster *gna* that makes up the following syllable. By contrast, the final three syllables of the foot flow smoothly, broken only by a nasal consonant, *ṇ*. A foot cannot break across a word, but it can break anywhere else. Because the lines are so short, the *muktachanda* creates a range of possibilities for enjambment and unusual stress, just as do the *ovī* and *abhaṅga.*

Anil lived and worked as a judge in Nagpur—where Muktibodh would himself reside from 1950 to 1957—and *Bhagnamūrti* was translated in 1958 by Muktibodh's friend and schoolmate Prabhakar Machwe, with some assistance by Muktibodh's own brother, Sharachchandra Muktibodh.[55] Although he was younger than his brother by four years, Sharachchandra's first collection of poetry, *Navī Maḷvaṭ* (A New Path) was published in 1949, fifteen years before Muktibodh's first collection. A second collection, *Yātrik* (Pilgrim), was published in 1957. Almost all of the poems in these collections use Anil's *Bhagnamūrti* meter. In a long afterward to *Navī maḷvaṭ* written in 1964, Sharachchandra credits the creation of this meter to Anil.[56] He also emphasizes the connection between *muktachanda*-based free verse and the *ovi/abhaṅga* tradition of Marathi poetry, noting, "it would not be overly optimistic to believe that someday *muktachanda* will receive the same respect and acceptance as *ovi* and *abhanga*."[57]

Anil's innovative *muktachanda* meter was specifically made for a new form of long, modernist poem, and was rapidly adopted by Muktibodh's own brother. It makes sense, therefore, to wonder whether Muktibodh—Gajanan Madhav Muktibodh, that is—was similarly influenced, despite writing in Hindi.[58] The *muktachanda* of *Bhagnamūrti* and of Sharachchandra's modernist poetry could be seen as supplying precisely the paratactic structure that Muktibodh seems to be grasping at in essays such as "Ek lambī kavitā kā ant," which, in its modular, endlessly rearrangeable lines and variable line length, might allow for a dreamlike, disconnected logic, even as it provides a formal framework on which to build the larger structure of the poem.

As I discussed earlier, Muktibodh came to prominence in Hindi poetry with the 1943 release of *Tār saptak* (A Heptad of Strings) an epochal anthology of seven poets that is canonized as the beginnings of modernism in Hindi poetry.[59] Perhaps surprisingly, not all of Muktibodh's poems for *Tār saptak* are written in free verse; about half of the poems use Hindi meters popular in the post-*chāyāvād* poetry of the 1930s. Those free verse poems, however, are consistent in their form of variable lines that can be broken into four-to-six syllable units. For instance, "Dūr tārā" (Distant Star), which considers the connection between the path of a star and the conscience of the individual, makes use of free verse, and in particular enjambment, for its effects. Consider the first stanza, which acts as a clue to the form:

tīvra-gati
ati-dūr tārā,
vaha hamārā
śūnya ke vistār nīle meṃ calā hai.

Racing away
ever-distant star,
gone off into
our absence's abundant blue.[60]

Three short lines followed by one long line: you could read this either with the first three lines broken apart, or with the final line an amalgamation of the shorter ones. I prefer the latter, given the rhythmic connections between the three: "tīvra-ga**ti**/ a**ti** dār **tārā**/ vah ham**ārā**." The final line breaks these rhythmic connections, but presents instead a line that neatly combines the syllables of the prior two: the eleven syllables of "ati-dūr tārā / vaha hamārā" leading into "śūnya ke vistār nīle meṃ calā hai." The transition of the shorter lines to the longer lends a sense of breath or expanse, in contrast to the rapid, enjambed breaks of the shorter lines. Furthermore, the syllabic organization contrasts with the real differences between vowel sounds, so that the short *a* and *i* sounds contrast against their longer counterparts before stretching out in the final line.

In Muktibodh's later poems, namely, those written in the rest of the 1940s, the influence of the *muktachanda* can be indexed to the development of form that would result in his later works. At the moments in which his poetry departs most decisively from the post-*chāyāvād* ideal—poetry which was progressive in theme, and more explicitly metrical in form—Muktibodh makes greater use of the *muktachanda* possibilities of free verse. For instance, a poem such as "pīlā tārā" (Yellow Star), written between 1944 and 1948, can be seen as a continuation of the themes of "dūr tārā"; the *muktachanda* rhythm shines through in its opening stanza:

apnī hī parchāīṃ-sā jo dhuṃdhlā hai
pīlā tārak
vah ho na sakūṃgā,
kṣamā karo.

smudged like your own shadow
little yellow star
i can't become,
forgive me.[61]

The rhythmic setting of "dūr tārā," in which a shorter line leads to a longer, is here reversed, with a longer, segmented line concluding with the dirgelike *pīlā tārak*. Like a grim nursery rhyme, the cascading, grand statement of cosmic significance of the star collapses, as if under its own weight, into declarations of incapability. If free verse was imagined as an expansion, a dam bursting, then these lines feel like the opposite, free verse as a whispering denial of lyric potentiality. In this way, "pīlā tārā" marks a turning point in Muktibodh's work: in contrast to "dūr tārā," the idea of a self as participating in the cosmos is denied and scrubbed away.

In later poems, as this confessional style comes to predominate, the *muktachanda* rhythms remain prominent, as in the 1953 "pahlī paṅkti":

pahlī paṅkti na ban pāyī jab—
nūpur-svar bhar, chanda tham gaye āṃgan meṃ hī
kahāṃ ruk gayī darvāze par,

When the first line doesn't take shape—
the ringing anklets of meter freezing at the threshold,
the words stopping at the door,[62]

Here, the "awkward" syntax of Muktibodh, sometimes referred by his critics, makes more sense when considered as forming units of a *muktachanda*-influenced line, with the grammatical particles *na* and *jab* pushed to the end of the units, and the words *pahlī, ban, nūpur chanda, āṃgan, kahāṃ,* and *darvāze* emphasized instead. The effect is to create a driving, pulsing rhythm across the three lines. The influence of the *muktachanda* in this way appears in Muktibodh's poetry as a defining feature of the long poem, to greater and greater extent as this form comes to dominate his works.

As this overview of Muktibodh's earlier works demonstrates, the Marathi *muktachanda* exerted an influence on Muktibodh's poetics because it was available at the exact moment in which he was attempting to create a form for his long poems, a poetics that include both narrative breadth and lyric intensity. While, to my current knowledge, he never commented on this aspect of his work, an analysis of his use of line, stress, and syllabic lengths makes a strong case for the importance of this form to his development as a poet. Although this analysis only touches on the larger question of the geography of literary form, it shows the history of South Asian modernisms to be one of influences moving across literary cultures of South Asia, in addition to participation in global literary movements. Certainly, writers in Hindi and Marathi were well aware of the shift to free verse in European languages, but the process through which free verse became dominant was one based on a complex series of decisions and negotiations with multiple literary traditions.

For Muktibodh, although the end result was a strikingly modernist long poem, both the motivating factors and the poetic resources utilized to create this form were specific to his own time and place. His long poems can be read both as an intervention in the debates over realism and modernism that dominated Hindi literature after independence and as an articulation of a shared literary culture across North Indian literary modernisms. In this case, the influence of Marathi poetics can point towards one answer for how Muktibodh's long poem was able to respond to a problem of image and narrative in postindependence Hindi modernism. In the literary history of Hindi, this indicates an alternate interpretation of the twentieth century—Hindi not in competition with the other languages of India, as is often portrayed, but actively engaged and interactive across the wide geographic space in which it was used.

The Formal Structure of the Long Poem

As I have shown above, Muktibodh developed a form of long narrative poetry that, once developed, he used throughout his career. This long poem has a metrical system that, as a distinct form of free verse, allowed Muktibodh to compose long, disjointed poems that nevertheless held together as a cohesive rhythm and form. What were the poetic potentials opened up by this form? What did it allow him to do that no other form could? Given his frequent distinctions made between the short lyric and prose fiction, why did he continue to extend and develop the long poem? To begin to answer these questions, I will turn to "Aṃdhere meṃ" (In the Dark). Easily Muktibodh's most famous poem—in fact, it is his only long poem to be translated into English in its entirety—and subject to several monograph-length works of criticism, "Aṃdhere meṃ" has a long reception history and outsized place in Hindi literary history. But "Aṃdhere meṃ" forms an ideal test site because, more than any of Muktibodh's other long poems, it is most engaged with forming its narrative from the disjuncture between everyday life and the nightmarish allegories that find allegorical expression in Muktibodh's work. This may, in fact, be part of the reason for its enduring appeal. It also tests my theory that the long poem is uniquely able to do the work of creating paratactic, fantastic narratives that are nonetheless engaged with the political and social reality that Muktibodh wished to depict. For "Aṃdhere meṃ," the balance between rhythmic regularity and the shifting sands of fantasy are crucial to create the feeling of a waking dream, regularly punctured by unreal visions that dominate the poem.

As its name might suggest, "Aṃdhere meṃ" takes place over the course of a single night—occasional references to time hint at a narrative structure that never fully comes into shape. Similarly, the poem references the structure of Shelley's "The Mask of Anarchy" in its depiction of a dream state and its nightmare depiction of the political present—complete with a parade that includes not only military and repressive forces, but also the intelligentsia.[63] The poem describes a long night in which a narrator wanders through an unnamed Indian city, strongly implied to be Nagpur, between dreamlike experiences and moments of clarity. These experiences become increasingly intense before culminating in a moment of apocalyptic violence just before daybreak. The poem ends with the speaker searching for the guru that he has intermittently sought throughout the poem. Although noted for its allegory of contemporary Indian life, the narrative relies just as much on the grounded experience of its speaker as on its more fantastic elements.

The poem begins with brief, staccato lines:

zindagī ke . . .
kamroṃ meṃ aṃdhere
lagātā hai cakkar
koī ek lagātār;
life's . . .
dark chambers:
walking in circles
someone, endlessly;[64]

These short lines are staggered across the page, producing a visual isolation that also evokes the *muktachanda* heritage of Muktibodh's long poem. These lines can be read as one line of four syllables, two of six and one of five: the quintessential rhythm of the *muktachanda*. The tension created between the enjambment of the lines and the syntax of the sentence enacts the drama of the poem. An enjambed syntactic relation between *zindagī ke* and the following line is created, joined together by the ellipsis. The shift between life—the word used, *zindagī*, is banal and quotidian—and dark rooms, the place of dreams and nightmares, will be repeated throughout the poem. The next two lines introduce an element of menace, of an encounter of some sort, of the tension created by pacing in a small room:

āvāz pairoṃ kī detī hai sunāyī
bār-bār . . . bār-bār,
vah nahīṃ dīkhtā . . . nahī hī dīkhtā,
kintu, vah rahā ghūm
tilasmī khoh meṃ giraftār koī ek,
bhīt-pār ātī huī pās se,
gahan rahasyamay andhakār dhvani-sā
astitva janātā
anivār koī ek,
aur, mere hṛday kī dhak-dhak
pūchtī hai—vah kaun
sunāyī jo detā, par nahī detā dikhāyī!

his feet sound out
again and again . . . again and again,
don't see . . . can't see
but still he wanders
a prisoner in the enchanted cave
from across the walls it comes to me
an echo, from across the black mysterious depths
someone
announces himself
unstoppable
and, the beat of my heart
asks—who is he
I hear, but cannot see[65]

The poem suddenly erupts—a prisoner in a "fantastic cave" sounds out from somewhere across the walls. The phrase references the prisoner in a magical cave of *Candrākāntā*, a widely read nineteenth-century novel that appears frequently in Muktibodh's works.[66] Here the lines roughly double in length, and the diction shifts into high, romantic, *chāyāvād*-era language, strongly influenced by Sanskrit, that stretches out the reading with long vowels: "gahan rah**as**yamay **andh**ak**ā**r dhvani-**sā**."[67] Words and phrases begin to repeat themselves, and the tension in the lines builds up to an exclamation, followed by:

itne meṃ akasmāt girte haiṃ bhītar se
phūle hue palistar,
khirtī hai cūne-bharī ret
khisaktī haiṃ papaṛiyāṃ is tarah—
khud-ba-khud
koī baṛā cehrā ban jātā hai,
svayamapi
mukh ban jātā hai divāl par,
nukīlī nāk aur
bhavya lalāṭ hai,
dṛṛh hanu,
koī anjānī an-pahcānī ākṛti.

And then suddenly falling away from within
the plaster cracking and bursting open
sandy lime falling out
skins sloughing off—
on its own
a massive face appears
a self-generated
a face appears on the wall,
with a pointed nose
and a splendid forehead,
a straight jaw
of some strange and unrecognized figure.[68]

Repeatedly in "Aṃdhere meṃ" a shift occurs with a sudden, jerking transition: "suddenly," "at once," "meanwhile." After the building anticipation of the opening lines, the walls of experience literally break apart. The diction abruptly shifts into a highly classicized, Sanskrit register. The word *khud-ba-khud,* "on its own," derived from Persian, is followed by *svayamapi,* a word derived from Sanskrit with an almost identical meaning, but one that is far less common in the spoken language. The figure, as it appears in the wall, is removed from the everyday not only in its unreality, but in its own linguistic presentation to the reader. But despite the shift in diction—which includes more words of greater length—the meter remains consistent. The poetics of the long form contains massive shifts in tone and texture while still maintaining a consistency of reading. As abrupt and complex as the poem appears to the reader, this allows for an experience of flowing along with a stable tempo.

If the rhythm established in the first lines of "Aṃdhere meṃ" was discarded, if each of the eight major sections of the poem took up a different structure, for instance, then the rhythm would matter less. But the opposite is true: the *muktachanda* rhythm referenced in the opening lines of the poem repeats itself, again and again, across the length of the work as a whole. The third section of the poem begins with the lines:

samajh na pāyā ki cal rahā svapna yā
jāgrati śurū hai.
diyā jal rahā hai,
pītālok-prasār meṃ kāl gal rahā hai,
ās-pās phailī huī jag-ākṛtiyāṃ
lagtī haiṃ chapī huī jaṛ citra-kṛtiyoṃ-sī
alag va dūr-dur
nirjīv!!
yah sivil lāins hai. maiṃ apne kamre meṃ
yahāṃ paṛā huā hūṃ.
āṃkheṃ khulī huī haiṃ,
pīṭe gaye bālak-sā mār khāyā cehrā
udās ikharā,
saleṭ-paṭṭī par khīṃcī gayī tasvīr
bhūt-jaisī ākṛti—
kyā vah maiṃ hūṃ?
maiṃ hūṃ?

i don't know if i'm dreaming or
already awake.
the lamp is burning,
in the yellow glow time softens and melts,
all the scattered forms of the world
like printed outlines
utterly distinct
lifeless!!
this is civil lines. i'm lying here
in my room
eyes open
my beaten child's face
lean and depressed
a picture drawn on a chalk board
like a ghost—
is that me?
is it me?[69]

This is a key moment of the poem, in which an initial vision of a mythical *manu* figure, and an invocation of the magical world of *candrakāntā* and of the *tilismīy kahani* (magical tale) has suddenly broken like a fever. In the following stanzas, the fantastic will appear not only as a grandiose, explosive force but as a creeping nightmare, with the appearance of a full military parade. The remainder of the poem will turn between the relations between these different forms of fantasy and the cold shocks of return to the waking world. The pressure is on these lines, then, to pull the reader back into the narrative of the long poem and establish a sense of fragile, jagged calm. The poem is able to do this by, again and again, returning to and departing from the established *muktachanda* line. The second line, which announces waking, is composed of precisely six syllables. The following line features another six syllables, before rhyming with the following, longer line (jal rahā hai / gal rahā hai), in a move that creates a syntactic relation between the two lines, but also pushes the shift into the unreal: in the soft light of the lamp, time itself begins to soften like wax or oil, as the visual world takes on the flattened, superficial appearance of stencils or silhouettes. After culminating with the exclamation of "nirjīv!!" (lifeless), the tension breaks with another line that can be broken into two *muktachanda* clauses: "yah sivil lāins hai. maiṃ apne kamre meṃ" (This is Civil Lines. I am in my room). The flat, declarative statements, spoken as if in a cold sweat, grind the action to a halt, clearing a space for the self-reflection that follows.

Both because Muktibodh never commented on this aspect of his poetics and because Marathi and Hindi have different sound systems and literary traditions, I cannot claim that my interpretation of Marathi *muktachanda* is the sole means through which one can approach "Aṃdhere meṃ" and other long poems. As I mentioned, recent work has made a compelling case for reading the history of *ghanākṣarī*, the syllabic meter used by Nirala, in Muktibodh's work, and the conversation of "Aṃdhere meṃ" with Jayshankar Prasad's *Kāmāyanī* is made clear by the repeated invocation of *manu*, the hero of that poem. But considering the long poems through the *muktachanda* draws our attention to the background of these works in the multilingual space of Central India, and the complicated sources for free verse in modern Indian literatures. It also offers a solution to the riddle posed by Muktibodh's criticism; through taking the compressed, dense verse form of the *ovī-abhaṇga* and expanding it to form a long, modernist narrative poem, the *muktachanda* forms a parallel to Muktibodh's desire to create an allegorical poetic structure, which would not be bound to the narrative expectations of prose.

Allegory Itself

"Aṃdhere meṃ" begins in the night, with the vision of a strange, monumental figure. As its narrative proceeds, it enters into and emerges from a range of unreal spaces, snapping between fantasy, nightmare, and what the poem depicts as a cold, clammy reality of insomnia. But whereas other long poems, such as "Brahmarākṣas," present a fully formed story drawn from myth, "Aṃdhere meṃ" is rooted in the city—an urban space vaguely similar to the Nagpur in which Muktibodh spent most of the 1950s.[70] The Nagpur of "Aṃdhere meṃ" is a terrifying, oppressive place, in which the speaker of the poem enters and sees magical, nightmarish scenes. In the most well-known of these scenes, he sees a strange procession marching through the nighttime streets:

proseśan?
nistabdh nagar ke madhya-rātri aṃdhere meṃ sunsān
kisī dūr baiṇḍ kī dabī huī kramāgat tān-dhun,
mand-tār ucc-nimn svar-svapna,
udās-udās dhvani-taraṅgeṃ hai gambhīr,
dīrgh lahariyāṃ!!

gailarī meṃ jātā hūṃ, dekhtā hū rāstā
vah koltār-path athvā
marī huī khiṃcī huī koī kālī jihvā
bijlī ke dyutimān diye yā
mare hue dāṃtoṃ kā camakdār namūnā!!

kintu dūr saṛak ke us chor
śīt-bhare tharrāte tāroṃ ke aṃdhiyāle tal meṃ
nīl tej-udbhās
pās-pās pās-pās
ā rahā is or!
dabī huī gambhīr svar-svapna-taraṅgeṃ,
udās tān-dhun śat-dhvani-saṅgam-saṅgīt
samīp ā rahā!!

aur, ab
gaislāiṭ pāṃtoṃ kī bindūeṃ chiṭkīṃ,
bīcoṃ-bīc unke
sāṃvale julūs-sā kyā-kuch dīkhtā!!

aur ab
gaislāiṭ nilāī meṃ raṃge hue apārthiv cehre,
baiṇḍ-dal,
unke pīche kāle-kāle balvān ghoṛoṃ kā jatthā
dīkhtā,
ghanā va ḍarāvnā avcetan hī
julūs meṃ caltā.
kyā śhobhā-yātrā
kisī mṛtyu dal kī?

ajīb!!
donoṃ or, nīlī-gais-lāiṭ-pāṃt
cal rahī, cal rahī.
nīnd mem khoye hue śahar kī gahan avcetnā meṃ
halcal (pātālī tal meṃ
camakdār sāṃpoṃ kī uṛtī huī lagātār
lakīroṃ kī vārdāt!!
sab soye hue haiṃ.
lekin, maiṃ jāg rahā, dekh rahā
romāñckārī vah jāduī karāmāt!!)

procession?
silently, in the still midnight dark of the city
the muffled beat of a band, off somewhere
sounds from a dream rising and falling on soft strings
rolling echoes, waves of sadness
rolling waves!!

i walk out onto the balcony and watch the street,
a path of coal
some dead black tongue stretched out
sparkling electric lights or
the shining teeth of the dead!!

but, far across the street
at the base of the stars shivering with cold
a dark shining
coming, coming closer
closer!!
those muffled dream sounds
the music of a thousand echoes crashing together
coming closer!!

and, now
the points of the gaslights burst into view
between them appears
something, something like a dark procession!!

and now
endless faces light up in the blue gas light

a marching band
behind them march massive black horses
even in dark and terrifying unconsciousness
is this the parade
of a death squad?

bizarre!!
the lines of the blue gaslight
marching on either side.
in the thick oblivion of the city lost in sleep
(in the underworld
rise up these writhing endless snakes
the tangled lines of calamity!!
all are sleeping.
but i am awake, yes, watching
the bloodcurdling magical feat!!)[71]

Muktibodh's image—which would eventually be included in Mani Kaul's film—of the procession marching through the silent streets evokes the familiar wedding band of the Indian city only to present it as a nightmarish, threatening spectacle. These lines take the innocuous scene and twist it into a nightmare by emphasizing the uncanniness, in isolation, of the elements of the modern city. By placing the procession in the space of a dream, the poem defamiliarizes the everyday of the modern city. The electric lights and blacktopped road, while probably in existence for at least thirty years, would still be unevenly distributed in Central India.[72] Each source of light—the street lamps, the stars, and the gas lamps—are frozen in the darkness. The poem uses the language of a fantastic story to further evoke the "dream-sounds" of the band. The frequent exclamation points of the lines and the language of the fantastic story serve to heighten the symbolic language of the poem, and remove and disorder the elements of the speaker's everyday life.

The dramatic set pieces, such as the parade that chases the speaker down the street, may seem at first—and are at times considered in Hindi criticism—overwrought, fantastic escapes from the problem of the political. Certainly, Muktibodh spent a large chunk of his career as a critic arguing against this interpretation, and his supporters, from Shamsher onwards, have insisted that the allegorical in Muktibodh's work is an attempt to confront the unevenness of contemporary Indian society. Muktibodh, as we saw in his own criticism, would endorse this view. But at the moments in which the imagery became the most intense, it extended beyond the often-restrictive framework placed upon it, into something that would be at place in one of the fantastic stories that the poem constantly evokes. Consider, for instance, the following scene, in which the narrator suddenly finds himself confronted with a statue of the nationalist political leader Bal Gangadhar Tilak (1856–1920):

sapāṭ sūne meṃ ūṃcī-sī khaṛī jo
tilak kī pāṣāṇ-mūrtī hai ni:saṅg
stabha jaṛībhūt.
dekhtā hūṃ usko parantu, jyoṃ hī maiṃ pās pahuṃctā
pāṣāṇ-pīṭhikā hiltī-sī lagtī
are, are, yah kyā!!
kaṇ-kaṇ kaṃp rahe jinmeṃ se jharte
nīle ilekṭron
sab or gir rahī haiṃ cingiyāṃ nīlī
mūrtī ke tan se jharte haiṃ aṅgār.
muskān pattharī hoṭhoṃ par kaṃpī,
aṃkhoṃ meṃ bijlī ke phūl sulagte.
itne meṃ yah kyā!!
bhavya lalāṭ kī nāsikā meṃ se
bah rahā khūn na jāne kab se
lāl-lāl garmīlā rakt ṭapaktā
(khūn ke dhabboṃ se bharā aṃgarkhā)
māno ki atiśay cintā ke kāraṇ
mastak-koṣ hī phūṭ paṛe sahsā
mastak-rakt hī bah uṭhā nāsikā meṃ se.
hāy, hāy, pita: pita: o,
cintā meṃ itne na uljho
ham abhī zindā haiṃ zindā,
cintā kyā hai!!
maiṃ us pāṣāṇ-mūrti ke ṭhaṇḍe
pairoṃ ko chātī se barbas cipkā
ruaṃsa-sā hotā
deh meṃ tan gaye karuṇā ke kaṃṭe
chātī par, sir par, baṃhoṃ par mere
girtī haiṃ nīlī

bijlī kī cingiyāṃ
rakt ṭapaktā hai hṛday meṃ mere
ātmā meṃ bahtā-sā lagtā
khūn kā tālāb.

standing high on the level ground
this lonely, lonely statue of tilak
still, insensate . . .
but at the moment i approach
the base of the statue begins to tremble and move
what, what is this!!
every grain trembles and showers
blue *electrons*
blue sparks falling in every direction
burning sparks flying from the body of the statue.
a smile trembles on lips of stone,
a smoldering bloom of electric life in the eyes.
and then, what is this!!
from the nostrils of that noble face
how long has blood been flowing
warm, red blood, drip by drip
(the overcoat slowly covered with bloodstains)
as if from worry, from stress
the skull has suddenly burst open
brainblood pours from the nostrils.
pitaḥa, pitaḥa, oh *pitaḥa,*
try not to worry
we're still alive, aren't we,
why worry!!
helplessly, i grab hold
of those cold legs
of a stone statue
almost crying
my whole body trembles with compassion
on my chest, on my head, on my arms
fall blue
electric sparks
the blood drips into my heart
as if it floods my soul
a pool of blood.[73]

In this passage, history, contemporary society, and Grand Guignol fantasy combine. The statue of Tilak—most likely a depiction of one that still stands besides an artificial pond in the center of Nagpur—marks the passage, to Hindi readers, as somewhat exotic; although Bal Gangodhar Tilak is a reliable member of the pantheon of nationalist leaders, he is particularly associated with Maharashtra. This locally resonant object, by first coming to life in a shower of blood, before erupting in fountains of blood after, presents a potent image of the anxieties of postindependence life that have been animating the poem as a whole. But this passage, and other similar passages in "Aṃdhere meṃ," rely upon the sense of normalcy, even of calm, that pervades other passages. As he puts it in "Ek lambī kavitā kā ant," images follow upon each other as in a dream. This passage is more than a simple allegory for postindependence disappointment, although it is certainly that as well. It is also a space where various elements of the fantastic—memories of Frankenstein, fantastic romances from the nineteenth century, a gothic vision of a mid-sized Central Indian city—can enter and intermingle within a unique narrative framework. This is the framework that was created by the long poem.

The placement of this moment is crucial. The speaker finds himself in the chamber of his mind roughly in the midpoint of the poem. He has just fled from the demonic possession described above and, after listening to the song of a wandering madman below a banyan tree, has fled again, blindly, through the city. After this moment in the cave, he will again wander through the city, in a series of adventures that will culminate in a violent cataclysm. Here, then, at the center of the poem, the action pauses in order to emphasize not only the dreamlike quality of the narrative, but the artifice of the poem itself. "Aṃdhere meṃ" has a way of reminding its readers of its own construction, with the frequent asides to the dream, the use of metaphors drawn from typography itself, and the emphasis on repeated, fairy tale–like phrases. This sequence makes this connection explicit, before the next section of the poem promptly begins with "sīn badaltā hai" (the scene changes).

The finale of the poem, after the dissolution of the final dream, returns to the idea of the guru that began the poem. After a series of encounters in the city, the speaker finds himself in the midst of violent revolution, in a vision of almost apocalyptic disruption, punctuated by the repeated line "kahīṃ āg lag gayī, kahīṃ golī cal gayī" (A fire started here, bullets flying there).[74] This vision suddenly breaks at morning, and the speaker finds himself once again in his room. The nightmare seems to be at an end. But it is at this moment, in the concluding stanza of the poem, that the speaker remembers once again the guru that had originally sent him on his journey:

vah mere pās kabhī baiṭhā hī nahīṃ thā,
vah mere pās kabhī āyā hī nahīṃ thā,
tilismī khoh meṃ dekhā thā ek bār,
ākhirī bār hī.
par, vah jagat kī galiyoṃ meṃ ghūmtā hai pratipal
vah phaṭe-hāl rūp.
vidyullaharil vahī gatimayatā,
udvigna gyān-tanāv vah
sakarmak prem kī vah atiśayatā
vahī phaṭe-hāl rūp!!
param abhivyakti
avirat ghūmtī hai jag meṃ
patā nahīṃ jāne kahāṃ, jāne kahāṃ
vah hai.
isīlie maiṃ har galī meṃ
aur har saṛak par
jhāṃk-jhāṃk dekhtā hūṃ har ek cehrā,
pratyek gatividhi,
pratyek caritra,
va har ek ātmā kā itihās,
har ek deś va rājnītik sthiti aur pariveś
pratyek mānavīya svānubhūt ādarś
vivek-prakriyā, kriyāgat pariṇati!!
khojtā hūṃ paṭhār . . . pahād . . . samundar
jahāṃ mil sake mujhe
merī vah khoyī huī
param abhivyakti anivār
ātma-sambhavā.

he never sat with me,
he never came to me,
i saw him in that magical cave,

once and for the last time.
but at every moment he moves through the alleyways
in his ragged form.
bursting with lightning
a tensed knot of knowledge
exploding with a love that calls to action
that ragged form!!
the supreme expression
ceaselessly he wanders the earth
who knows where he'll be
where he'll be next.
so i look into every alley,
every lane and street,
i look at every face,
every event
every character,
the story of every soul,
every country political situation circumstance
every ideal born out of humanity
process of discernment, action-bound consequence!!
i search the plateaus, the mountains, the seas,
where i will find
that which i lost
my inevitable, supreme expression
born out of the self.[75]

As I mentioned above, the guru appears rarely in the poem, primarily at the beginning of the poem and at the end. The poem begins with his appearance in the room of the speaker, but for the rest of the poem the speaker is wandering through a nightmarish world of the city, interspersed with moments in the cave of the imagination. Now, the speaker resolves to seek out the guru, but in such a way as to indicate that ultimately the guru is not a person per se, nor even a collective entity as is implied by the lines "I peer at every face / on every street." Rather, the guru here is the imaginative and conceptual faculty of the speaker himself. In this way, my reading departs from interpretations in which "Aṃdhere meṃ" depicts a search for political identity with a larger metasubjectivity. The final lines, which complete a poem that has featured multiple instances of the speaker enacting the revolutionary capability of the imagination, depict the guru not as someone hidden away, but as an expression created out of interaction between the mind of the speaker and his engagement with the world.

Conclusion

The long poems of Gajanan Madhav Muktibodh, even as they are presented as formless responses to history or as a moment in the reception of an Anglo-American modernist model, stand as a formal triumph and a successful experiment in genre formation. The primordial men, fascist marches, and living statues of "Aṃdhere meṃ" exist in a carefully calibrated literary form, one that seems to remain consistent over more than twenty years of literary production, even as the scope of these works grew more ambitious. In spite of what he seems to have perceived, and certainly presented to the world, as an incomplete project, Muktibodh's long poem stands as a monumental achievement in Hindi modernism. Both literary critics and writers have long recognized and analyzed this long poem as the basis for a committed literature that departs from the dictates of formal, social realism, and, although the long poem was never historicized as emerging from a distinct historic conjuncture, as I have done here, it was nonetheless recognized as the basis for a distinct modernist poetics in Hindi.

What can the long poem tell us about South Asian modernisms in the twentieth century? Muktibodh's persistent invocation of the novel and the *mahākāvya* insists on the connection between his poetic form and a larger ecosystem of genre and form. Although, as I have shown, Muktibodh does not explicitly draw his long poem from an engagement with classical Sanskrit poetics—and indeed, in his criticism, sharply criticizes such a move in an earlier work, *Kāmāyanī*, which he analyzed extensively—he is keenly aware of the place of his own work within a larger literary history. One path forward, then, would be to view the long poem as a single moment within a larger history of generic experimentation, in which the classical epic, discourses of realism, and generic structures such as the novel, the short story, and the lyric interacted in a complex ecosystem across multiple languages.

Similarly, the crucial influence of Marathi poetics, far from a sign of weakness in Muktibodh's Hindi, indicates the need to consider Hindi literature within a larger system of North Indian literary cultures, including not only Marathi, but also Bangla and Urdu, in addition to literary registers, such as Braj Bhasha, subsumed today under the category of Hindi but considered as distinct literary languages throughout the nineteenth and twentieth centuries. Muktibodh's long poem shows us that the "multilingual local" of literary interaction, shown in Francesca Orsini's recent work to typify North Indian literary cultures, also defines what are seen as distinct modernist literary cultures. This last point is especially important when considering the literature of the 1950s. Muktibodh's work cannot be considered outside of the historical circumstances of this time, including not only the literary politics that we associate with the Cold War, but also the particular language politics surrounding Hindi. Muktibodh himself has stated that he decided to write in Hindi due to its "universal scope." The language was, by this time, given a constitutional primacy and fully separated from the related Urdu. However, its ascendence would be short lived, and by 1965, it would be placed in a permanently temporary official status.[76] How did this idea of Hindi's relation to universality, then, inform both Muktibodh's creation of the long poems and Hindi literary criticism's response to it?

These and other questions posed by the analysis of the long poem demand a reading that takes into account literary form and its role in a larger analytic framework and historicization. In this way, a consideration of the work of Muktibodh points towards a further exploration of how writers in South Asia were often moving in parallel, rather than in response, to changes in world literature, and how they made use of specific histories of literary form to engage with problems common among different literary modernisms. This points to the necessity of not only moving away from a center-periphery model of world literature in which writers are merely responding to changes in a universal system from a peripheral location, but of embracing the variety and imagination of writers in a specific circumstance making use of the diverse resources around them.

Conclusion

The Afterlives of Muktibodh

> My friends said to me, "No one comes back from Delhi alive."
> I thought to myself, "Just like Muktibodh."
>
> —Harishankar Parsai

The year of 1964 began with riots in Calcutta, the relaxation of dry laws in Maharashtra, police firing on BEST workers in Bombay, and a coup in Zanzibar that led to hand-to-hand combat with Indian shopkeepers in Dar es Salaam.[1] In the aftermath of the Sino-Indian war of 1962, an early headline described the initiation of a new transmitter that would "combat Chinese propaganda."[2] In Moscow, Ghanaian students, angry over mistreatment and abuse by the police, staged a protest at the Red Square.[3] Nehru's health began to decline, and urgent editorials called for his rest.[4]

These trends—complicated postcolonial politics intersecting with the evolution of the Cold War, the onset of what would later be called "disillusionment," intimations of Nehru's mortality—would come to dominate the year. In April, after years of tension between Congress- and Soviet Union–aligned members and those aligned with China, a walkout of members of the Communist Party of India led to a split, and the formation of the Communist Party of India (Marxist). This was the first major split in the CPI, soon to be followed by the emergence of the Naxalite movement and the foundation of the CPI(ML).[5]

In the world of Hindi—the language in which Muktibodh wrote—the major tensions echoed and paralleled current events.

The literature of the postindependence period had dramatically shifted, with key works in the 1940s, into a recognizable "modernist" idiom, which by the end of the 1950s was often referred to as, in poetry, *nayī kavitā,* and in the short story, *nayī kahānī.* Works associated with these two schools claimed to speak to the new realities of the decade, but, by 1964, terms such as these were already being historicized, criticized, and generally superseded. Major works assessing the period would be written by the end of the 1960s, but, in 1964, the first journal appeared that made a clean break from the 1950s—by calling itself *akavitā,* or "nonpoetry." This "nonpoetry," as much as it was mocked in mainstream publications, claimed a rebellion against an earlier modernism, influenced by the Beats—Allen Ginsburg had famously visited three years before—and the Hungry Generation in Bengal.[6]

Nehru would die in May, following a sharp decline in his health seemingly prompted by the Sino-Indian war two years earlier. The news was easily the most important event of the year; the tensions and anxieties in India that had been building up, in retrospect, began to spill over. Around the world, journalists described India as rudderless without its leader, plunged into a "nightmare world," as the *Guardian* put it.[7] The death of Nehru would be seen as the moment in which history shifted away from the possibilities—from nonaligned solidarity to five-year plans—of the immediate postindependence period.[8]

Surprisingly, despite the epochal importance of Nehru, in the Hindi literary sphere this event was rivaled by another death. Gajanan Madhav Muktibodh, teaching at the time at a small college in Chattisgarh, had suffered a stroke in March 1964. His circle of friends, desperate to improve his medical treatment, prevailed first upon the state chief minister, and then, through the assistance of the famous poet Harivansh Rai Bachchan, upon the prime minister himself. With the personal intervention of Lal Bahadur Shastri, the poet was brought to the All-India Medical Institute and put under the care of its director and one of the most well-known physicians in the country, Khushwant Lal Wig.[9] Despite this attention, unprecedented in the Hindi literary world, Muktibodh passed away on September 11. His illness, death, and funeral were written about in every major Hindi journal and newspaper, as well as major English dailies such as the *Times of India.* An article published shortly before his death pictured the poet, unconscious, surrounded by three other poets, forming a tableau of contemporary poetry.[10] The popular newsmagazine *Dharmyug* featured a full-page picture of his funeral.[11] One of the carriers of his bier was the artist M. F. Hussain, who walked barefoot, and continued to do so for most of his life thereafter.[12]

What prompted such a massive outpouring of sympathy and interest in a poet who, prior to his illness and death, had only recently begun to emerge from a small circle of literary enthusiasts? Clearly, for Hindi literature, the death of the poet seemed to parallel the death of Nehru. But whereas, with Nehru, India lost a last link to the optimism and possibility of the independence movement, with Muktibodh, the Hindi literary world seemed to acknowledge a darkening future. Commentators, some of them close friends such as Harishankar Parsai, described the drama of Muktibodh's death as a synecdoche of the corruption and tensions in Hindi, in which a newly emerged literary elite was happy to ignore a middle-class poet until he was written about positively in the *Times of India* and aided by the prime minister. Other writers saw in Muktibodh's plight the increasing weight of Delhi, adding drama to Muktibodh's belated, unconscious arrival.[13] One could ask, as well, whether the response to Muktibodh's death didn't parallel an anxiety about the status of Hindi itself, from a language that could imagine itself speaking on behalf of the nation to an increasingly regional, even marginalized identity.[14]

This sense of Muktibodh as an outsider, a rebellious, impoverished critic of the placid institutionalism that was present on both the right and the left, remains at the center of Hindi literary culture. The image of the neglected, poverty-stricken poet from the small towns, the symbol of the alienated modernity of the Hindiphone lower middle class, is at the moment of its creation counterposed against the largest levers of power in Nehruvian and postindependence India. It should not be a surprise, therefore, that the legacy of this poet, in whom all the schisms of the time were dissolved, should be the subject of continuous contention and debate. The powerful image of Muktibodh, which came into being almost at the moment of transition from the Nehruvian era to the economic stagnation and political instability that defined the rest of the 1960s and 1970s, became a structural force in thinking through the legacy of independence, Cold War literature, and Nehruvian models of development.

Despite, or perhaps, because of this centrality, the legacy of Muktibodh has been fiercely debated almost since the moment of his death. At stake is the question of whether Muktibodh's works can be understood as actively political or rather addressed to a postcolonial epistemic crisis. This question, central to so much of literary debate, becomes the question of how to read Muktibodh's fantastic, politically committed work. These debates include the most prominent critics of postindependence Hindi, such as Namwar Singh and Ram Vilas Sharma, as well as the network of literary journals and small magazines that collectively continue to shape the Hindi reading of Muktibodh.

Alienation or Existentialism

The first important critic of Muktibodh, in the sense of critical appreciation that attempted to analyze him in the context of Hindi literary history, was his contemporary, Shamsher Bahadur Singh (1911–1993). Shamsher himself occupies a crucial place in the story of Hindi modernism: although he was only anthologized in the second *Tār saptak* anthology, he in fact had been experimenting with modernist poetics at the same time as Agyeya and others, and had arguably been more involved in translating Anglo-American and European literary history into Hindi criticism[15]

As I discussed in the previous chapter, Shamsher had engaged with Muktibodh's work prior to his death, and his criticism forms some of the most important early analysis of Muktibodh's long poems. In his preface to *Cāṃd kā muṃh ṭeṛhā hai*, Shamsher extended this analysis. Shamsher, in arguing for "Aṃdhere meṃ" as an allegory of contemporary life, established the image of Muktibodh as the central prophet of Hindi poetry, even as he undercut Muktibodh's artistry by frequently categorizing his work as excessive and his style as rough.[16] Because of the prominence of Shamsher's introduction, this piece had a huge role to play in later understandings of Muktibodh, and pushed his long, allegorical poems to the center of Muktibodh's reception in the next decades.

In the following decade, Muktibodh's centrality to Hindi literary criticism would only increase; he was the subject of commemorative conferences as soon as two years after his death, and the first of many special issues devoted to his work appeared in the prominent journal *Ālocnā* (Criticism) in 1968.[17] This issue featured a series of new appreciations of Muktibodh, and could be seen to mark the incorporation of Muktibodh's work into literary history.

Namvar Singh (1926–2019), who was quickly rising as one of the most prominent critics of his generation, had taken over editorship of *Ālocnā* one year previously, in 1967.[18] He would follow up editing this special issue by discussing Muktibodh extensively in *Kavitā ke naye pratimān* (The New Standards of Poetry). *Kavitā ke naye pratimān* is intended to be an extensive treatment of *nayī kavitā,* alongside Singh's earlier, and equally magisterial, *chāyāvād.*[19] In his preface to the first edition, Singh makes clear that he viewed that initial moment of *nayī kavitā* as limited. In placing Muktibodh at the center of this moment, he was also indicating its end: "Muktibodh fulfilled the ordinary poetry of his time, and, through challenging its limits, activated their creative specialities, as a result of which a true evaluation of contemporary literature became possible."[20] Muktibodh established essential ideas about *nai kavita,* and its crucial difference from *chāyāvād.* But in Singh's insistence on the social content of his work, particularly through what he defined as the dramatization of alienation, he revealed the limits of what Singh sees as a hidebound, solipsistic modernism that came to dominate by the end of the 1950s.

Kavitā ke naye pratimān was not only an attempt to create a theory of Hindi modernism and its history, but it was just as much both an attempt by Namvar Singh to engage with the literary criticism of Sahi and other "socialist" critics and an attempt to adapt Anglo-American New Criticism.[21] Singh takes up the idea of the *laghu manav* and the importance of reflected experience as shown in this earlier generation of critics.[22] For Singh, these ideas are crucial in moving beyond a *chāyāvād*-centered idea of criticism. This body of criticism, for Singh, was unable to accept not only the formal changes of modernism, but also the idea that literature should be addressed, not to the depiction of emotional states, but to the depiction of experience based on engagement with the real world. This difference is crucial for Singh because, as much as *chāyāvād* was responsible for forming an idiom for poetry, it failed to account for the historic social shifts that followed independence. Thus, he states repeatedly that *naī kavitā* moves from the outside in rather than the inside out.[23] Singh notes that although critics from both generations relied on the idea of *anubhūti*, or experience, for a *chāyāvādī* poet such as Prasad, this implied that the feeling would be described through description of a form, whereas for a *nai kavitā* poet such as Agyeya, the form, or object, was to be suddenly illuminated through feeling.[24] This meant that *nayī kavitā* could be presented as a profound form of realism.

In Singh's narrative, the modernist poetry associated with *nayī kavitā* "quietly compromises" with the aesthetic prerogatives of *chāyāvād* neoromanticism.[25] What, in the poets of *Tār saptak* and the early issues of *nayī kavitā*, is a preoccupation with form becomes, by the time that poets like Kunwar Narayan (1927–2017) become prominent, a concern with *āsthā*, or faith.[26] The poetry of the later 1950s gradually shifts from a concern with the experienced world, to the nature of experience itself to, eventually, a primary concern with the self. Muktibodh stands out in this context not only for his poetry but his criticism, which, in the essays collected in *nayī kavitā kā ātmasaṅgharṣ* (The Internal Struggle of New Poetry), criticized precisely this tendency in modernist poetry to withdraw from concern with the world. In addition to Muktibodh's critique of his contemporaries, his poetry, in Singh's reading, gradually expresses the violence and political repression that was taking hold by the end of the 1950s, and the larger sense of conformism that followed a more liberation-oriented sense of poetic realism in the 1940s. But it is worth noting here that the idea of Muktibodh as a prophet of the violence of the Indian state is largely absent here in the first edition of *Kavitā ke naye pratimān*; instead, the distinction of Muktibodh lies, for the most part, in his position vis-à-vis the aesthetic debates of the 1950s, and in particular his critique of the growing conservatism among modernist poets over the course of the first two decades of independence.

Similarly to his situating Mutkibodh's criticism and aesthetic thought as a reaction to an earlier era of poetry, Singh approaches Muktibodh's poetics within the story the emergence of *nayī kavitā* from, and in reaction to, *chāyāvād* neoromanticism. Through *Kavitā ke naye pratimān*, Muktibodh's poetry is cited in terms of its rejection of self-centered, individual reflection, in favor of processes of dramatization of the self in order to engage with society. For this reason, in his analysis of "Aṃdhere meṃ," Singh emphasizes not necessarily Muktibodh's allegory of contemporary history, but his address to the middle classes. In a brief afterword to the book and analysis of the poem, Singh argues that the self is split into two, in order to describe the alienation of the middle classes:

> The depiction of the "I" in the poem is divided into two personalities for dramatic effect; there is the "I" who is the protagonist of the poem, and there is the "he" who is the obverse of that protagonist. This division in fact is not merely dramatic effect, but rather is based on self-alienation [*ātma-nirvāsan*]. The protagonist of "In the Dark" is a self-alienated individual, whose symbol [of his alienation] is his residence in caves. Like Dostoevsky's "underground man," this individual, terrified of external circumstances, resides in a magical cavern.[27]

Singh rejects the possibility that the *guru* of "Aṃdhere meṃ" is meant to be read directly. Rather, the driving narrative of the poem, with its frequent slippage between dreaming and wakefulness, is read by Singh as a "search for identity," or *asmitā kī khoj*, with a dramatically bifurcated narrative voice showing the alienation of the middle classes under postindependence capitalist expansion.

Kavitā ke naye pratimān was received as one of the most important critical works of its generation, not least because it synthesized a series of seemingly disparate aesthetic perspectives and brought together a Marxian analysis of literature with emerging techniques of analysis. Furthermore, it was seen as establishing a solid ground for evaluating modernism in Hindi, freeing literary criticism from any lingering attachments to *chāyāvād* aesthetic norms. At the same time, however, initial reviews accused Singh of *rūpvād*, or formalism, citing not only his extensive use of New Critical methods of analysis, but also in his privileging of poets, such as Agyeya, who were by the late 1960s seen as irredeemably hostile to any progressive analysis of literature.[28] However, because Muktibodh was indisputably at the center of *Kavitā ke naye pratimān*, Singh's analysis of Muktibodh gravitated towards the center of debate. Nemichandra Jain, for instance, a close associate of Muktibodh's who would later edit his collected works, praised *Kavitā ke naye pratimān* for its innovation and comprehensiveness, but accused him of relying on Muktibodh, a clearly committed poet, to make claims regarding poetic language that Muktibodh would not himself have supported.[29]

The most aggressive and extensive response to *Kavitā ke naye pratimān*, however, can be found in the work of Ram Vilas Sharma (1912–2000). Fifteen years his senior, Sharma had established himself at an earlier moment in literary history, contributing to Premchand's reception in the 1930s and making some of the earliest arguments that Premchand should be considered, alongside Maxim Gorky, as a social realist writer. Sharma went on to occupy important institutional positions on the left, most notably his chairmanship of the AIPWA from 1949 to 1953. However, by the end of the 1960s, Sharma began to be associated with the orthodox criticism beginning to be attached to the progressives, in large part due to his critique, not only of Singh's criticism, but of the position of Muktibodh that was becoming clear in literary history.[30]

Sharma, himself a contributor to the initial *Tār saptak* anthology, later wrote his own monograph on Hindi modernism, titled *Nayī kavitā aur astitvavād* (New Poetry and Existentialism). Its first essay—originally published in 1969—explicitly argued against Namwar's idea of Muktibodh as a poet of alienation, and against the depiction of middle-class alienation as progressive literature. Sharma argued that Muktibodh should be understood as expressing not alienation and the search for identity, but the tension between committed art and escapism. In Sharma's interpretation, this escapism is an essential feature of *nayī kavitā* separate from its aesthetic innovations. The inner struggle of Muktibodh, therefore, is not evidence of a "revolutionary romanticism," as Singh puts it, but the temptations of mysticism:

> Muktibodh was far away from that happy world, and so mysticism created a great complication. He believed that the mind could be joined with the sun in such a way that the mysteries of both the universe and of human society would be simultaneously revealed, and that he could retrieve from the cave of inner consciousness such gems that the poverty of the filthy slum would at once disappear. And then he smashed these dreams and cursed his dreaming mind.[31]

For Sharma, the "existentialism" of Hindi modernism, in elevating the experience of the self, was a repetition of the mysticism of *chāyāvād* to which, in part, the earliest progressive poets had responded.[32] This mysticism is repeated in Muktibodh's poetry through an elevation of the self and his dreams—dreams that are explicitly, in Sharma's formulation, meant to allegorize not the alienated middle-class self but rather, through drawing upon a rich well of mystical symbolic language, the total transcendence of historical materialism itself. It was for this reason that Sharma saw Muktbodh's fantastic poetry as escapist. Rather than reveal any new truth, Muktibodh's work cycled back and forth between a dream of transcendence and a shattering despair that followed that dream. Muktibodh "itched for a knowledge which was always developing" but needed "complete knowledge; and such knowledge can only be given by mysticism."[33]

In referring to "complete knowledge" and "gems" that could be retrieved from the "cave of inner consciousness," Sharma based his critique, at least partially, on the imagery from "Aṃdhere meṃ." As I argued in the previous chapter, the poem, rather than present fantastic imagery as a solution in and of itself to the problems depicted in the poem, places the imagination, and specifically the poetic imagination, as central. The poetic imagination in "Aṃdhere meṃ" is the precondition for further political consciousness, rather than a direct depiction of political action. The guru of the poem, who appears at first as a kind of imprisoned superman, is transformed by the end of "Aṃdhere meṃ" into the expressive power of the speaker.

For Sharma, however, what he saw as the mysticism of Muktibodh's poetry was an unacceptable deviation from political commitment. Although Sharma, an astute critic, analyzed a wide range of possible interpretations of Muktibodh's imagery, he ultimately took exception not only to the content of Muktibodh's poetry, but to the entire tradition of *nayī kavitā* that it represented.[34] In this criticism, Sharma responded directly to the argument made by Singh Singh and Vijaydevarayan Sahi, which held that the poets of *nayī kavitā* were responding to the breakdown of the ideals of the nationalist movement.[35] In Sharma's literary history of postindependence literature, *nayī kavitā* was, first off, an essentially reactionary creation of the 1950s, in which poets rejected the emotionalism of *chāyāvād* without understanding the ways in which their own poetry was conventional in its rejection of society.[36]

Sharma's treatment of Muktibodh was a direct challenge to Singh Singh's entire model of literary history, and so he naturally responded with an afterword to *Kavitā ke naye pratimān* for the 1974 second edition, which consisted of a second, extended reading of "Aṃdhere meṃ."[37] For Namvar Singh, Muktibodh represented the possibility of a critical, imaginative left poetry that would engage with the political concerns of the lower middle class while rejecting the proscriptive tenets of realism that were becoming associated with progressivism. "Aṃdhere meṃ," representative of Muktibodh's poetry in general, succeeded in allegorizing contemporary life, and most importantly the alienation of the modern subject from itself. In his second treatment of "Aṃdhere meṃ," Singh extended his earlier argument in two primary ways. First, whereas *Kavitā ke naye pratimān* was largely concerned with debates in the 1950s, and more than anything else with the evaluation of *nayī kavitā* according to the literary standards of *chāyāvād*, this second treatment was concerned with defending Singh's interpretation of Muktibodh against both a charge of formalism and Sharma's rejection of the entire concept of alienation. Citing Marx's *Economic and Political Manuscripts*, while also possibly being influenced by Lukacs's recently translated *History and Class Consciousness*, Singh argues that Muktibodh's poetry should be understood as a search for identity, an *asmitā kī khoj*, and that this identity is a precondition for the identification of the middle classes with the class consciousness of the proletariate.[38] In echoing Lukács's model of the metasubjectivity of the proletariate, this is therefore one of the first and most important moments in the reception of what we today refer to as Western Marxism.

The second important change in Singh's afterword is that Muktibodh's poetry is more explicitly linked to a political allegory, and to the growing political violence and tension in India. The years between 1968 and 1974 were certainly crucial in the history of disillusionment, as I will more explicitly discuss in the next section. But Singh also responds here to the idea that Muktibodh's depiction of violence, and the general role of the fantastic and allegorical in his poetry, is an example of escapism. At stake, unsurprisingly, is the status of mysticism in Muktibodh's work.

Singh argues that Muktibodh's work responds to the gradually increasing violence in Indian society—as he puts it, what was once "a fairy tale" gradually becomes real and openly expressed in "Aṃdhere meṃ."[39] What for Sharma is mysticism and escapism is therefore, for Singh, oriented towards the social. He writes that Muktibodh's work should be understood not as interested in mystery but, in fact, in historicity, or *aitihāsiktā*, "which is not mysticism, but is rather the enemy of mysticism."[40]

Singh argues that Muktibodh's work should be considered not mystical but historical because its allegorical content refers not, as Sharma puts it, to a transcendent, supermaterial plane, but to actual historical forces in contemporary India. He concludes:

> There is no need to say that whatever *romantic* dream is present in "Aṃdhere meṃ" is based on a consciousness of the developing progressive forces of its age. In the final section of the poem these progressive forces suddenly appear armed for revolution. The dream is made even more vivid and colorful in light of the nightmares that preceded it, whose basis was the "triumph of the party of the dead" of regressive [*hrāsonmukh*] forces. Clearly this dream of Muktibodh does not contain Shelley's gauzy haziness, because it is illuminated by the feelings and ideas that are shaped by progressive forces. Despite this, if anyone finds this dream hazy or obscure, they should understand that their eyes have been dazzled by the terror of regressive forces, and that they have not fully felt the dawn of progressive forces. From this point of view, we could go so far as to call Muktibodh a *romantic*, but this romanticism is, in the words of Gorky, a revolutionary *romanticism* or a *romanticism* which contains within it heroism.[41]

The romanticism of Shelley, long a touchstone for left aesthetic thought, appears here tied to the long debates in Hindi over mysticism. As I discussed in the previous chapter, Shelley and his work looms over "Aṃdhere meṃ," which features a long depiction of a parade that is openly influenced by "The Masque of Anarchy." But Singh's argument here, which becomes crucial to the next generation of Muktibodh scholars, is that Muktibodh's long poems, and especially "Aṃdhere meṃ," need to be incorporated into any left aesthetic model of literature. in response to Sharma's dismissal of Muktibodh, Singh elevates him to the center not only of the transition from neoromanticism to modernism, but of the evolution of committed literature in Hindi after independence.

The work of Namvar Singh, in addition to the ceaselessly increasing importance of Muktibodh over the course of the 1970s, prompted a final response by Ram Vilas Sharma, included in the 1978 second edition of *Nayī kavitā aur astitvavād*. This piece, twice as long as his previous essay on Muktibodh, goes into far greater detail both on Muktibodh's work and with the points of debate with Singh's own interpretation of Hindi literature. Sharma responds to Singh's argument that Muktibodh was depicting the alienation of the middle classes by arguing that Muktibodh was, instead, himself personally torn between the transcendent and the real. The long, fantastic depiction of repression and revolution was nothing more than a desire, on Muktibodh's part, for a nonpolitical, *nonhistorical*, moment of revolution. And, whereas Singh was at pains to argue that Muktibodh's dreams were intimately tied to progressive forces, Sharma saw the fantastic in Muktibodh's work as an example of Muktibodh's split goals. Going further, in what would later prove to be the most controversial and incendiary aspect of his argument, Sharma directly argued that Muktibodh was beset by mental illness.[42] In one section, Sharma would directly argue that Muktibodh could be diagnosed with schizophrenia, writing that "the capacity of Muktibodh for dreaming became such a fundamental aspect of his character that he was no long able to depict reality without first transforming it into a dream."[43] Although Sharma granted that Muktibodh was genuinely committed to a committed literature, he flatly rejected the creative possibility of the allegorical in his work, arguing instead that it should be seen as evidence of a range of mental instabilities, and ultimately as a step away from realism generally.

Sharma's argument was frequently attacked and, as we shall see shortly, his point of view became representative generally of a conservative, orthodox progressivism, in response to which a new generation of left critics would compare his perspective on Muktibodh to the famous debate between Brecht and Lukacs that was then coming into the English world via translation.[44] Ironically, however, because he had little investment in arguing for Muktibodh's work as allegory, Sharma presented one of the most detailed accounts of the imagery of Muktibodh's work. Because Sharma was not interested in interpreting Muktibodh's imagery as representing a current political moment, let alone the possible radicalization of the middle classes, he was able to range widely across the imagery of Muktibodh's work, presenting aspects of it that appear as "excessive" or otherwise irrelevant to other critics.

The debate between Namvar Singh and Ram Vilas Sharma is crucial not only because it established the parameters of Muktibodh's reception, but because it showed that his legacy was central to the way that Hindi literary history was beginning to understand the period following independence. In some ways, such as the focus on realism as depicting a certain range of progressive possibilities, these debates echo an earlier moment's focus on useful literature as opposed to mysticism. And, as critics soon noted, aspects of this debate came to be seen as parallel to that which took place at other moments between realism and modernism more generally. But in other ways, this debate shows how the paradigm of, to use Premchand's phrasing, "idealist realism" (*ādarśonmukh yathārthvād*) began to break down following independence, as a diverse range of critics began to search for new ways to depict the reality of postindependence India. The reevaluation of poetry from the period was crucial, because it signaled a decisive shift from the politics and aesthetics of the nationalist period. Muktibodh, in turn, gravitated to the center of these debates not necessarily because his work was a dramatic departure from the standards of his time, or even because he addressed his criticism to both sides of the progressive/experimentalist debates of the 1950s, but because his work demanded attention both to the standards of the *chāyāvād* period and to the poetry of the future.

Ratlam and Bhopal

The debates I have described between Namwar Singh and Ram Vilas Sharma played out, in magazines, journals, and different editions of their books, over the course of the 1970s. Both Singh and Sharma, however, were largely responding to a paradigm of literature that had been formed two decades earlier. The stakes at hand, over the evolution of modernist poetic idiom and the legacy of *chāyāvād*, the split between experimentalists and progressives in Hindi literary discourse, and the role of experience and perception in poetry, were very much rooted in the shifts in Hindi poetry that took place following independence. Even as their debates played out, however, a new generation of literary critics were reevaluating many of the parameters that Namwar and Sharma took for granted, in response to the social, literary, and political shifts that took place during the 1970s.

Some of these shifts had far outside of Hindi literature itself. The most prominent of these include the birth of the Naxalite movement and the development of nonparticipatory Marxist politics more generally.[45] In the case of Hindi, this had the particular impact of refocusing attention on the plight of the rural poor, including an early response to issues of caste—even if the more explicit discourse of Dalit literature would only become prominent in Hindi in the 1990s.[46] Another profound, although frequently taboo, impact was through the eighteen months of Indira Gandhi's Emergency declaration from 1975–1977. The Emergency created lasting rancor among Hindi writers, depending on their support, and presented a dark vision of India that echoed through the 1980s at least.[47] As a result of these and other events, Muktibodh's prominence continued to increase, especially as "Aṃdhere meṃ," with its vision of city streets dominated by militarized police, a hypocritical and coopted intellectual class, and open violence began to seem less allegorical and more prophetic. Similarly, a romanticized image of Muktibodh, mythologized as the rebellious outsider and more akin to the angry young man of the 1970s, began to take hold. As a result, by the end of the decade, Muktibodh was increasingly the subject of hagiography as much as analysis, and debates over his legacy expanded to take on not only the fate of *nayī kavitā* in Hindi literature, but the fate of Hindi literature more generally.

These disparate events and forces converged with Muktibodh's legacy, and the continued efforts to collect and publish his works, to produce a remarkable moment of his reception in 1979 and 1980. Over a brief period, a second major collection of Muktibodh's poetry, the publication of his collected works, and the release of a film based on his works by the noted director Mani Kaul, *Satah se uṭhtā ādmī*, were released in quick succession. Both Muktibodh's collected works and Mani Kaul's film were financed by the Madhya Pradesh state government, in initiatives spearheaded by Ashok Vajpeyi, who had first met Muktibodh as a young student at Sagar University and now, as minister of culture for the state, had placed Muktibodh at the center of a new institutional vision of regional literature in Hindi. These releases were accompanied by a conference that drew in a series of major figures in Hindi literature, recorded in the journal *Pūrvagraha*, which was associated with Ashok Vajpeyi and his cultural efforts in Madhya Pradesh. At the same time, and to an extent in response to this, another conference was organized by the journal *Kaṇk*, published from the small town of Ratlam and by the end of the decade associated with the populist, Naxal-adjacent left. Thus, these two conferences, and the journals associated with them, present a spectrum of Hindi literature at the time, split between increasing provincial support and control over the arts, led by Congress-affiliated governments during and following the Emergency, on the one hand, and the growth of the "little magazine" in Hindi, frequently adjacent to a driven-underground left, on the other.[48] But, despite a seemingly clear split between these positions, looking closely at this moment shows a dynamism of conversation that crosses between these political positions and cultural camps.

Kaṅk (Hawk), was begun in 1971 in the small city of Ratlam, located in Madhya Pradesh on the intersection between the Northern Railway, to Bhopal and Delhi, and the Western Railway heading to Bombay. In its first issue, *Kaṅk* emphasized these *mofussil*, small-town roots, memorializing a young, local writer who had recently committed suicide, and aligning itself with the burgeoning body of writers elsewhere in the Hindi-speaking region who rejected the institutionalization of Hindi in Delhi and other large cities. Over the course of the 1970s, however, the journal shifted towards the left: a 1975 issue, published just before the declaration of Emergency, was devoted entirely to the subject of Mao.[49] By the end of the decade, the journal was strongly associated with *janvādī* literature, a term that means "people-ism" and succeeded the use of the term *pragativād*, which had become discredited through its association with doctrinaire leftist writing in the 1950s.[50]

Kaṅk's special issue on Muktibodh was a natural outgrowth of the journal's interests. Muktibodh's background in the smaller cities of Central India was becoming more and more of interest, and his growing reputation guaranteed that he would frequently be discussed by a journal such as *Kaṅk*. At the same time, however, the difficulty of Muktibodh's poetry, the focus of his address on the middle classes as opposed to either the urban or rural proletariat, and his increasing importance to poets who were seen as opposed to the left, also meant that this special issue is a crucial site to see how left-oriented critics and writers in Hindi were responding to changes in literary history in the 1970s. The articles and conversations collected in this issue were dynamic, pointed, and at times polemical, providing a record of veiled arguments among themselves and open accusations against their opponents. These opponents included, most prominently, Agyeya, who had transformed over the course of the 1960s into a villain on the left, and who was accused of having been openly supported by the CIA through his activities with the Congress for Cultural Freedom. But they also included critics on the left, such as Ram Vilas Sharma, who were seen as too dismissive of Muktibodh's revolutionary potential. For the critics of *Kaṅk*, the obvious importance of Muktibodh to literary history, and his clear and growing influence on poets such as Dhumil, Alok Dhanwa, and Chandrakant Devtale, necessitated an analysis of his work.[51] At the same time, Muktibodh's allegorical poetry and nightmarish depictions of the small Indian city presented a challenge, since they seemingly ignored the aesthetic standards of *Janvād*, which emphasized accessible language and depiction of rural oppression. Many of these critics, therefore, were attempting to thread a needle.

One of the primary concerns of these critics, raised again and again, was Muktibodh's perceived identification with the middle classes. For these critics, the difficulty of Muktibodh's verse, and the sustained interest with clerks, schoolteachers, and other members of the middle class in the 1950s, had to be explained in a way that emphasized Muktibodh's political commitment, while avoiding what they considered a "formalist" approach that would rely entirely on the subject of alienation and identity. There were several responses to this. Some critics acknowledged the difference of Muktibodh from a poet such as Nagarjun, whose pioneering depictions of rural life throughout his career had culminated in a prominent position of protest against the Emergency.[52] But they argued that Muktibodh's address to the middle class was made necessary by the proscriptivism of left literature in the progressive period. Canchal Chauhan, for instance, stated:

> Dr. Ram Vilas Sharma refused to recognize the demands of the time and cast everything away—any poem written on a subject other than a farmer or worker was trash; his criticism was an analysis not of class but of individuals. After Dr. Sharma, Dr. Namvar Singh was the victim of formalism and restricted himself to seeing only awkwardness, irony, tension, playfulness and sensuality. One extremism ignored changing aesthetics, and the other bid farewell to Marxist aesthetics altogether and took shelter in formalism. Contemporary populist criticism developed through avoiding these two extremes. We understand that the writer who emerges from India's lower middle class is the friend of the proletariat, and that it is not beneficial to ignore the reality of his artistic interests or developed consciousness and merely lecture him to write in simple language, or to write an *ālhā* epic poem. The important thing is that Muktibodh understood this group and encouraged them to meet with the proletariat, and through addressing them [the lower middle class] and telling them that your freedom will be with the proletariat, and that you should therefore transform yourself, your interests are joined with the interests of the proletariat. This advice is given repeatedly in his works.[53]

As this long passage shows, the evolution of Muktibodh's work is balanced against the position, by the 1970s, that left literature needed to change in response to the excesses of the "extremist views" of both Ram Vilas Sharma and Namwar Singh. Muktibodh's writing, with its concern for the "artistic interest or developed consciousness" of the lower middle class, can thus be perceived as inherently political, without needing to be explained in terms of the allegorical structure presented by Namwar Singh. Other critics present at this conference, including Shamsher Bahadur Singh, would support this position, arguing that Muktibodh was addressing a middle-class audience that was "comapratively less conscious" than that of the 1970s.[54]

This model, however, presents certain issues, because it does not address the clear and increasing prevalence of the fantastic in Muktibodh's work, a tendency that only increased as his work increased in length in the final decade of his life. In the same piece as is quoted above, Chauhan argues that Muktibodh's use of fantasy, and the critical apparatus he developed to support that use, should be seen in terms of the "objective condition" of the period, as opposed to the one prevailing in the 1970s. This line of argument holds that Muktibodh had no choice but to veil his criticism of Nehruvian society in fantastic, allegorical imagery. Such a position would continue be developed after this point and still appears frequently.[55]

Some critics, such as Murli Manohar Prasad Singh, presented a more unorthodox view of Muktibodh, one that was bolstered by connecting his legacy with a series of figures who were becoming more widely available in translation. Indeed, by the 1970s, a network of modernist writers outside of the Anglo-American tradition, such as Alexander Blok, Vladimir Mayakovsky, and César Vallejo, were becoming more widely read in Hindi, through both English and Hindi translation.[56] As a result, the fantastic in Muktibodh's work could be seen as parallel with some of the trends presented by writers such as Blok, with whose work Singh frequently compared Muktibodh's.[57] Murli, in turn, argues for an allegorical reading of Muktibodh's work, noting, for instance, the importance of the Korean war in understanding his short story "Claude Eatherly," and generally rooting Muktibodh's turn towards the fantastic in the context of the general corruption of the middle classes.[58]

Despite the diversity of opinion among these critics, they were unified not only in their opposition to, and revision of, the work of Namwar Singh and Ram Vilas Sharma, but also in their opposition to the body of critics, such as Ashok Vajpeyi and Shrikant Verma, whom they saw as explicitly opposed to their own committed politics. Chanchal Chauhan, criticizing such views, wrote:

> The imperialist, capitalist system has produced perversions in society which are the defining features of this century. They are all visible in the twentieth century. The human being who fights against this, the socialist system which oppresses him, the freedom struggle of the third world which has erupted, none of this appears to him [Varma]. He either believes them meaningless, or perhaps he believes imperialism-capitalism to be the single truth. In such an atmosphere, his fundamental concern is that "mankind should find release from the socialist system, which is formed from false understandings of Marxism." And if for this reason he finds in Muktibodh all those perversions, then we should not be surprised—that very darkness, that very manic, broken, helpless individual, that very geography of hell.[59]

Shrikant Varma was at the time a prominent member of the Congress Party, and had been closely involved with Muktibodh's career; he was responsible for the editing of *Cāṃd kā muṃh ṭeṛhā hai,* as well as publishing Muktibodh in his journal *kṛti* in the early 1960s.[60] But Varma was coming to be perceived, on the left, as associated with a pessimistic poetry that rejected the politics in Muktibodh's work. The idea of "perversion" in the interpretation of Muktibodh reveals, in part, the dangers of the fantastic in Muktibodh's work—that it offered a great deal of ground for interpretation that would seem to be evacuated of political potential.

If there was one point of criticism in particular on which all the participants at *Kaṅk* might have agreed, it would be the work of Ashok Vajpeyi with *Pūrvagraha.* The special issue of *Kaṅk* devoted to the conference on Muktibodh ends with a description of *Pūrvagraha* and the conference on Muktibodh that it organized.[61] The brief article describes a series of altercations with the organizers of the conference, focused in particular on Mani Kaul's film *Satah se uṭhtā ādmī,* which was released as part of the festival.[62] The piece describes how, when Mani Kaul was pressed by a local critic on the "social import" of the film, Ashok Vajpeyi attempted to intervene, at which point Vajpeyi was told "Why should we question you—we only pity you!" presumably mocking Vajpeyi's insistence on his own importance in the making of the film. As the journal reports, "The easy atmosphere at once became uneasy, and shouts of '*get out*' resounded through the wealthy Shyamla hills neighborhood of Bhopal!"[63]

Pūrvagraha, since the early 1970s, had emerged as one of the most prominent literary journals in Hindi, but also as a harbinger of several new trends in literary history and the institutionalization of literature. The journal was officially published by the Madhya Pradesh Kala Parishad, the official state art institution, but was edited and spearheaded by Ashok Vajpeyi. Vajpeyi entered literary life as a teenager, and at the age of twenty-three joined in editing *Cāṃd kā muṃh ṭeṛhā hai.* Over the following decades, however, Vajpeyi would become, as a civil servant, one of the most important arbiters of literary culture in Hindi, beginning first in the state of Madhya Pradesh, and eventually at a national level.[64] During the 1970s, Vajpeyi made Bhopal, then a newly formed state capital and more known as a center for Urdu literature, into a center for a new understanding of Hindi literature and a new form of regionalism.[65] Under Vajpeyi's tenure and hosting of a range of conferences, eventually held in the purpose-built center for the arts, Bharat Bhavan, Vajpeyi created a fusion of the local and the international that remains extremely influential.[66] The many literary initiatives spearheaded by Vajpeyi launched the careers of many of the prominent Hindi writers of the late twentieth century, perhaps most prominent that of Vinod Kumar Shukla, who received an inaugural Gajanan Madhav Muktibodh fellowship in 1976.[67]

As the title of that fellowship indicates, Muktibodh was central to Vajpeyi's reimagination of Hindi literature. In addition to the establishment of a memorial in his name, Vajpeyi was responsible for securing funding for the publication of his collected works, and for the making of Mani Kaul's film, both released in 1980 and the occasion for the conference. This was not simply a moment in the reevaluation of Muktibodh, but, indeed, a crucial moment in his canonization. For the writers of *Kaṅk,* the overarching question was Muktibodh's relation to politics, but for the writers of *Pūrvagraha,* Muktibodh's fantasy and his idea of the alienated middle class becomes crucial for understanding the turn towards myth and history in Hindi writing, while also giving an indication of a new, Madhya Pradesh–based regional identity. In fact, the elevation of Muktibodh could be seen in part as a response to the "regionalization" of Hindi, something particularly evident here. By emphasizing Muktibodh as a writer of the small towns of Madhya Pradesh, *Pūrvagraha* was able to articulate an idea of Hindi, and even a Hindi cosmopolitanism, that was not necessarily bound to the central power structure, or a national role for Hindi that was no longer possible.

The conference on Muktibodh was therefore a major media event to the extent that it was reported on in major English-language media as well.[68] The conference included major, established figures in Hindi, and the articles resulting are still widely cited in Muktibodh scholarship.[69] Other articles engaged explicitly with the debates over Muktibodh's political position, with one, for instance, arguing that Muktibodh had become largely disenchanted with the left in India by the time of his death.[70] On the whole, however, these critics were not as interested in directly debating Muktibodh's ideological position as they were in emphasizing his ability to transcend such distinctions. If, for the *Kaṅk* poets, there was an effort to embed Muktibodh within a left modernist tradition of writers such as Mayakovsky, these *Pūrvagraha* poets were interested in crafting a literary history of Hindi modernism with Muktibodh, and his dark fantasies of alienation, at the center. For instance, the novelist and critic Ramesh Chandra Shah (born 1937) took up the question of why Muktibodh seemed to portray the totality of Indian life not in the expected form of the novel, but in his long poems. Shah's argument both reveals an anxiety over a perceived failure of Muktibodh, and by extension of Hindi literature, to produce a great novel and in the process shifts the interpretation of the long poem. Whereas, for earlier critics such as Shamsher Bahadur Singh, Namwar Singh, and Ram Vilas Sharma, Muktibodh's long poem was the apex of his work and compared to a vast mural, for Shah, and also for Varma, the long poem was symptomatic of the postcolonial modernity that shaped Muktibodh's writings.[71]

The essays collected in *Pūrvagraha* were crucial in forming an image of Muktibodh, not as a symbol for the revolutionary potential of the middle classes as in *Kaṅk*, but for the disillusionment, or *mohbhaṅg,* that would come to characterize this period across South Asian literatures. In this light, Muktibodh emerges as a tragic figure, emblematic of a larger idea of postindependence India as a time of disappointment and the search for meaning and tradition in a society shattered by the experience of colonialism. The Muktibodh presented in *Pūrvagraha,* in sharp contrast with his reevaluation in *Kaṃk,* was not assimilable to a turn towards the popular in Marxism, but he also did not fit within a classical mold of *nayī kavitā,* which would privilege the artist's own interpretation of experience. Rather, the Muktibodh of *Pūrvagraha* was rooted in the fractured societies of the small towns of Central India, and his work articulated the unique modernity of the Indian lower middle class. As we see throughout the reception of Muktibodh, the analysis of his life and works is a way through which thinkers working in Hindi were able to shape a literary history of the twentieth century.

A useful contrast between the two journals can be found in their covers. *Kaṅk* featured throughout abstract illustrations by the painter Bal Samarth, who lived and worked in Nagpur throughout his life. The cover itself features a line drawing of Muktibodh, in a realistic style, with the poet, in his characteristic clothes and in good health, looking thoughtfully into the middle distance. Beneath the drawing is an abstract image of groups of people, composed of interwoven lines that form monochromatic figures. The tension of the issue, between the populism of *janvād* and the "revolutionary romanticism" of Muktibodh, is made plain. *Pūrvagraha,* on the other hand, has for the cover of its special issue on Muktibodh an image by Akbar Padamsee (1928–2020). Padamsee, already well-known as a prominent member of the progressive modernist school of painters, presents a watercolor of Muktibodh, seemingly drawn from photographs taken in the final few months of his life. A bare, cadaverous skull, formed from soft, indistinct greys and blacks, Muktibodh's face appears in darkness, with the jawbone shaping a dark shadow across his cheeks. One eye appears clear and focused, the other broken up, blurred and fractured, as the image is crackled into fine lines. The image would seem to present the grey, disillusioned, and alienated individual of postcolonial Indian society.

Figure C.1. Cover image of *Kank* 1980. *Source*: *Kank*.

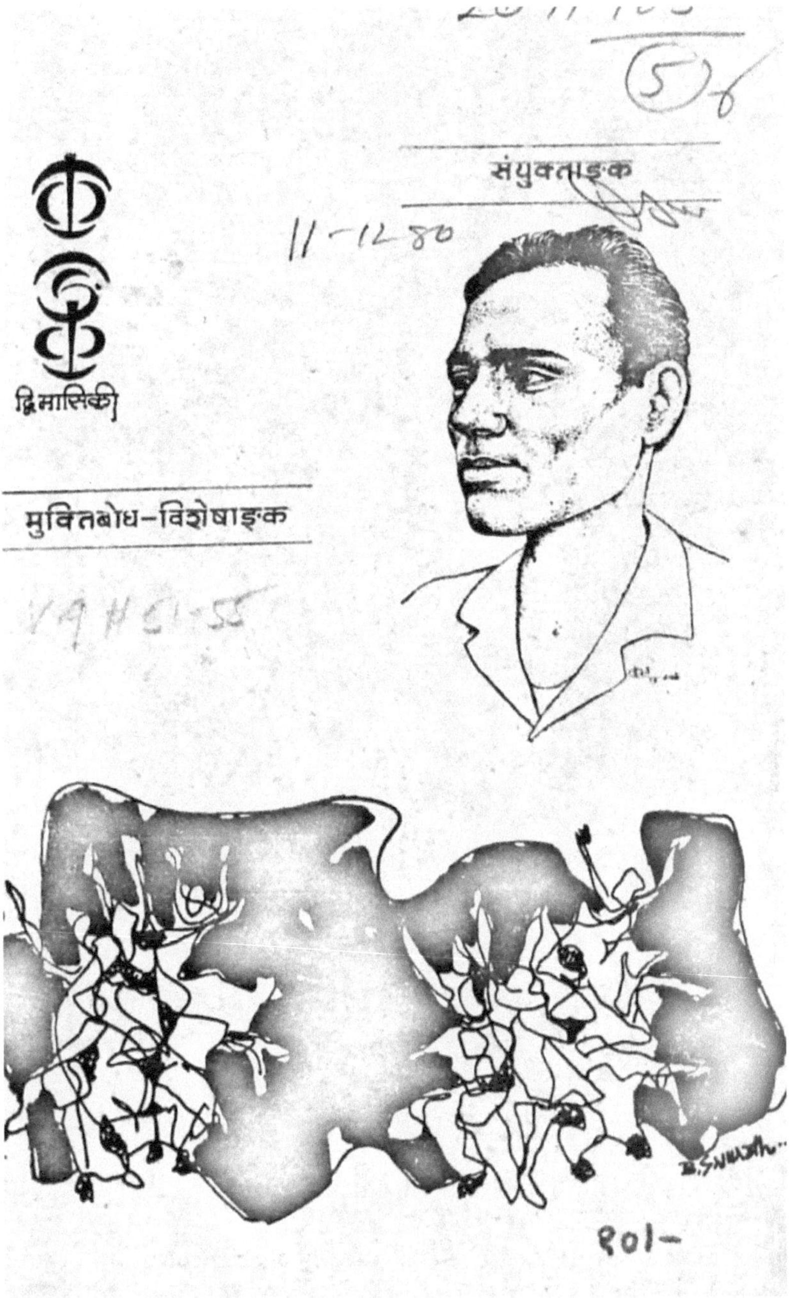

Figure C.2. Cover Image of *Purvagraha* 1980. *Source: Purvagraha.*

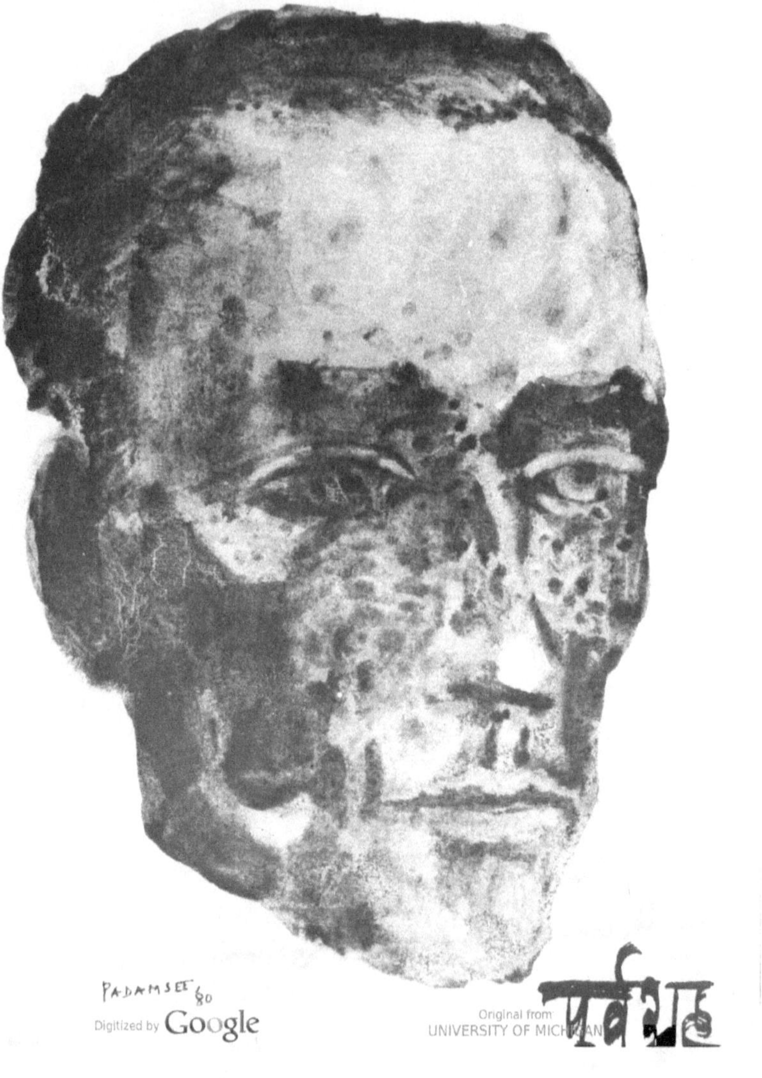

The Idea of Muktibodh

This book has argued for a historically specific Muktibodh. By emphasizing the particularities of his linguistic and family background, and of his career in Madhya Pradesh, and situating his interests firmly in the context of the world of pre- and postindependence India, an image of Muktibodh has emerged that is impossible to imagine outside of the context of the long 1950s in which he developed his work. The most particular example of this is Muktibodh's interest in science, which draws so much from the tenor of its time, even as it pulls the material of that time into a space of radical critique, where the present is forced to account for itself in the well of the Brahmin's ghost. The intellectual contradictions faced in "Brahmarākṣas" were utterly particular to Muktibodh's own anxieties about caste and education while simultaneously rooted in the intellectual history of his own time.

Understanding the particular historical circumstances in which Muktibodh worked makes clear both Muktibodh's own contribution to the literary history of Hindi and his place in its intellectual history. Muktibodh is typical of the first generation of Hindi modernists in that he was strongly influenced by the poetry of the 1920s and 1930s; indeed, he would grapple with the legacy of *chāyāvād*, and especially the interpretation of Jayshankar Prasad's long poem *Kāmāyanī*, for most of his career. He is also deeply embedded in the time and place in which he worked, from the turn to the left among Hindi writers in the late 1930s and early 1940s to his interest in questions of internationalism in the 1950s. Muktibodh's career is also deeply affected, however, by his particular background as a Marathi speaker and the area in Central India in which he worked. An examination of Muktibodh's career reveals the importance of a location such as Nagpur, one of the largest cities of Central India, and the unique Hindi-Marathi bilingual literary culture that it supported. Muktibodh is both a typical figure in modern Hindi literature and a representative of changes in regional literary cultures, as well as the literary expression of the lower middle class.

Muktibodh's reception arguably hinged on the question of his background and its relation to his ideology. I have argued, however, that these negotiations have resulted in an image of Muktibodh that obscures his accomplishments. First, because Muktibodh has been understood primarily in terms of his position in the lower middle class and because his work has been debated primarily in terms of its possible political readings, his own accomplishments are often less deeply analyzed, especially in terms of his innovations and his theorization of literary form. Second, the emphasis on Muktibodh's position in the lower middle class and the debate over the implications of that position for his political allegiances obscure the ways in which he was deeply and consistently engaged in thinking through the framework of the international.

If I have argued that Muktibodh needs to be understood as operating within his own time, however, this begs the question: What can Muktibodh tell us now? What is the relevance of his work to our attempts to understand contemporary India? How can this figure, who seems to be so prophetic to readers of Hindi literature in his time, speak to us today? The time of which he was a part seems to be more and more distant and irrelevant. Nehru cast a long shadow over the postindependence period and defined many reigning themes of state-led development and an independent foreign policy. Today, he has often come to be seen as an irrelevance. Recently, there have been attempts to remodel the Nehru Memorial Museum and Library, founded after his death in 1964. One possibility, stated only in indefinite terms, would be to redesign the museum so that it focuses instead on contemporary Indian governance. The idea of Nehru in this way is to be effaced. In other ways, aspects of Muktibodh's life continue to seem prophetic. The banning of the history textbook, and the court cases and processions that accompanied it, seemed to bring to life the nightmares of "Aṃdhere meṃ"; today, capricious bannings under organized public pressure have become ordinary, and acts of violence against intellectuals more generally, have become commonplace.[72]

In this way, Muktibodh's fantasies continue to remain relevant and alive. He continues to be analyzed in part because his works remain a vital model for Hindi literature. But Muktibodh is also important because he is a key figure in mid-twentieth century literary and cultural history. This period, extending from just before independence to the disillusionment with that independence that set in in the 1960s, saw the development of crucial paradigms that remain vital today. The conversations and debates that Muktibodh took part in and the literary models that he developed have formed defining moments in Hindi modernism. This in turn means that as this period begins to become an object of historical inquiry rather than contemporary criticism, the understanding of Muktibodh in Hindi will begin to change as well.[73] This criticism builds on the shift I described, which took place in the late 1970s and early 1980s, towards viewing Muktibodh as representative of a particular, lower-middle-class modernity. This new appreciation of Muktibodh, also historicizes Muktibodh's contributions to literature and criticism, looking at Muktibodh as a participant in intellectual history. I hope that this work will be a contribution towards this trend.

On one level, this book is an attempt to historicize Muktibodh's contributions to Hindi literature, so that they can be seen as developing out of the particular times, locations, and interests within which he worked. In that way, it is a contribution to the study of modern Hindi literature, and in particular to the study of Hindi literature after independence. But I also hope to have demonstrated the intense vitality of this period and the ways in which Muktibodh's work can be seen as a unique record of Hindi's engagement with a global stage. From his location in Central India, and without ever leaving the country or even spending significant time in a major Hindi-speaking city, Muktibodh insisted on his work's ability to reimagine the world. In this way, it reflected the time in which he lived, an unprecedented period for Hindi literature. For the first time, Hindi could claim to speak on an international stage as the hegemonic language of the nation. That this period of imagined hegemony was so short-lived—by the mid-1960s it would be not the single national language but only part of a three-language compromise—and riven with so many contradictions while it existed, makes it all the more important to understand its effects on literary culture at its apogee. Muktibodh is key to those effects, in part because his internationalism was so locally rooted. Rather than participate directly in the international through travel or movement, Muktibodh reimagined the framework in which the international took place. He did so through creating a literature, and its theorization, that emphasized the interconnections between the imagination and the outside world, thus unifying the most important aporias of literature as he understood them. The result was a body of work that provided the most important modernist model for a Hindi literature that could, through its imaginative landscapes, confront simultaneously the world of the Cold War and postindependence India, and it remains today a crucial model in Hindi for imagining the interplay between the self and world.

Appendix

Full Translations of "Brahmarākṣas" (The Brahmin Demon) and "Aṃdhere meṃ" (In the Dark)

Brahmarakshas

that way from the city towards the ruins
an abandoned, silent, *baoli;*
inside,
in the clammy dark
settled depths of the water . . .
steps, drowned
in the surrounding stagnant water
like the point—
you can't get to the bottom of it
but it's deep.

around the stepwell
its branches tangled
a silent *audumbar* tree.
on the branches
owl's nests hanging
abandoned, brown, round.

Poems reprinted with permission from Rajkamal Prakashan Pvt. Ltd., New Delhi.

the sensation of a hundred virtuous deeds long ago
has settled into a wild, green, raw smell
and hangs in the air
forms a suspicion
of some unknown, dissipated greatness:
a rattle catching in the heart.
leaning over the lips of the well
on elegant green elbows
sits a *ṭagar* valerian
with its white star blossoms.

next to it
a flash of red—
my own oleander . . .
it calls me to danger
where the well's dark open mouth
stares up at the empty sky.

a *brahmarākṣas* has penetrated
the voidblack depths of the baoli;
up from within resounds, echoing against itself,
a mad, babbling sound.
the great reckoner
the filth of the body
every moment
scrubbing at
the shadow of offense—day and night
to cleanse—
the *brahmarakshas*
scrapes his body
with the claws on his hands, smooth,
slapping water across arms chest mouth
cleaning and cleaning
and yet
still filthy
still filthy!!

and . . . from his lips
an amazing *stotra,* some enraged recitation—

or perhaps a flood of pure sanskrit obscenity,
brows knotted together into
glittering strands of criticism!!
in the insane streaming waters of that unbroken
  bath . . .
the sensitivity of life itself blackens!!

however, when on occasion
the flying particles
of crooked sun-rays
bounce across the walls of the *baoli*
and happen to reach the water,
the brahmarakshas believes that the sun
has bowed to him and said 'namaste.'
if rays of moonlight,
somehow forgetting their proper path,
should collide against the walls,
the *brahmarākṣas* assumes
that the moon,
head lowered in reverence,
has accepted him as its *guru* of wisdom.

covered with thorns as his body and mind is,
he blossoms with the experience
that even the heavens
have humbly accepted his excellence!!

and then, with a brilliance doubly terrifying
this discerning mind
takes in everything—
sumero-babylonian myths
sweet and noble vedic hymns
all the *sūtras* from that time to today
vedic verse, mantras, *theorems*
and all of the propositions,
marx, engels, russell, toynbee,
heidegger and spengler; sartre—even gandhi—
from all these prince-i-ples
he composes an entirely new exposition

the brahmarakshas bathes in
the vacant, thickened depths
of the ancient stepwell.

. . . rumbling, ringing careening
these echoes rise up from the depths, and so
in the new turning of these rising sounds
each word collides with its response
in struggling with its image, form
becomes perverse action
and a sound battles against its echo.

on the lip of the well
held up on elegant green elbows
the *ṭagar*, with its white starflowers, listens
                    to the echoes!!
the tender flowers of the *karaundi* listen
that ancient *audumbar* fig listens as well
and i am there, listening
to the *tragedy*,
recited in insane symbols,
bound within the well.

X X X

a tall, tall staircase disappearing in darkness
                    its steps . . .
towards a marvelous inner space.
ascending descending
again, up and down, a stumble
sprained ankles
lashes across the chest.
the struggle between good and evil—
                    more terrible
is the war between good and better
a narrow, obscure success
a grand and noble failure!!
. . . these agonies
of liberal plenitude

are so very precious . . .
noble, ethical esteem
formed through a vision
of geometric mathematical balance
the appearance of a subtle, ethical
   self-consciousness . . .
. . . since when has it been easy
to satisfy such liberal plenitude
these secret tales, so humane, so precious!!
the sun emerges
a blood-red river of thought
spreads across the walls;
the moon rises
his wounds now oozing,
he ties clean white bandages
on that agitated forehead.
the stars spread out across the shores of the sky
all the points
of countless decimals
spread out across the twisted battleground of math
murdered, he finds his purpose
sprawled out . . .
the chest and limbs, splayed out,
of a scientist.

the self is a kind of delicate crystal palace,
with a staircase
and lonely steps
difficult to climb.
leave him
to his equations
completely resolved
balanced in feeling, balanced in action.
in the search
for an action equally balanced
and logical in feeling
addressing every priest and thinker
in his search for a *guru*
he's stumbled away!!

but times change and now he traded in fame
. . . wealth from good, profitable work,
while from within that wealth his heart and mind
and, from within that self overcome by wealth,
the shadow of truth
                    continued to burn.

but the consciousness
within the self
was inherently out of sync . . .
a despairing mind
tracing out the footsteps of greatness!!
if only i had met him then
i would have felt his pain
told him his value
his greatness!!

ground between
two hard stones,
inside and out,
such a sad, pathetic *tragedy*!

in the baoli
still he recites
in mad symbols
how in the palace
he wrote out his math
and died . . .
                    like a dead bird
                    in a thorned darkness of
   undergrowth
gone forever
that gem, unknown and now gone for ever
why!!
why did it happen!!
i would like to become
the tear-stained student of the brahmarakshas,
so that i could deliver that unfinished labor,
the source of all his pain,
to some collected, whole conclusion.

In the Dark

1

life's . . .
dark chambers:
walking in circles
someone, endlessly;
his feet sound out
again and again . . . again and again,
don't see . . . can't see
but still he wanders
a prisoner in an enchanted cave
from across the walls
deep and mysterious echo of darkness
announces the identity
of someone
unstoppable
and, the beat of my heart
asks—who is he
i hear, but cannot see!
and then suddenly falling from the wall
plaster cracking and bursting open
sandy lime falling out
skins sloughing off—
on its own
a massive face appears
self-generated
a face appears on the wall,
with pointed nose
and splendid forehead,
straight jaw;
some strange unrecognized figure.
who is he who appears but
will not be known?
who is this *manu*?

out of the city, over the mountain, a lake . . .
darkness everywhere,
still water,

but, bubbling up suddenly from within
a white shape on the black glass of the water
a great foggy face diffuses
and smiles,
introduces itself;
but, i am stunned,
and do not understand.

and now!!
around the lake, the dark forest
flashes with green sparks, suddenly
electricity dances on the canopy of the trees
the branches bend and sway
scream, heads crashing together when suddenly
the stone door of a magical cave
hidden within the dark of the trees
cracks open
. . . . . .
enter an odd torch, bright red flame,
thick red mist
into the black of the inner cavity;
in the mist, before me, a man bathed in bloodlight
mystery made visible!

seeing this face radiating light,
my limbs break into a strange shiver.
fair-skinned, bright eyed, calm face
seeing this beloved form of respected love and
  kindness
i feel an extraordinary doubt,
seeing this noble long-armed one at once produces
a deep suspicion.

that mysterious person
is my still ungrasped expression,
a totality
a complete manifestation
of my personal potentialities, inherent brilliance,
  genius,

the tension of knowledge that seeps into the heart,
the icon of my soul.

but, why is he wearing tattered clothes?
why is his white face dirty?
how did he get such a massive wound across his
  chest?
why has he endured the pain of imprisonment?
why this terrifying condition?
who fed him?
who gave him water?
and why, after all this, is there a smile on his face?
where did he find this awesome strength?

serious questions, even dangerous,
and so from the thick
jungles came a wind into the cave
and, with a gust, blew the candle out . . .
caught in this darkness
a life sentence!
the dark bandage of some black '*dash*'
has been tied around my eyes
i've been impaled on a standing exclamation point
                                        thrown
                                        unconscious
                                        into the black pit of a decimal.

2

shivered emptiness
echoes bubbled up in the dark,
wrinkles of voice on the mouth of emptiness,
on my chest, pushing down my head,
waves of frothing words
intolerably sweet!!
yes, the knocker keeps
banging against the door.
someone is calling to tell me my own thought,
calling (caressing the heart

as if at some difficult moment suddenly
pressing lips against lips, craving
to say some true thing in a simple way, and then
as soon as i hear it i am deflated . . .
like that, the chain bangs and bangs against the door)

midnight, in all this darkness, who's there?
surrounded by mist dejected and desperate with
   anticipation
face like lightning—that face filled with love—
innocent—
i know that face out there!!
that's the one, yes it is!
who saw me in the magical cave.
carelessly
he appears,
without a single thought for my convenience.
wherever he wants, whenever he wants
whatever form
pulling on whatever symbol;
he signals, he convinces
he sends shocks into the heart!!
oh dawns bloom on his face,
mountain peaks glint on his cheeks,
radiating waves of peace in his eyes,
look at him, and feel the love rise!
i feel like—opening the door
and embracing him in my arms,
bringing him into my heart
melting down, holding him and merging into him.
but, i'm here, lying
covered in wounds
in the terrifying darkness of this pit;
not even the strength to lift myself up
(it's true as well that
i'm enamored of my weaknesses)
and so, i delay my love
avoid him,

fear him.
he sits me down on the highest peak
on a dangerous, rocky ledge;
he leaves me in a frightful state.
he says—'cross the abyss between the mountains,
cross that rope bridge
go on your own to that far mountain peak.'
Listen, brother, mountaineering is the last thing i need,
i'm afraid of heights;
let the door knocker ring!!
let the bubbles of echoes rise up in the darkness,
those people . . . anyways
you'll leave the way you came.
i'll lie in this cave.
surrounded by my pain!!
what should i do, what shouldn't i, tell me;
the world-critique swims in this dark emptiness
(can't bear it)
his great frenzied perception
in the dark expanse (can't bear it)
this map of the future
flashing inside me shapes of lightning
i can't bear it!
no, no, i can't leave him
come what may i'll have to bear it.
massage my weak knees again,
stumbling i
get up to open the door,
wipe the weird bloodless emptiness off my face
with my hands,
feel my way forward
in the dark,
feel the ground with my feet,
point out the directions with my hands
experience the world with my breath,
my head feels the sky above me,
my heart beats out a guess at the darkness,
eyes sniff out theories,

the only deep sense is touch.
in the soul, a terrible
consciousness and sensation of knowledge bursts into flame.
thoughts scatter.
i feel my way forward,
balancing myself,
feeling for the door,
rusted shut, i force it
force the
hinge, open the door,
peek outside . . .

the road is empty, a weird spaciousness
cold darkness.
with tired eyes they watch the world
weary stars.
again thought and again sorrow
again worry
growing pain as if far off, there in the distance
the dark peepal tree guards the way.
the distant, distinct barking of dogs
shivering in the lonely waves of the winds
mixing with the echoing cry of jackals.
the farnesses shiver, the distances ring
(outside there's no one, there's no one outside)

and then a cry in the dark emptiness
the bird of night
says:
'he's gone,
and he won't come back, won't even come
to your door.
he's slipped away into the village, into the city!
look for him now
search for him now!
he is your complete, supreme expression,
you are his student (albeit truant)
he is your guru,
your teacher . . .'

3

i don't know if i'm dreaming or
already awake.
the lamp is burning,
in the yellow glow time softens and melts,
all the scattered forms of the world
like printed outlines
utterly distinct
lifeless!!
this is civil lines. i'm lying here
in my room
eyes open
my beaten child's face
lean and depressed
a picture drawn on a chalk board
like a ghost—
is that me?
is it me?

two in the morning,
cries of jackals in the far-off forest,
the wheels of a train
coming closer wailing and screeching
a terrifying thought of an impossible event,
an unconscious premonition,
that somewhere will be a *rail accident.*
calculations of worry
glittering on the slate of the sky
outside my window.
. . . . . .
oh tolstoy
how do you appear before me
amidst the stars
roaming and pausing
as you view the earth.

perhaps, like tolstoy
a certain man

another,
the far end of a thread within me,
the central perception
of my unwritten novel
like a strangled, smothered cry
perhaps, like tolstoy.

procession?
silently, in the still midnight dark of the city
the muffled beat of a band, off somewhere
sounds from a dream rising and falling on soft strings
rolling echoes, waves of sadness
rolling waves!!

i walk out onto the balcony and watch the street,
a path of coal
some dead black tongue stretched out
sparkling electric lights or
the shining teeth of the dead!!

but, far across the street
at the base of the stars shivering with cold
a dark shining
coming, coming closer
closer!!
those muffled dream sounds
the music of a thousand echoes crashing together
coming closer!!

and, now
the points of the gaslights burst into view
between them appears
something, something like a dark procession!!

and now
endless faces light up in the blue gas light
a marching band
behind them march massive black horses
even in dark and terrifying unconsciousness

is this the parade
of a death squad?

bizarre!!
the lines of the blue gaslight
marching on either side.
in the thick oblivion of the city lost in sleep
(in the underworld
rise up these writhing endless snakes
the tangled lines of calamity!!
all are sleeping.
but i am awake, yes, watching
the bloodcurdling magical feat!!)

a strange *procession,*
a solemn *quick march* . . .
in black dress, embroidered with metallic thread
a sparkling band—
skeletal, bilious, noble
bound in a net of intestine, banging their terrible
drums
deathly melodies coming in waves
their echoes writhing on the road.
i think i've seen some of
the faces of this band,
in fact, some of them appear to be well-known
journalists
of this very city!!
how on earth did these illustrious names wind up in
this band!!
behind them marches
a forest of bloody points
long lines of footsteps in rhythm
tank formations, *mortars, artillery,* united,
slowly this terrifying parade creeps forward
the stone faces of the soldiers
angry, scarred, disfigured!!
perhaps, i've seen them somewhere before.
perhaps, some of them are known to me!

and what's this behind them!!
cavalry!!
khaki military dress on pitch-black horses,
with faces half in sindoor and saffron,
half black as tar, horrible
terrifying!!
holding in their hands straightedged swords
shimmering!!
on each, a bandolier from shoulder to waist.
on the waist, a pistol in a leather holster,
a sharp edge in the angry focus of their eyes,
colonel, brigadier, general, marshal
more commanders, more officers
their faces familiar somehow
i've seen them in the newspapers
seen their articles
i've read their poems even
now! i see
eminent critics, thinkers, brilliant poets
ministers, industrialists and scholars
and now the most famous murderer of the city
domaji ustad
has become their balban[1]
no, no!
they appear in the bodies of ghosts and ghouls.
their inner nature as demons
bubbles out clearly
hidden motives
have bloomed into visibility,
this is the triumph of the dead.

(the pinwheel of ideas
spins in the head)

and then up from the *procession*
eyes swollen with rage,
as if plunging their bloody bayonette
into the heart,
a cry has broken out on the street—

'shoot the bastard, blow him away
we had slipped away
from the eyes of the world
sneaking along when
he spotted us
in the dark of midnight
he's seen it all
kill him, finish him off for good.'

running madly through the street!!
i run from my balcony covered in sweat!!

suddenly the dream breaks apart
images
shatter.

waking i remember that dream,
remember again the faces of darkness,
and, it's clear to me that the terrifying
dead souls of the city
step out every night,
but, by day
they sit together, plot their schemes
in their offices, their centers, their homes.
no, i saw them in their naked truth,
and i will pay a harsher price for it.

4
suddenly
a bell somewhere rings four
my heart races
a sad, dull mind like an anthill
distracted.
the scuttling of endless pitch-black *hyphen-dash* lines
scattered everywhere.
i'm lying in my room.
the black beams of the ceiling
crush my heart
in the courtyard there's a broken pipe

sputtering out its stream of water.
but the body is weak
the heart melts in the dark.

at once i sense the world,
the wide world of the newspaper,
strangled, surrounded, tension everywhere,
on the tree stills the leaf
the army has seized the streets
the pulse of my mind
counts the beats of time.
and what is all this?
the repression of a people's revolution
martial law!!

my nerve fails and my feet race through the alleyways,
running out of breath,
the era has stuck out its tongue,
someone is chasing after me.
i run in terror,
turn after turn
far away the crossroads,
maybe there's no patrolman
there for now.
before me appears, like a darkened stupa,
a terrifying banyan—
isolated, desolate,
the home of the poor, their only roof,
in the dark pit of its roots sleep
a few homeless beings.
drowned in the dark
their faded rags hanging from the branches
the only wealth
of a mendicant lunatic.
yes, it's a madman who lives there.

but, it's a strange night tonight!
the same lunatic madman
today is suddenly
enlightened, radiant with wisdom and understanding.

he abandons his madness
and with a fullthroated voice
sings some verse, some song
animacognitive!!
spectacular, man,
who knew that you could find him here
in this city of military propaganda!
who knew that his mind could awaken even here!!

(this voice, raised by compassion to the heights of
aesthetic bliss,
is presented here in prose translation)

'o idealist mind,
o intellectual mind,
what have you done?
what life have you lived?
you've become a glutton, soulless
stretched out as a canopy at a wedding of ghosts
laid out as a bed of corruption,

dressed in the tassels of sorrow,
lost day and night in your thoughts,
a lonely mind, suffering alone,
this life without action has become a bunker

what have you done?
what life have you lived?

tell me why you are running,
when you've turned your face from compassion!
you've become a stone;

you've taken so, so much
given so, so little
the nation is dead—and still you're alive!!

you drove away the father of public welfare,
crushed the mother of compassion,
raised *terriers* of selfishness,

renounced . . . the feeling of responsibility,
killed . . . the comtemplations of the heart!
broke open the forehead of wisdom,
cut off the hands of logic,
awoke, stuck, caught,
sunk in your own muck!!
tempered discernment in the oil of selfishness
and eaten your ideals.

what have you done?
what life have you lived?
taken too much, and given back so little,
the nation is dead, but you're still alive!'

my head feels warm,
this is why i'm confused.
my dreams are filled with critique,
my thought is a flock of scattering images.
interiority—a restless mist,
what should i do, who should i talk to,
where should i go, delhi or ujjain?

like the father
of the sage shunashepa,
the cursed ajigarta,[2]
his own self lost to him,
found only sometimes at night
during the day raving
disturbed mentality.

my god
what has he sung,
what has he brought into the world,
manifest,
i stand before myself
my own shadow, thick and deep
an argument breaks out and

one slaps the other.
just madness,
a pointless critique.

a terrifying darkness . . .
as if the *martial law*
was only made for me,
as if my inactive consciousness called forth the crisis,
as if this accident
caused by me.

head spinning, my head is spinning . . .
however sharp the dialectic of action and event
in the world outside,
the interior dialectic
is just as pointed
thought comes from thought.
today this madman took away my calm,
robbed me of my rest.

i'm standing next to this banyan.

this face of mine
washed in this unfathomably dark water
this mind washed
from the bottomless darkness
of broken house, still and bent.
in the dim light of night
a massive, sombre heaviness
with an odor
as if in ruins a garden
of roses and jasmine, in the darkness of night,
releasing their fragrance, every moment their
   fragrance.
but where is that garden,
in the dark i cannot see.
only their scent everywhere,
but in that wave of scent

a pain hidden, a hidden worry
writhing
writhing.

5

suddenly a feeling!!
from behind a stranger has placed
a hand on the shoulder.
startled and terrified
a shiver runs to my head,
no, no. falling from above
a banyan leaf on my shoulder,
a signal? a sign?
has someone sent a letter?
a letter from the soul of the banyan?
which is it?

i run in terror,
turn after turn
the sound of gunfire
rising like a golden dawn over the buildings.
i run in terror,
turn after turn.
turns the earth, turns the sky
and then, i see the stone steps
of a boarded-up house, there
i sit down quietly, head in hands!!
head spinning,
dizzy . . . whirlpools,
in their swirling eyes i see
like a dream—
far beneath the surface of the earth
a dark and lonely
cave.
in the darkness of this vast pit
glittering stones cutting through the blackness
radiant *radioactive* gems too are scattered across the walls,

falling on them is a powerful waterfall.
natural water rushing in,
slipping and flowing in waves
over the electric burning rubies
rays of light bursting up from the depth of the water,
the radiance of these gems with their forms of color
breaking
against the rough walls of the cave!!

i find myself inside this cave,
with eyes dazzled and seduced, i watch these electric
flashes,
take the radiant gemstones into my hands
look upon them with overcome . . .
suddenly i see
these are not gems refracted with light
they are my own
experience, pain, discerning conclusion,
and ideas coming together into gems of bloody fire
the living water softening them moment by moment
their movement of their rays moistened
their sparkle dampened!!

i made them a home in this cave
drove them away from worldly things
forbade them from serving the people,
banned them
pushed them into the pit!!
they were dangerous
(children are begging) and . . .
this isn't the time,
we have to hold the line.

6

the *scene* changes,
a crossroads, wide, silent, dark,
in the center an abandoned ochre clock tower,
an ancient dome,

time pacing in dark winds.
the four clock faces are yellow in the night,
four separate movements of the minute hand,
four separate corners,
four distinct signs,
(four separate movements in the mind)
on poles, the necks of electric lines drooping,
around lightbulbs burning with shame
restless wings of insects
flying in circles
buzzing angrily.
at the base of the tower
bird shit and straw!
sitting in a crack in the dome, the old
birds of impossibility
watch over everything with their sharp gaze,
as if terrifying
intentions
sparkle in their eyes.
abandoned crossroads,
scattered movement, scattered speed
an evil desire paces in patrol.
a terrifying soldier, with impossibly tired movement
suddenly in the darkness
the rigid lines of his coppery face illuminated
as he lights his cigarette.
the stony wrinkles
in the momentary flame of the match
terrify.
but each time the color changes on his face,
as if something unexpected . . .
who knows what will happen, who knows!!
he stares . . .
their rifles pointed with bayonets
a ground of soldiers
stands in formation, a curved triangle
in the center of the square!!
on one side

a *tank* troop, their soldiers yawning at attention,
but still standing!!

i run in terror,
turn after turn.
running, my chappels slap
as they hit the ground.
the muck under my feet is pulled up
spatters against my face and on my chest,
i'm nauseous from the shame.
the dark encircling alleyways
attack my face, attack my eyes.
a strange air, stale and humid
the trapped breath of the alley.
i run in terror,
turn after turn.
vague shapes appear,
fear? a home? can't say
suddenly a street of black tar
long and wide and dark and cold
restless eyes look in every direction.
no one's there,
no one at all.
in the dark sky, the pictographic eyes of stars
sparkling.
my heart sputters in its lamp.
something pulls me to the center of the road.
i move bound by magic.
standing high on the level ground
this lonely, lonely statue of tilak
still, insensate . . .
but at the moment i approach
the base of the statue begins to tremble and move
what, what is this!!
every grain trembles and showers
blue *electrons*
blue sparks falling in every direction
burning sparks flying from the body of the statue.

a smile trembles on lips of stone,
a smoldering bloom of electric life in the eyes.
and then, what is this!!
from the nostrils of that noble face
how long has blood been flowing
warm, red blood, drip by drip
(the overcoat slowly covered with bloodstains)
as if from worry, from stress
the skull has suddenly burst open
brainblood pours from the nostrils.
pitaḥa, pitaḥa, oh *pitaḥa,*
try not to worry
we're still alive, aren't we,
why worry!!
helplessly, i grab hold
of those cold legs
of a stone statue
almost crying
my whole body trembles with compassion
on my chest, on my head, on my arms
fall blue
electric sparks
the blood drips into my heart
as if it floods my soul
a pool of blood.
and then a knocking in the chest
a banging sound in the head!! the bones crack and
break!!
a powerful thought!!
discernment moves the sharp plane
the blade moves
someone is shaving off my very being
a terrifying resolve awakens within me,
some great and heavy stubbornness rises up.

and then the sky trembles and crackles
with the sound of gunfire
electricity shot into my legs.
in a corner of those dark cave alleyways

i sit exhausted
to think and plan.
from over the thatched roofs of homes drowned in
  darkness
a faint cry, a quiet sobbing
trembling in the darkness, trembling from a distance
an animal nature in those waves of sighs
terrifying shivering pain

i am trying to listen closely when
what do i see—
in front of me
wrapped in a jute sack
someone, huddling
in the cold
shivering, shaking!! he'll die!!
and then he opens his mouth and at once
his tousled hair,
his ears then
he opens his mouth, mutters
something
but, i can't hear it
i look closely—he's known to me,
i've seen him often, examined him a few times
but could never capture him.
no, it can't be . . .
i suppress the thought as soon as it rises in the mind
the courage to think has escaped me entirely.
that face—that face, its gandhi *jī*!!
but lame like this!!
astounding!!
no, no, he must be some kind of detective
disguised for investigation
operating quietly
undercover.

finding before me a god drowned in the black of darkness
i approach him with great humility
like a bolt of lightning

he says—'beat it, run for it,
ours is the face of the past
you have to move forward.'
but, i kept looking at that face.
with its wrinkles formed of long resolve
the weight in his words.
he said—
'the world isn't a pile of garbage, where
some rooster pecking its way up the hill
some chicken
if it crows loud enough
becomes the messiah.'
he said—
every quantum particle of a lump of clay
is a quality,
only the qualities of the people make possible
the goals of the future'
those solemn words advanced forward,
who knows what he said!!
i was perturbed!

suddenly the skeleton of the soul has risen up
the carcass of the statue.
glasses on the nose, stick in the hand,
jute blanket on his shoulder, and a child in his arms.
astonishing!! astounding! a child!!
with a smile this resplendent man said—
'he's fallen sound asleep with me.
take him carefully, keep him safe.'

i am about to say something, when there
isn't any one there, no one at all.
and the darkness
is deeper than ever, more alone than ever!
in this alleyway the child clings to me silently,
holding on to my chest and shoulder, a tiny little
   vault of the sky
his touch is soft gentle filled with love
but, i feel a heavy weight.

the scent of the future and the dark distances,
i take the stars of the sky along with me
and move along
cross into the abyssal depths.

suddenly the infant on my shoulder breaks out in a sob
but, but, this voice is familiar!!
i've heard it several times before,
bursting with the momentum of explosive rage,
a deep complaint,
a terrifying anger.
i'm afraid someone will hear.
then we two won't be able to stay anywhere at all.
i quiet it, rock it back and forth,
then i begin to sing to it
half-forgotten lullabies spring to my lips!
but however much i try to quiet it
it cries out in anger even more, continuously!!
a wet shower of coals burns against me.

but, somehow i am happy.
(it's doing something
I never could do all my life)
i pat and stroke its little baby back,
the soul is moist.
the feet move forward, the mind moves forward.

i drown in my thoughts, in deep thought
a lake of blood in the depth of the heart,
brilliant gems drowned in the blood,
hematic rays burst out,
there are resolutions drowned in that blood,
and these resolutions
walk with me.
i walk through the dark alleys.

and then i find myself in the dark
with nothing on my shoulder!! that infant
has gone away somewhere,

and now in its place
only a bouquet of sunflowers.
those golden flowers shed their rays of light
on my shoulders, my head, my cheeks, my body,
and on the road, their atoms radiating in all
  directions.
how wonderful!!
and then i passed into a new lane and saw
an open door.
dark stairs.
somewhere a lamp burning.
i move forward
carrying that bouquet on my shoulders
what is this, where should i go?
no no
it's a rifle now
what
a heavy rifle,
what a thing!!

a large, open room, a dark breeze,
peer out the window, stars stitched into the dark
an icy breath, abandoned
everything in the room thrown and smashed.
lying on the floor
arms spread out, and finally laid flat.
i shine a *torch* on his face and—
the hair on his forehead matted with blood,
a bullet hole between the eyebrows,
patches of blood on the cheeks
a thin line dried on the lips,
the glasses broken, the nose straightened out.
this was the solitary
man i knew, there, yes
the truth is just a feeling
he was an artist
of the darkness in the alleys, a weight in his heart
but, a personality without capacity for action
propelled his solitary existence.

his pure world of gentle
humanist hearts
was just a dream.
these dreams and knowledge and experiences
which animated him stayed in his heart,
he never managed to share them with anyone.
his silence drowned in the waters of nothingness
and it was never of any use.
but somehow, who knows what happened
but someone suspected him and
he was murdered at the hands of the killers.
he had a yearning for freedom
with his efforts
he was beloved by all,
radiant in himself.
he was murdered,
it was the death of an era,
the death of life's ideal!!
suddenly i hear a mocking voice.
it asks—what have i done so far,
running and fleeing in every direction.
(it's no use blaming yourself now)
what's important—to seek out my friends
find these new companions
activated radiant with truth–consciousness–sensation!!

i descend the steps,
when suddenly i am surrounded by hideous forms,
captured by something like a *machine,*
terrifying shapes surround me,
i am confronted by a force ready for oppression.

suddenly my heart stops—what is this!!
a terrifying sensation.
they grab me by the collar and squeeze my throat.
a slap breaks my eardrum
rips the skin off my cheek.
building in my ear
a horrifying roaring ringing

swimming in my eyes
blood-red butterflies; blue sparks.
before me rising and falling apart dim
hazy circles,
their irised centers expanding outwards
and in that space i see
massive *towers* crashing down
curled smoke and pale yellow flame.
i begin to panic—
suddenly, on a desolate barren mound
someone breaks into sobs, someone crying
someone running to help.
(internal elements appear once again to be
in a process of restructuring and reorganization)

the scene changed, the image switched
i'm dragged into the black emptiness
of a deep dark room.
they sit me on a broken stool.
they're breaking open my skull.
massive hammers falling
on a steel spike.
now they've pulled off the large plate of the skull.
they are searching—
which impulses drive which ideas
in the mental processes,
which pulses in which vessels,
which quiver in which vein,
where is the photo-camera in which
material images of ideas emerge,
the receptacles of true dreams
the material needed for a dynamic explosion!
somewhere inside hidden deep
in the bunker
find the hidden printing press.
the place where secretly ideas are printed
into pamphlets (handed out)
find the leader of this organization
perhaps, his name is faith,

where's the boss of this gang
where's the soul?
(and, i hear an irritated high
scraping voice)
screen him . . . *mister* gupta,
cross examine him thoroughly!!

even as the flashing whip
has torn off the flesh
and raised a line of bloody brown welts on my back
my spirit is supple,
i pull the ringing strings
of my sensibility into control
pull them all together
gather this pain
in my mind, forcing it
into a small nail
fastening it together into something strong
like a rock.
with my bare hands
i smash the rock into powder,
throw the powder into the dust.
the mind moves beyond the boundary of the body
into some other world
a strange moment,
i am simply magic,
only electricity
even as i am bound in this cave,
with these monsters surrounding me
but i have gone miles away
i fall back quietly in the form of a letter
into a pocket
that pocket . . .
of a shattered mind.

with one voice, one rhythm,
a soft thrill of sympathy!!
we are nowhere,
our mind is everywhere.

our interiority!
an inner network of electricity
running through living wires,
a terrible mass of burning wire,
the earth outside a brown
and barren scab.
even as it burns our mind is cold as ice;
we bring a terrible storm, bur our chest
is completely still.
grasping our terrible power
our souls are dressed in dirty rags.
for all of our strange forms
our lives move along a single path.
free!!
i've been released!!
now the shadow faces follow behind,
the dark shapes still with me,
wherever i go, wherever i stay, wherever i move,
the mysterious glances beneath the eyebrows
pierce me like bayonets—
their gazes an obsidian goad.

now i must search for my companions—
black rose and jet chrysanthemum,
dark jasmine,
shadowy lotus in the water of caves
in the lake beneath the earth
for who knows how long
sending signs in their blooming
beaming out their message!!

and then far on the horizon
appears to me
falling from the naked branches of lightning
white blue pearlescent golden roseate flowers;
hands emerge suddenly
begin to gather these flowers of flame.
i can't take my eyes away from them;
suddenly out of some odd impulse

i begin to gather the sparkling stones
from the earth, choosing
trying to form them into flowers
of lightning. refraction—
my stones too radiate in every moment.
these too are shining gems of scattered light.
they are just like those flowers of electricity
they too are products of effort,
but, my dissatisfaction runs deep,
these expressions of words—a sign of absence.
however vivid these spectacles of poetry may be,
they are cold.
my flowers too are radiant,
but frozen and frigid.
i must embrace the burning arms
with their restless blue flame of lightning
must perform a dance just as destructive
i must roam with them in the sky
i don't have the color of lightning's glory
i am a terrible black cloud
but i am seized with a grand passion
a composure born of infinite inspiration.
these colored pebble-flowers of mine
won't do at all!!
what can i say,
in my mind burns
truth-consciousness-sensation—true and false—
the veins of my head swelling with tension
day and night.

now we must take up
all the dangers of expression.
every fortress and monastery must be destroyed.
we will have to cross over the high mountain peaks
then we will find
the swaying depths of the blue lake
in which, at every moment, trembles
a red lotus,
i will have to penetrate

the icy cold blue water
the magical lake must await me.

7

the moon has risen
over the long strips of cloth hanging above the alleys
its crooked beams fall
the neem tree
beneath it
on an earthen platform, in the blue
moonlight a lamp glows
like a dream made real.
the empty scrubby gardens
of ruined mansions are fragrant
with blooming jasmine, timid in their youth
they don't like the fixed stare of the stars.
i run with terror,
turn after turn
on the other side of broken walls
a heated conversation
the mind is active, strength in the heart
shades of war between truth and power,
but, all my weaknesses still with me.
suddenly i find—
quietly through the tunnellike alleyways
sombre and firm,
an army of youth
absolutely silent
possessed of something deep inside
a far burning somewhere within.

a strange experience!!
even as i walk ahead
of these lines of people,
i find myself behind, alone,
the devant garde.
but, another rush and

from behind more
joining me!
astounding!! astonishing!!
the fists of the people are clenched.
from the tips of their fingers rays,
bright red,
what's this!!
those are my own diamonds of fury,
my own gens of discernment,
encouraging the people as they walk in the dark.
but i am alone
joined only by myself in my intellectual rumination.

i am running through the alleys in the dark;
when i see someone
giving out pamphlets,
some hidden force
quietly it speaks to my heart!!
i read it carefully.
astonishing!!
my own secret ideas
repressed feelings and experiences
smoldering pain.
what is all this!!

i see the sky between those black lines
a sky ganga spread out across the sentences
a map glimmers in the pattern of words
and in those clusters of stars blooms a garden
champa flowers
and between those flowers
a solution to the problem of life itself.

as i read the pamphlet i float in the wind,
i roam across the heavens,
even as i remain on the earth,
present and conscious everywhere
i lend a hand at every task,

every crossroads, at the corner of every road
i stand at the road
celebrating, believing, convincing!!

and then the distances of the chronotope
the map of my own country suspended
the water of the soft rays of dreams
transformed into stones
dense and bright,
these are stones of resolute action
which will form icons of dreams
smiling and benevolent
whose rays of shining action
will spread across the entire universe!
truly, now i see
the boundaries of life
spreading beyond even the reach of suns!!
i am transformed,
i am not in the habit of speaking in poetry, but i will say
the current society can't last forever.
a heart tied to capital cannot change,
the believer in a liberated individual
cannot cheat the idea of freedom,
the mind of the people.

8

suddenly my heart stops, what is this!!
a terrifying smoke rises from the city,
bullets and fire.
the streets are filled with corpses,
the fury of invisible flames
in the wind.
together we roam, together we live,
together we sleep, eat, drink,
the people unified in thought and purpose!!
troops roam about,
with their stony faces and their khaki dress,

unrecognizable truly
bullets and fire!!

all are quiet, writers are quiet and poets are quiet
thinkers, artists, philosophers are quiet;
they think this is all talk
only rumors.
they are all parasite-intellects to the bloodsucking class
neutered and caught in a net of consumption,
they have only a superficial idea of the question
the path is unknown to them
their voices silent
a heartlessness has taken them
bullets and fire.

the faces of the big newspaper publishers
are hidden in their grand mansions.
conversations are created,
news is created,
comments are created all to torment the people.
the intellectual class is bought and paid for,
their ideas are for sale.
ink is smeared across these great faces.
neutered faith
is hidden in the gutter of the alleyway
bullets and fire.

beneath clouds of poisonous smoke every time
personal analysis,
a hundred interviews in a subtle moment.
dreams filled with illusions break apart.
rays of wisdom flow in the blood
the idol of the world itself is toppling over
bullets and fire.

from the loose rocks on the road,
a stream of water from the mountains
bubbles up.
in lumps of claw

burns the fire of devotion
in the grain of dust
trembles the
dangerous
unstruck sound
the sheep jump
from the roofs of the building!!
the poles are ripped out
flying in the wind.
grandfather's staff is of no use in this maelstrom,
uncle's lathi dances in the sky.
even the cribs of the babies fly through the air
waving and flying wildly.
every object becomes an individual bomb
the ultimate bomb, a missile, yama.
in the empty sky they
soar and break apart inevitably.
this is not a story, this is true, every word!!
bullets and fire!!

a blacksmith, filled with strength,
has lit a burning mandala from cow manure
flames leap up from it
like the heavenly petals of the lotus,
a chunk of iron
set within that burning line
blooms into
blue and red golden sparks.
some strong ones
are stretching across a wooden frame
a bright red strip of iron
beating it into shape,
now in its form
fit for the spirit
from the strength of these devoted workers
a burning tire!!
now the age has well and truly changed,
bullets and fire.

a pale sky, sparks flying through the air
the forest of life is burning now
in its terrible burning light
rivers of pain flow from the ancestors
in the waters
the countless centuries
come to consciousness
and transmit their images in every moment.
rivers of pain
in which are drowned, for age after age
the fierce colors of the worry of fathers
the restless depths of their pain and discernment,
in which are drowned the curses of the workers.
the tears of mothers.
drinking that water,
the youth become active
waging war each in their own way
as if they are also surrounded by petals of flame
seated in the burning lotus.
energies flow with their own committed speed.
bullets and fire!!

X X X

suddenly the dream breaks
images dissolve and i am again alone.
heart and mind are both pierced and wounded
but, within the pain
settles the flowing essence of light.[3]
i will search for those dreams
even as the mind is filled with the pain of facts.
a strange puzzle.
the mind roams across feelings and wounds
the soul filled with a sparkling thirst.
i see the whole world in golden images
as if last night at some moment suddenly
i fell in love with a beautiful face
for the rest of my life!!
as if at that moment
such gentle arms

took me in their embrace
that dream touch, the memory of that kiss,
comes to me now!!
who was that unknown beloved?

the morning light enters the room
golden sunlight in the gallery,
will i truly meet such a love?
why do i now feel this deep
pain of affection?

in every direction electric movement
magnetic attraction.
every object has its own light,
as if different flowers
bloom in different environments,
each meaning has its own explanation,
mixing together
the writers of great works on the desk
observe my mental actions,
when suddenly the light enters my room,
the mind flutters in the wind from the sky.
i rise, i go out and stand on the balcony.
suddenly that individual . . .
before me
in the alleyways, on the streets, in the crowds
moving.
the people i saw in the cave.
the heart races
when a cry bursts from the mouth
spontaneously . . .
he appears, he appears
he disappears among the people . . .
my arm hangs waving in the air!!

he is the sole pinnacle of my undiscovered
  enlightenment
the ultimate expression . . .
i am his student

he is my teacher,
my guru!!

he never sat with me,
he never came to me,
i saw him in that magical cave,
once and for the last time.
but at every moment he moves through the alleyways
in his ragged form.
bursting with lightning
a tensed knot of knowledge
exploding with a love that calls to action
that ragged form!!
the supreme expression
ceaselessly he wanders the earth
who knows where he'll be
where he'll be next.
so i look into every alley,
every lane and street,
i look at every face,
every event
every character,
the story of every soul,
every country political situation circumstance
every ideal born out of humanity
process of discernment, action-bound consequence!!
i search the plateaus, the mountains, the seas,
where i will find
that which i lost
my inevitable, supreme expression
born out of the self.[4]

Notes

Introduction

1. Muktibodh, "Aṃdhere meṃ," 2:382–83. Unless otherwise noted, all translations are my own.

2. Tolstoy occupies a central position not only in the cultural history of India through his importance to Gandhi, but also in Soviet internationalism. Works by Tolstoy were universally included in Soviet gifts to major cultural figures in India; see Clark, *Eurasia without Borders*, 197.

3. Among these, the most important are probably the criticism of Ramchandra Shukla and the debates between Pant and Nirala over the proper form of Hindi free verse. Shukla, who also put in place the paradigm through which Hindi literary history is still understood, accused *chāyāvād* poetry not only of being unduly influenced by Bengali and English poetics, but of engaging in what he called *rahasyavād*, or "mysticism." See Wakankar, "The Moment of Criticism in Indian Nationalist Thought." In Shukla's view, *rahasyavād* implied a departure from the ideals of social reform and uplifting poetry that he enshrined in his literary history by elevating Tulsidas as the preeminent Hindi literary figure and rendering Kabir as not a poet at all. In this way, Shukla brought *chāyāvād* into the grand, composite narrative that was the still-forming history of Hindi, but rhetorically linked it to what he saw as the worst excesses of obscurantism and rhetorical mannerism, both of which he saw similarly as low points.

4. Muktibodh wrote a manuscript for a novel that was lost, and to my knowledge never read. "Vipātra" is composed of a long, stream-of-consciousness experience of a teacher in a small college, as this loosely autobiographical figure attends a party, joins his colleagues for a walk through his city, and eventually attempts to place his experiences in some kind of theoretical framework. Some evidence indicates it is unfinished. See Muktibodh, *Muktibodh Samagra*, 4:258.

5. Muktibodh, *Muktibodh Samagra*, 5:267.

6. Many, if not most, of Muktibodh's long poems feature a search for a teacher or guide, who will lead the speaker towards revolutionary or liberating knowledge. "Aṃdhere meṃ" and other poems end with this search unfulfilled, but ongoing, after an initial revelation of the guru's existence. This search implies an impulse of the utopian in his work, a search that, unfulfilled, can be read as tragedy. David Scott's influential idea of the tragic dimension of the postcolonial may point towards an interpretation; see Scott, *Conscripts of Modernity*, 7–8. Muktibodh's insistence on an unending poem, a poem that cannot be finished—a feature that he points out of his own writing and is a trope in the criticism of Muktibodh—points towards an insistence on the utopian possibilities inherent in his continued impulse forward; as Nicholas Brown puts it, "the narrative of decolonization cannot simply end in tragedy" (Brown, *Utopian Generations*, 168). The invocation of science fiction and an explicitly universal framework of his work, from within a context of the shrinking space of address of the Hindi language, may also underline a utopian impulse; see Jameson, *Archaeologies of the Future*, 3–4.

7. I will discuss the trajectory of Muktibodh's reception in the conclusion.

8. Throughout the book, I will be treating the period of time between India's independence and the death of Jawaharlal Nehru as a single unit of time—the long 1950s. In part, this is because this period ends not only with the death of Nehru, but the death of Muktibodh, the central figure of this book. But these seventeen years were also marked by a range of conditions in the cultural, political, and social life of India that set them apart, from the growth of the Indian state and its institutions and the politics of nonalignment, as well as narratives of change that cover this time, such as the assumption of a national role for Hindi, followed by the advent of modern language politics and the split of the Communist Party of India following the Indo-Chinese war in 1962. Recent historical research has begun to reshape our idea of this period, something especially urgent after the rise to power of the modern BJP and the dismantling of many of these Nehruvian institutions. See Menon, *Planning Democracy*, 1.

9. On the modernist and postmodernist long poem, see Perloff, "From Image to Action"; Dickie, *On the Modernist Long Poem*; Friedman, "When a 'Long' Poem Is a 'Big' Poem"; McHale, *The Obligation Toward the Difficult Whole*; Gillott, *Reading the Modernist Long Poem*. I will discuss the definition of Muktibodh's long poems further in the first chapter.

10. In addition to Ram, "The Scale of Global Modernisms," see Tanoukhi, "The Scale of World Literature"; Smith, "Scale Bending and the Fate of the National." An overview of Neil Smith's influential work on scale can be found in Jones et al., "Neil Smith's Scale."

11. See Jain, *Mahāguru Muktibodh Jummā Taiṇk Kī Sīḍhiyoṁ Par*. The multilinguistic environment of Central India requires further study.

12. A range of accounts of Muktibodh's life are collected in Varmā, *Lakṣit Muktibodh*. This remains the most important source for most biographical information on Muktibodh's early life. On Sharaccandra Muktibodh, see Joshi, *Sharachchandra Muktibodh*. A recent collection of reminiscences on Muktibodh's life collects many pieces that were otherwise difficult to obtain; see Muktibodh and Jośī, *Tummeṃ Maiṃ Satat Pravāhit Hūṃ*.

13. The formation of *Tār saptak* is discussed in Lotz, "Rāhoṁ Ke Anveṣī." A recent biography of Agyeya promises to contribute a great deal of new information on the history of this text; see Mukul, *Writer, Rebel, Soldier, Lover*. Although many aspects of the creation of this seminal anthology and its originality in comparison with lesser known poetic experiments remain points of debate in Hindi literary history, the crucial impact of this anthology on Hindi literary discourse and historiography, not least through Agyeya's preface to *Tār saptak* and the two anthologies that followed it, places it at the center of any understanding of Hindi modernism.

14. The events surrounding these publications are described in Singh, "Ek Vilakṣaṇ Pratibhā." They are also briefly discussed in Rosenstein, *New Poetry in Hindi*, 35.

15. Muktibodh's death closely followed that of Jawaharlal Nehru, perhaps increasing the resonance of this event. It also coincided with an increasing sense of dislocation of Hindi, as attention began to shift towards the lower-middle-class writer. It may be argued as well that this shift was related to the rapidly shifting status of Hindi itself.

16. On networks between qasbahs, see Robb, *Print and the Urdu Public*, 73–77.

17. See in English Lotz, "Romantic Allegory and Progressive Criticism"; Lotz, "Long Poem or Unending Poem?"; Gautam, "Conflict of Callings"; Dadawala, "Gajanan Madhav Muktibodh and the Passing of Soviet India," and Ghosh, *The Deed of Words*. In German, see Lotz, "Poesie, Poetik, Politik"; Barbara Lotz was able to visit several archives that are no longer available, particularly the offices of *Nayā xūn* (New blood) in Nagpur, and her research is foundational to my own study. The bibliography on Muktibodh in Hindi is vast and continues to increase, as he remains both a popular writer and a deeply canonized figure; representative works include Vajpeyi, "Bhayānak khabar kī kavitā"; Varmā, *Lakṣit Muktibodh*; Cakradhar, *Muktibodh kī kāvyaprakriyā*; Śarmā, *Muktibodh kī ātmakathā*; Naval, *Muktibodh, jñān aur saṃvedanā*; Devtale, *Muktibodh: kavitā aur jīvan-vivek*; Jain, *mahāguru muktibodh jummā taiṇk kī sīḍhiyoṁ par*; Ahmad, *Muktibodh ke māhaul meṃ*. The approach and aftermath of Muktibodh's hundredth

birth anniversary in 2017 prompted a large number of shorter pieces and special issues, such as Apoorvanand, "The Worker of Poetry," and *Ālocnā* issue number 55 in 2015.

18. On the history of the 1970s and the Emergency, see Jaffrelot and Anil, *India's First Dictatorship*.

19. The most important translation into English is Muktibodh, *In the Dark*. Other notable translations include Muktibodh and Mehrotra, "At Every Step"; Muktibodh and Mehrotra, "The Error"; Muktibodh and Mehrotra, "The Zero"; Dharwadker, "The Future of the Past," 1:142–51; Muktibodh, "Brahmarakshas."

20. Upon the formation of the Republic of India, Hindi was scheduled, according to the constitution, to become the sole language of administration, but this proposal was permanently postponed following protests from speakers of languages in South India, primarily Tamil. On the Tamil language movement, see Ramaswamy, *Passions of the Tongue*. On the politics of Hindi, see Rai, *Hindi Nationalism*. The unique constitutional status and trajectory of Hindi in the twentieth century does not mean, however, that it was not subject to the forces of vernacularization created during the colonial period, as Mani argues; see Mani, *The Idea of Indian Literature*, 19.

21. For a representative account, in English see Machwe, *From Self to Self*; the trajectories of such writers followed the tracks of the Cold War world, so that some would move through New York and Iowa, while others would travel to Moscow and Tashkent, depending on their affiliations. For comparable examples outside of Hindi, see Pue, "Ephemeral Asia"; Zaitseva, "Gained in Translation." As the history of these two Urdu writers demonstrates, these travels were also shaped by the complex histories and geographies of specific languages.

22. In South Asian studies, the concept of the vernacular, as opposed to a "cosmopolitan" language, often draws from the work of Sheldon Pollock, especially Pollock, *The Language of the Gods in the World of Men*. Pollock created a framework for understanding the shift from Sanskrit to literary cultures in what are today the modern languages of India. In a colonial and postcolonial context, the concept of the vernacular relates instead to the growth of South Asian language literatures, and the complex relationship between these languages and English. See Mani, *The Idea of Indian Literature*, 7–11; Patel, "Vernacular Missing"; Orsini, "Present Absence." For a critique of the assumption that vernacular literatures are inherently non-cosmopolitan and locally oriented in the context of modern Tamil poetry, see Shankar, *Flesh and Fish Blood*, 4–8.

23. Shankar has argued against this model of the vernacular and the cosmopolitan, primarily through citing figures such as Ka Na Su in

Tamil; see Shankar, *Flesh and Fish Blood*, 5–6. While he effectively argues that such a writer is deeply engaged with questions of Anglo-American modernism, I would argue that writers in South Asian languages must be considered not only as transcending or scrambling this dichotomy, but also as shaped by and operating within it, and at times using it for their ends. These writers are also placed in positions of vernacular languages in part through processes of translation, or their lack.

24. Among other travels, Agyeya spent several years at the University of California, Berkeley, where he taught Hindi and collaborated on translation projects. See Mukul, *Writer, Rebel, Soldier, Lover*, 386. Agyeya is also often posed as the opposite to Muktibodh, despite their frequent collaboration and interaction, because of his access to cultural capital and his perceived position on the right, as opposed to Muktibodh's progressive position. See Trivedi, "The Progress of Hindi, Part 2," 997–98; Mani, *The Idea of Indian Literature*, 104–5.

25. This picture is further complicated by the debate over Muktibodh's legacy, in which critics argued over whether his writings should be seen as more or less affiliated to left aesthetics and politics. Those who objected to viewing Muktibodh solely in terms of Marxist aesthetic principles often emphasized his connections to an essential Indian identity, aligned with the push towards nativism, or *desīvād*, in Hindi, Marathi, and other languages. See Nemade, *Nativism*; Nerlekar, *Bombay Modern*, 261n56.

26. Although Muktibodh is often discussed exclusively in terms of his politics, these politics are rarely viewed in an international perspective. For an attempt to do so, see Dadawala, "Gajanan Madhav Muktibodh and the Passing of Soviet India." Through its analysis of Mani Kaul's film on Muktibodh, Dadawala frames Muktibodh's reception in terms of the long afterlife of what he calls "Soviet India"; my own study, while similarly emphasizing the Cold War context of Muktibodh's writing, focuses on the way in which it was articulated at the level of literary form, and similarly focuses on his reception in terms of the aesthetics of the long poem, rather than the symbol of Muktibodh.

27. For an overview of this distinction, see Rosenstein, *New Poetry in Hindi*, 8–15.

28. In the Urdu context, for instance, see Dubrow, "The Aesthetics of the Fragment."

29. See Esty, "Realism Wars," 317. On the broader history and scope of these debates, besides Esty, see Jameson, "Antinomies of the Realism-Modernism Debate"; Cleary, "Realism after Modernism and the Literary World-System"; Lye, "Afterword."

30. On Andrei Zhdanov and his influence on the early progressives in colonial India, see Coppola, *Urdu Poetry, 1935–1970*, 62–74. Zhdanov, as

second secretary of the Communist Party, was largely responsible for formulating the doctrine of Socialist Realism, which was extremely influential in South Asian cultural politics. Today, Zhdanov is often read through the work of critics, such as György Lukács, who adapted his ideas, along with those of Karl Radek, to his own, preexisting idea of realism and theory of history. See Clark, "The Soviet Project of the 1930s to Found a 'World Literature' and British Literary Internationalism," 410–11.

31. On the military and political history of the Cold War, see Leffler and Painter, *Origins of the Cold War*; Westad, *The Global Cold War*.

32. See Clark, *Eurasia without Borders*; Popescu, *At Penpoint*; Kalliney, *The Aesthetic Cold War*.

33. On the history of the CCF, see Scott-Smith, "The Congress for Cultural Freedom, the End of Ideology and the 1955 Milan Conference"; Saunders, *The Cultural Cold War*; Rubin, *Archives of Authority*.

34. See Shringarpure, *Cold War Assemblages*, 111. Shringarpure's assessment of postcolonial studies, I would argue, is an important addition to the foundational work of Gayatri Spivak on the modern American academy, particularly regarding the Cold War politics of language, expertise, and area studies; see Spivak, *Death of a Discipline*, 2–8.

35. The reason for this is, of course, outside the focus of this book, but relates both to the linguistic terrain of Africa and to the nature of Cold War cultural politics, which played out more in metropolitan literatures. A telling exception of the non-English work of Ngũgĩ wa Thiong'o, who famously disavowed the use of English after becoming a prominent writer; see Thiong'o, *Decolonising the Mind*. The topic is discussed in Popescu, *At Penpoint*, 15–16.

36. Although modern literatures in Africa were certainly subject to pressures similar to those faced by India during the Cold War, their position vis-à-vis state power was often different. The sheer number of writers, and the prior establishment of literatures during the colonial period, may have also played a factor.

37. See Mani, *The Idea of Indian Literature*, 4.

38. See Zecchini, "What Filters through the Curtain."

39. On *Quest*, see Pullin, "Money Does Not Make Any Difference to the Opinions That We Hold," 391.

40. See Djagalov, "Progress Publishers"; Kalliney, *The Aesthetic Cold War*, 85–86.

41. See Orsini, "Literary Activism."

42. As will be discussed in the fourth chapter, Muktibodh has been perceived as a rough, outsider artist among some of his most perceptive critics. See Singh, "Ek Vilakṣaṇ Pratibhā," 20. In English, in a move that leads to the same result, his poetry is often described as untranslatable; see Dharwadker, "The Future of the Past," 1:142.

43. The demarcation between these two super-generic modes may draw, in part, from colonial discourses disparaging poetry; see Mani, *The Idea of Indian Literature*, 9; Ebeling, *Colonizing the Realm of Words*. Similarly, both Simon Gikandi and Dinesh Chakrabarty have discussed the ways in which, in part as a result of this history, prose is often asked to take up different forms of representation as opposed to poetry, which might portray a more emotional relationship with the nation during the nationalist period. See Gikandi, "Realism, Romance, and the Problem of African Literary History," 320; Chakrabarty, *Provincializing Europe*, 151–55.

44. Warwick Research Collective, *Combined and Uneven Development*, 16. The Warwick Research Collective (WReC), drawing on the work of Löwy, claim that what they call "numinous narration," including magical realism and fantasy, "suggest that it is easier to explore questions about '(semi-)peripherality' in the world-literary system through reference to 'modernist' and 'experimental' modes than through reference to 'realist' or 'naturalist' ones." See Löwy, "The Current of Critical Irrealism." One of the most important critiques of this position is found in the special issue of *Modern Language Quarterly* edited by Colleen Lye, Jed Esty, and Joe Cleary. See Esty and Lye, "Peripheral Realisms Now," 274. While I agree with this position with regard to trends in the contemporary American academy, I would also note their point that "we do not need a new realist antimodernism to overcome the blind spots of a recent modernist antirealism" (280). A figure such as Muktibodh, whose critique of realism and literary projects intersects at so many points with problems of both modernism and realism at a global scale, demands careful attention to the assumptions underlying global history; not least, in the case of the work of WReC, an emphasis on the novel as the primary genre of world literature.

45. Cheah, *What Is a World?*, 212.

46. The early conception, articulated by Mikhail Bakhtin and György Lukács, of the novel as a "modern epic," has been historicized in the work of Ian Watt and Michael McKeon in terms of the emergency of the novel in conversation with a range of prose forms, and changes to the class structure, in early modern England; see Bakhtin, *The Dialogic Imagination*; Lukacs, *The Theory of the Novel*; Watt, *The Rise of the Novel*; McKeon, *The Origins of the English Novel, 1600–1740*. The novel is also claimed to have a unique relationship to colonial modernity and nationalism; see Anderson, *Imagined Communities*.

47. Ramazani, *A Transnational Poetics*, 3. See also Ramazani, *Poetry in a Global Age*.

48. Mukherjee, *Realism and Reality*, 7.

49. See Kaviraj, *The Unhappy Consciousness*; Joshi, *In Another Country*; Shandilya, *Intimate Relations*; Dalmia, *Fiction as History*.

50. See Orsini, *Print and Pleasure*; Dubrow, *Cosmopolitan Dreams*.

51. See Mani, *The Idea of Indian Literature*, 23–25; Mufti, *Enlightenment in the Colony*, 182. Mufti's claim that the emphasis on the short story in Urdu is countered by Mani, *The Idea of Indian Literature*, which argues that the short story performs a more wide-ranging function with regard to the conception of Indian literature itself.

52. On *nayī kahānī*, see Roadarmel, *A Death in Delhi*; Mani, "What Was So New about the New Story? Modernist Realism in the Hindi Nayī Kahānī."

53. Mary Pratt has discussed the short story as a genre in terms of its dependency on the novel, according to which the short story is in a hierarchical relationship with the superior novel; see Pratt, "The Short Story," 96. Mani has argued, however, that "the novel operated in concern with the short story," due to its coexistence and interaction with a range of prose genres. See Mani, *The Idea of Indian Literature*, 23.

54. See Pritchett, *Nets of Awareness*, xiv–xvii; Busch, *Poetry of Kings*, 220–25.

55. On the history of *kāvya* and its conventions, see Bronner, Shulman, and Tubb, *Innovations and Turning Points*; on the conventions of the *mahākāvya*, see Patel, *Text to Tradition*, 19.

56. Culler, *Theory of the Lyric*, 349–50. For a useful critique of Culler, see Perloff, review of *Theory of the Lyric*.

57. Jackson and Prins, *The Lyric Theory Reader*, 2–3.

58. Jackson and Prins, *The Lyric Theory Reader*, 7. In addition to the works discussed below, see Terada, "After the Critique of Lyric"; Kaufman, "Lyric Commodity Critique, Benjamin Adorno Marx, Baudelaire Baudelaire Baudelaire." Much of the impetus for the revision of the lyric follows critical debates following New Criticism; see Hošek, Parker, and Parker, *Lyric Poetry*.

59. On *Kāmāyanī's* impact, see Lotz, "Romantic Allegory and Progressive Criticism," 213–14; Lotz's essay also discusses the *Punarvicār* extensively. *Kāmāyanī* is also discussed in Sahota, *Late Colonial Sublime*, 204–7.

60. Kantor, "South Asian Magical Realism," 88.

61. I am drawing my use of the term from Rashmi Sadana's work, Sadana, *English Heart, Hindi Heartland*. On the intersection of the Hindi movement with caste, see Mukul, *Gita Press and the Making of Hindu India*; Gajarawala, *Untouchable Fictions*.

62. On the early history of Hindi, see Fārūqī, *Early Urdu Literary Culture and History*; Busch, *Poetry of Kings*. For a basic overview of the early history of Hindi, see McGregor, "The Progress of Hindi, Part 1." On the differentiation of Hindi from other literary languages of the area,

see Rai, *A House Divided;* King, *One Language, Two Scripts;* Dalmia, *The Nationalization of Hindu Traditions,* 146–217; Rai, *Hindi Nationalism.* The early history of Hindi can be seen as one of exclusion and isolation, as the language increasingly separated itself both from Braj and Urdu, the two competing literary languages, and from the range of other language forms, such as Bhojpuri, resulting in a literary language that was particularly disassociated from any one region in favor of identification with an abstract idea of the nation. This, arguably, shaped the way in which writers in Hindi considered the rapidly changing geography of the Cold War world. Recent work by Francesca Orsini has intervened in this history through emphasizing what she calls a "multilingual local" of exchange and complicated spatial relations among the literary cultures of North India; see Orsini, "The Multilingual Local in World Literature"; and her newly released book, Orsini, *East of Delhi.*

63. On the early novel in Hindi, see Orsini, *Print and Pleasure;* Dalmia, *Fiction as History.* Although a range of prose genres were adapted and transformed in the nineteenth century and became the basis of the novel in both Hindi and Urdu, prose literature such as the *dāstān* was not subject to the same kinds of regulation as poetic genres. Francesca Orsini has argued that, for this reason, the *dāstān* could be more easily adapted into the Hindu majoritarian framework of a novel such as *Chandrakāntā.* See Orsini, *Print and Pleasure,* 204–16. Although the seamless transition between the prose *dāstān* and the novel is surely overstated, prose literature is frequently perceived as unencumbered by both generic expectations and the colonial-era disparagement of poetic traditions. On the evolution of prose literatures in North India, in addition to Orsini's work, see Blackburn and Dalmia, *India's Literary History;* Khan, "The Oriental Tale and the Transformation of North Indian Prose Fiction"; Dalmia, *Fiction as History;* Khan, *The Broken Spell.* A key source for thinking through the novel in colonial in India remains Mukherjee, *Realism and Reality.*

64. Pant, *Pallav,* 51.

65. For an overview of this history, see Sarkar, *Modern India, 1885–1947,* 339–42.

66. See Djagalov, "Progress Publishers"; Kalliney, *The Aesthetic Cold War,* 85–86.

67. On the history of the AIPWA in Urdu, see Gopal, *Literary Radicalism in India;* Jalil, *Liking Progress, Loving Change;* Coppola, *Urdu Poetry, 1935–1970.* The history of progressive literature in Hindi is relatively less studied, in part because major figures such as Premchand published in both Urdu in Hindi. A brief discussion is found in Rosenstein, *New Poetry in Hindi,* 7–9. In Hindi, see Avasthī, *Pragativād Aur Samānāntar Sāhitya.*

68. Sahi, "Laghu mānav ke bahāne hindī kavitā par ek bahas," 305.

69. On the modernism of the *Aṅgāre* writers, see Dubrow, "The Aesthetics of the Fragment."

70. On *Tār saptak* and its impact, see Rosenstein, *New Poetry in Hindi*, 9–11.

71. For an equivalent movement in Marathi, see Deśpāṇḍe and Rājādhyakṣ, *A History of Marathi Literature*, 135–38.

72. See Sahi, "Laghu mānav ke bahāne hindī kavitā par ek bahas," 320.

73. On Hindi journals prior to independence, see Orsini, *The Hindi Public Sphere, 1920–1940*, 31–51; as well as Mody, *The Making of Modern Hindi*.

74. On the history of Hindi publishing, see Sadana, *English Heart, Hindi Heartland*; Mandhwani, "Saritā and the 1950s Hindi Middlebrow Reader."

75. On the foundation of the Sahitya Akademi, see Rao, *Five Decades*, 7–20.

76. On the history of the term *nayī kavitā*, see Varma, *Hindī Sāhitya Koś*, 1:311–14.

77. The original word in Hindi for progressive, *pragatiśīl*, which was used in the Hindi name of the AIPWA, was transformed by its critiques to *pragativād*, using a suffix, *-vād*, meaning "ism," to imply orthodoxy and prescriptivism. On the term and its history, see Varmā, *Hindī Sāhitya Koś*, 1:394–95.

78. See Pullin, "Money Does Not Make Any Difference to the Opinions That We Hold." On the formation of *Tār saptak* and the controversy over Agyeya's role in it, see Lotz, "Rāhoṁ Ke Anveṣī."

79. Varma, *Nayī Kavitā Ke Pratimān*, 132.

80. For an overview of Sahi and his work in English, see Tripathi and Naved, *The Hindi Canon*.

81. On Dharmvir Bharati's critique of progressivism, see Dalmia, *Fiction as History*, 299–327.

82. Sahi, "Laghu mānav ke bahāne hindī kavitā par ek bahas," 259.

83. Sahi, "Laghu mānav ke bahāne hindī kavitā par ek bahas," 316.

84. The term "modernism" presents a few problems for a study of postindependence Hindi literature. First and foremost, it was not a term used in Hindi itself, which used instead the terms *prayogvād* and *nayī kavitā* to refer to the poetry that is most influenced by what is now canonized as the Anglo-American modernism of Eliot and Pound. On the other hand, modernism is often conceived as indexed to the nation, so that it is often applied both to postindependence literature and to literature from the late nineteenth and early twentieth century, which used the same terms, such

as *ādhunik* in Hindi or *jadīd* in Urdu, to refer to itself as "modern." The issue is loosely comparable to the Hispanophone and Catalan use of the term "modernism" to refer to the literature of the late nineteenth century in peninsular Spain and the Latin-American world, and of "modernismos" links with Catalan nationalism. On the question of modernism in India, see Kapur, *When Was Modernism;* Chaudhuri, "Modernisms in India."

85. *Parimal* was a loose organization of writers formed in Allahabad in the 1950s; see Varmā, *Parimal: smṛtiyāṃ aur dastāvez.*

86. Muktibodh, *Racnāvalī,* 2:327. All translations mine unless otherwise indicated.

87. Adorno, "Translator's Introduction," xxi.

Chapter One

1. Muktibodh, "Brahmarākṣas," 2:368–69.

2. On stepwells, see Rooprai, *Delhi Heritage.*

3. The journey out of the city, towards an ambivalent space of ruins, is certainly a familiar one to postindependence literature. It is repeated across space and language, in works such as Arun Kolatkar's *Jejuri* and O. V. Vijayan's Malayalam novel *Khasakkinte itihasam* (The Legends of Khasak).

4. The syntax of the Hindi also has the effect of isolating the word *bhītarī* and creating a rhyme scheme of *bāvṛī, bhītarī,* and, in the fifth line, *jal kī.* Hindi, like many languages but unlike English, features a phonotactics with fairly regular vowel endings that lend themselves to rhyme.

5. According to the most recent edition of Muktibodh's collected works, *Muktibodh samagra,* the poem was revised up to 1962. The poem was published in *Kavi* in 1957; I was unable to access this issue to consult the poem.

6. See Lotz, "Long Poem or Unending Poem?"

7. Singh, *Racnāvalī,* 3:246. Shamsher's piece is discussed further in the fourth chapter of this book.

8. Varma, *Hindī Sāhitya Koś,* 2:120.

9. Dickie, *On the Modernist Long Poem,* 1.

10. See Dickie, *On the Modernist Long Poem;* Friedman, "When a 'Long' Poem Is a 'Big' Poem"; Gillott, *Reading the Modernist Long Poem.*

11. Eliot, generally, has an extensive influence in South Asian–language literatures; see Trivedi, "Eliot in Hindi Modes of Reception."

12. Dickie, *On the Modernist Long Poem,* 11.

13. See Perloff, "From Image to Action." On the postmodernist long poem, see McHale, *The Obligation toward the Difficult Whole.*

14. See McHale, "Telling Stories Again."

15. McHale, "Telling Stories Again," 250.

16. Sawhney, *Modernity of Sanskrit.*

17. I will discuss Muktibodh's monograph, *Kāmāyanī: ek punarvicār,* in the following chapter. On the term *neo-epic* and its use, see Sahota, *Late Colonial Sublime,* 13.

18. On the history of *kāvya* and its conventions, see Bronner, Shulman, and Tubb, *Innovations and Turning Points;* on the conventions of the *mahākāvya,* see Patel, *Text to Tradition,* 19.

19. On the revision of the *kāvyā* in modern literature, see Bose, *Modern Poetry and Sanskrit Kavya;* Sawhney, *Modernity of Sanskrit;* Sahota, *Late Colonial Sublime.*

20. For more on the history of the Brahmarakshas, see Chelnokova and Streltcova, "Brahmarakshasa in Modern Hindi Literature."

21. For a representative example, see Cakradhar, *Muktibodha Kī Kāvyaprakriyā,* 146. For other representative interpretations of the poem, see Jośī, *Ek kavi kī noṭbuk,* 11–19.

22. On the relationship between caste and the Left in India, see Menon, *Being a Brahmin the Marxist Way;* Vaitheespara and Venkatasubramanian, "Beyond the Politics of Identity."

23. On Nehru's idea of the scientific temper, see Arnold, "Nehruvian Science and Postcolonial India."

24. Muktibodh, "Brahmarākṣas," 2:369.

25. Muktibodh, "Brahmarākṣas," 5:220–24.

26. See, for instance, Singh, "Ek Vilakṣaṇ Pratibhā"; Singh, "Kālbaddh Aur Padārthmay."

27. A clear exception would be "ek ṭīle aur ḍākū kī kahānī" (The Story of a Hill and a Thief), in Muktibodh, *Muktibodh samagra,* 2:236–54.

28. The Jungian connection between the underground and madness is discussed in Bachelard, *The Poetics of Space,* 20.

29. Muktibodh, "Brahmarākṣas," 2:370.

30. See Chelnokova and Streltcova, "Brahmarakshasa in Modern Hindi Literature," 139–43.

31. See Chelnokova and Streltcova, "Brahmarakshasa in Modern Hindi Literature," 146.

32. See O'Hanlon, "Letters Home."

33. See Jones, *Urban Politics in India;* Singh, *Geography and Politics in Central India.*

34. Muktibodh's family background is discussed briefly in Singh, "Kālbaddh Aur Padārthmay," 34. One can argue that Muktibodh obliquely addresses his father in his poem "Ek arūp śūnya ke prati" (To a Form-

less Void), which takes up religiosity and features a menacing figure of a police chief.

35. Muktibodh, "Brahmarākṣas," 4:131.

36. Muktibodh, "Brahmarākṣas," 5:192.

37. Muktibodh, "Brahmarākṣas," 2:372.

38. See Daniyal, "At Delhi University's Vedic Chronology Seminar, Discussions on Flying Chariots, Mahabharat-Era TV."

39. See Subramaniam, *Holy Science*, 13–16.

40. Arnold, "Nehruvian Science and Postcolonial India," 361.

41. Arnold, "Nehruvian Science and Postcolonial India," 361.

42. Arnold, "Nehruvian Science and Postcolonial India," 361.

43. On the career of Jagdish Chandra Bose, see Nandy, *Alternative Sciences*.

44. Subramaniam, *Holy Science*, 200.

45. See Thomas, "Brahmins as Scientists and Science as Brahmins' Calling."

46. Muktibodh, "Brahmarākṣas,"2:372.

47. On the figure of the *ayyār* in Hindi literature and the magical space of the magician, see Orsini, *Print and Pleasure*, 413. The influence of *qissā-dāstān* literature on Muktibodh's work will be discussed further in chapter 3.

48. On the scientific vocabulary of Hindi, see Singh, "Science in the Vernacular?"

49. See "Yah Aṅk," in *Kalpana*, August 1964.

50. Muktibodh, "Brahmarākṣas," 2:373.

51. Mukherjee, *Final Frontiers*, 60–61.

52. On the allegorical structure of sufi romances, see Behl, *Love's Subtle Magic*. On the *Rāmcharitmās*, see Lutgendorf, *The Life of a Text*, 25.

53. See, for instance, "Mere sahcar mitra" (My Steadfast Friend), Muktibodh, *Muktibodh samagra*, 2:287–99.

54. Muktibodh, "Brahmarākṣas," 2:374.

Chapter Two

1. See, for instance, Althusser, "Darśan."

2. On Western Marxism as a concept, see Jay, *Marxism and Totality*, 1–21.

3. György Lukács provides another ideal example of the complications of writing an intellectual history of modern Hindi aesthetic thought. His vast influence through his theories of the novel and realism

were themselves influenced, from the 1930s onwards, by Soviet-aligned ideas that were also promulgated in India and available through English translation. And yet his influence arguably increased in the 1970s when his writings became increasingly available in translation in the *New Left Review*, and from there were translated into Hindi in journals such as *Ālocnā*, creating a new idea of the "Brecht-Lukács debate," which could then be applied to Muktibodh and Ram Vilas Sharma. The kaleidoscopic layers of translation, parallel genealogies of thought, and an iconic reception of Western Marxism complicate any attempt to understand how such a thinker was received in Hindi. On the Brecht-Lukács debate, see Bloch et al., *Aesthetics and Politics*; on Lukács's wider career, see Jay, *Marxism and Totality*, 81–127.

4. See Sharma, *Nayī kavitā aur astitvavād*, 186. The point has also been made in Lotz, "Romantic Allegory and Progressive Criticism," 225.

5. Brecht, *Schriften Zur Literatur Und Kunst*, 2:198.

6. Brecht, "Notes on the Realist Mode of Writing, 1940," 260.

7. Muktibodh, "Kāmāyanī," 5:211.

8. On allegory in Marxist aesthetics, see Jameson, *Allegory and Ideology*.

9. On the reception of British romanticism in general, and Shelley in particular, in left aesthetic thought, see Foot, *Red Shelley*; Kaufman, "Legislators of the Post-everything World"; Kaufman, "Red Kant, or the Persistence of the Third 'Critique' in Adorno and Jameson." On the larger question of the left lyric, see Moe, "Elegy's Generation."

10. See Clark, "The Soviet Project of the 1930s to Found a 'World Literature' and British Literary Internationalism," 409.

11. See, for instance, Dneprov, "Method and Style in Art"; Dneprov, "In Defence of the Aesthetic of Realism."

12. For an overview of this context, see Bloch et al., *Aesthetics and Politics*, 9–15.

13. In addition to being collected in the most recent edition of Muktibodh's collected works, these pieces were first collected in Muktibodh (ed.), *Jab praśnacinh baukhlā uṭhe* (When the Question Mark Becomes Frenzied).

14. The idea of *laghu mānav* is discussed in the introduction.

15. Muktibodh, *Muktibodh samagra*, 5:239.

16. Muktibodh, *Muktibodh samagra*, 5:239.

17. For an overview of literature on the middle class in India, see Joshi, "India's Middle Class."

18. Mayer, "The Lower Middle Class as Historical Problem," 417.

19. See Felski, "Nothing to Declare," 39.

20. Schleifer, *A Political Economy of Modernism*, 218–21.

21. See Deshpande, "Mapping the 'Middle.'"

22. Barbara Ehrenreich, *Fear of Falling,* 3.

23. See Jeffrey, *Timepass,* 5. See also Deshpande, "Mapping the 'Middle,'" 218.

24. Joshi, *Fractured Modernity,* 2.

25. Joshi, *Fractured Modernity,* 8.

26. See Mani, "What Was So New about the New Story?," 16.

27. On *āñcalik* literature in Hindi, see Gajarawala, *Untouchable Fictions,* 99–100; Trivedi, "The Progress of Hindi, Part 2," 1012. The term *āñcalik,* which literally means "of the hem," is drawn from Renu's first novel, *Mailā āñcal* (The Soiled Hem). It refers not to a specific border but to the rural countryside, both in terms of subject matter as well as linguistic diversity. Renu's work frequently features dialogue in the Maithili language, and the literature as a whole is associated with rural settings and nonnormative Hindi.

28. Mani, "What Was So New about the New Story?," 4.

29. See, for instance, Naval, *Ādhunik hindī kavitā kā itihās,* 472–73.

30. On the question of upper-caste resentment and the middle class, see Joshi, "India's Middle Class."

31. For a selection of Parsai's satires in English, see C. M. Naim, *Inspector Matadeen* on the Moon.

32. Recent scholarship on literary journals in India, especially those after independence, is rapidly expanding our sense of this history. On the little magazine in Hindi and in India generally, see Orsini, "World Literature, Indian Views, 1920s–1940s"; Nerlekar, *Bombay Modern;* Mandhwani, "Saritā and the 1950s Hindi Middlebrow Reader"; Orsini, "Literary Activism."

33. On the contemporary sociology of literature and the coding of Hindi as the literature of the small city, see Sadana, *English Heart, Hindi Heartland,* 14–21.

34. Varma, "Carcā," 59.

35. One could interpret his comment in terms of a sociology of taste, rendered in terms of habits and the repellant appearance of anxiety; see Bourdieu, *Distinction.*

36. I discuss differing conceptions of postindependence modernism in the introduction; as well as in the conclusion, in which I discuss Muktibodh's further reception and the debate between Namvar Singh and Ram Vilas Sharma.

37. These pieces can be compared to Coleridge's *Biographia Literaria;* see Pyle, *The Ideology of Imagination,* 42–43. An obvious reference point is also Dostoevsky's *A Writer's Diary,* but there is no clear indication that Muktibodh read this. See Dostoevsky, *A Writer's Diary.* Hindi weekly and monthly magazines frequently included a regular column that would

include light criticism, humor, and gossip, and Muktibodh's *ḍāyarī* may simply be modeled on these closer examples.

38. *Ājkal* was a magazine published by the Indian government beginning in 1945; see Śrīdhar, *Bhāratīya patrakāritā koś*, 1074–75.

39. Muktibodh, *Muktibodh samagra*, 5:37.

40. On the *bhadralok*, see Metcalf and Metcalf, *A Concise History of Modern India*, 88.

41. Recent work, such as Rahman, *Locale, Everyday Islam, and Modernity*, Boyk, "Collaborative Wit," and Robb, *Print and the Urdu Public*, has produced a new understanding of the *qasba*, in North India. This work has focused for the most part on Urdu literary culture, the practice of Islam, and the network of small towns primarily in Bihar and present-day Uttar Pradesh. Although the relationship between Muktibodh's career, his reception, and the development of regional identities in Central India is a central theme of the first chapter, and is often remarked upon in Muktibodh scholarship, it is most prominently explored in Jain, *Mahāguru muktibodh jummā taiṇk kī sīḍhiyoṁ par*.

42. See Sadana, *English Heart, Hindi Heartland*, 23–26.

43. Muktibodh, *Muktibodh samagra*, 5:28.

44. See Singh, "Ek vilakṣaṇ pratibhā," 2.

45. In claiming his experiences in this way, Muktibodh arguably echoes the false universalism of the middle class that he critiques. In this sense, the same problems of upper-caste, male universality return to disturb a definition of the lower middle class just as they do a more general idea of the middle class. For an interesting parallel, see Kidambi, "Consumption, Domestic Economy, and the Idea of the 'Middle Class' in Late Colonial Bombay."

46. The most important work of Lakshmikant Varma, *Nayī kavitā ke pratimān*, was itself an important source for the later, and more well-known, work, Singh, *Kavitā ke naye pratimāna.*, 1968. The phrase "cult of experience" was coined in Rahv, "The Cult of Experience in American Writing"; see also Jay, *Songs of Experience*, 267.

47. See Sharma, *Nayī kavitā aur astitvavād*, 1978, 38. Ram Vilas Sharma would mostly not consider Muktibodh in this light—he saw his work more as a problem of imagination and *palāyaṇvād*, "escapism," than of anxiety. This could relate to the gradual growth of the corpus of Muktibodh's writings; Sharma would have primarily been working with Muktibodh's long poems.

48. *Akavitā* [non-poetry] was a poetic movement which, as its name implies, rejected entirely poetic convention. A journal under the name published irregularly beginning in 1966 for at least four issues, and many

of the poets, such as Rajkamal Chaudhuri, were also associated with the Bengali Hungrealist, or *bhūkhī pīṛhī,* poets. See also Parmar, *Akavitā aur kalā-sandarbh.*

49. Muktibodh, *Muktibodh samagra,* 5:69.

50. Muktibodh, *Muktibodh samagra,* 5:72.

51. Muktibodh, *Muktibodh samagra,* 5:72.

52. Muktibodh, *Muktibodh samagra,* 5:73.

53. It is unclear whether Muktibodh is referring here to film; while the term *citra-kathā* is not commonly used to refer to the cinema, there is no reason why it could not be interpreted that way. Muktibodh at times refers to cinematic techniques, such as wipes, and scene changes, in his poetry, and wrote a handful of film reviews. See Muktibodh, *Muktibodh samagra,* 8:383–92. But *citra-kathā* could just as easily refer to comics or sequential art; in 1967, the famous series of children's historical and mythical comics, *Amar citra kathā,* would begin publication. On this, see Chandra, *The Classic Popular Amar Chitra Katha, 1967–2007.* Muktibodh's offhand reference here, whether it is taken to refer to film or sequential art, brings our attention towards his interest in the relation between individual image and narrative, which will be discussed extensively in the fourth chapter.

54. On the relation between realist fiction and reform, see Gajarawala, *Untouchable Fictions,* 35. On Premchand's definition of realism, see Coppola, *Urdu Poetry, 1935–1970,* 135–42.

55. Muktibodh's use of *rasa* vocabulary raises a range of questions that parallel his use of Marxist aesthetic terms such as realism, in that in both cases one must analyze the context of his usage and determine the genealogy of the concept in a specific instance. For instance, while one can read the use of *bhāv* here, straightforwardly, within the Sanskrit literary tradition or the Brajbhasha aesthetics that was modeled on it, it more likely is being drawn from Hindi criticism of the early twentieth century and reformulations of *rasa* in the context of Hindi literary modernity. For an overview of *rasa,* see Pollock, *A Rasa Reader;* on the reformulation of *rasa* in Hindi, see Ritter, *Kama's Flowers;* Orsini, *The Hindi Public Sphere, 1920–1940,* 142–57.

56. Muktibodh, "Vīrkar," 5:75.

57. See Varma, "Muktibodh kī gadya-kathā," 5. I will discuss Nirmal Varma's essay on Muktibodh more extensively in the third chapter.

58. See Varma, *Hindī sāhitya koś,* 2:119.

59. On the relevant cultural and social history of the 1930s, see Metcalf and Metcalf, *A Concise History of Modern India,* 175–202. On the influence of *advaitā-vedāntā* at the time, see Pauwels, "Diptych in Verse."

60. Muktibodh, "Tīsrā kṣaṇ," 5:81.

61. Ujjayini has a prominent role in Sanskrit literature and its modern-day memory, in particular due to its association with the poet Kalidasa. See Thapar, *Early India,* 145.

62. On the layout of the modern city, see Shaw, *Indian Cities,* 12–26.

63. Muktibodh, "Tīsrā kṣaṇ," 5:82–83.

64. Muktibodh, Tīsrā kṣaṇ," 5:84.

65. Caverns appear throughout Muktibodh's writing, including in "Aṃdhere meṃ," where the narrator frequently finds himself in an underground space. See Muktibodh, *Muktibodh samagra,* 2:393.

66. Muktibodh's idea of the fantasy bears strong similarities to Schelling's idea of *Einbildungskraft*; see Engell, *The Creative Imagination,* 80.

67. On the imagination as a magnetic force, see Engell, *The Creative Imagination,* 80.

68. Muktibodh, "Tīsrā kṣaṇ," 5:92.

69. On the relations between Fox, Caudwell, and the Indian left in the 1930s, see Clark, "Indian Leftist Writers of the 1930s Maneuver Among India, London, and Moscow."

70. On Caudwell, see Browne, "An Unclaimed Legacy"; Smith, "Balancing Accounts"; Thompson, "Christopher Caudwell."

71. For example, see Dneprov, "In Defence of the Aesthetic of Realism"; Dneprov, "Method and Style in Art."

72. See Jośī, *Ek kavi kī noṭbuk,* 12. Joshi writes that "it is no mere coincidence that the deepest and best *fantasy,* in poetry and in story, was possible in the decade and a half following independence. Perhaps during that time, *fantasy,* in comparison with any other form of realism, was more effective in understanding and, more importantly, expressing the truth of that era." Muktibodh is seen, by Joshi and others, as the founder of a fantastic literature that could perceive the hidden truth of a historical moment. But the engagement with nonrealist elements by these writers stands apart from Muktibodh's actual poetics, and an assessment of Muktibodh as essentially rejecting realism, or forming a kind of "peripheral realism," in the influential phrasing of the Warwick Research Collective, would be a simplification of the complex place of Muktibodh's work in the critical literary debates in which he took part. The importance of realism for Muktibodh indicates the larger role of the discourse of realism in Hindi literature writ large: as a means through which questions of genre, lyric and novel, the ghost of *kāvya,* and the legacy of the Nationalist Movement could all be brought to the surface and discussed. On idealism and peripheral realism, see Warwick Research Collective, *Combined and Uneven Development,* 57; Löwy, "The Current of Critical Irrealism."

73. On *Kāmāyanī's* impact, see Lotz, "Romantic Allegory and Progressive Criticism," 213–14; Lotz's essay also discusses the *Punarvicār* extensively. *Kāmāyanī* is also discussed in Sahota, *Late Colonial Sublime*, 204–7.

74. See Varma, *Hindī sāhitya koś*, 2:120.

75. See Muktibodh, *Muktibodh samagra*, 8:290–95. Shripad Amrit Dange was the chairman of the Communist Party of India from 1962 to 1980. Muktibodh's letter, written anonymously and in English, addresses a range of issues but is primarily remembered as a defense of the progressive aspects of *nayī kavitā*.

76. Muktibodh, *Muktibodh samagra*, 5:211.

77. Muktibodh, *Muktibodh samagra*, 5:213.

78. Muktibodh, *Muktibodh samagra*, 5:213–14.

79. Muktibodh, *Muktibodh samagra*, 5:218.

Chapter Three

1. On the adaptation of early novels, see Mukherjee, *Realism and Reality*, 3–19. Scholars including Ulka Anjaria, Toral Gajarawala, and Jennifer Dubrow have extended the basic work of Mukherjee to examine the ways in which realism is shaped by the specific historical contexts of colonial and postcolonial India, as a basis for rethinking a rigid definition of realism. See Anjaria, *Realism in the Twentieth-Century Indian Novel*; Gajarawala, *Untouchable Fictions*; Dubrow, "The Aesthetics of the Fragment." While I hope to build on this work in considering this specific instantiation, a key problem that I confront is that, even as a writer like Muktibodh often theorized realism in unique ways, he did so in a context in which a specific, often orthodox understanding of realism was still operative.

2. Premchand's speech was published in Hindi as Premchand, "Sāhitya kā uddeśya." Originally published in *Hans* in July 1936. In Urdu, it was published in *Zamānā* in July 1937, and is available as Premchand, "Adab Kī Gharaz-o-Ghayat." The original speech may well have differed from both the Hindi and Urdu publications, but no transcription of the speech is extent. See the note in Premchand, "Sāhitya kā uddeśya," 7:511.

3. Anjaria, *Realism in the Twentieth-Century Indian Novel*, 1.

4. Premchand, "Sāhitya kā uddeśya," 7:500.

5. On the revival of the *dāstān*, see Khan, *The Broken Spell*, 214–19.

6. I would like to emphasize that I am not claiming that Premchand was in any way naive or hypocritical in his position regarding these genres, or indeed on the revolutionary potential of realism. As Anjaria notes, Premchand's position must take into account the "stakes

of representation" through which realism becomes inherently metatextual. See Anjaria, *Realism in the Twentieth-Century Indian Novel*, 4–5.

7. Siskind, *Cosmopolitan Desires*, 62.

8. Siskind, *Cosmopolitan Desires*, 82.

9. Kantor, "South Asian Magical Realism," 88.

10. On Cheah's definition of a "normative theory of world literature, see Cheah, *What Is a World?*, 5–11.

11. In addition to Mani, the point is made—albeit only in regard to Urdu—in Mufti, *Enlightenment in the Colony*, 182.

12. Mani, *The Idea of Indian Literature*, 109.

13. On the *nayī kahānī*, see Mani, "What Was So New about the New Story?" An important anthology of *nayī kahānī* stories in translation remains Roadarmel, *A Death in Delhi*.

14. Mani, "What Was So New about the New Story?," 236. On Agyeya's short stories, see also Orsini, "The Short Story as an Aide à Penser."

15. Yādav, *Ek duniyā*, 29.

16. See Singh, *Kahānī*, 52–65.

17. For an introduction to and selection of Nirmal Verma's short stories, see Verma, *Indian errant*. A biography of Verma has recently been released; see Gill, *Here and Hereafter*.

18. Verma, "Muktibodh Kī Gadya-Kathā," 3.

19. On networks between qasbahs, see Robb, *Print and the Urdu Public*, 73–77.

20. The demarcation between these two supergeneric modes may draw, in part, from colonial discourses disparaging poetry; see Mani, *The Idea of Indian Literature*, 9; Ebeling, *Colonizing the Realm of Words*. Similarly, both Simon Gikandi and Dinesh Chakrabarty have discussed the ways in which, in part as a result of this history, prose is often asked to take up different forms of representation as opposed to poetry, which might portray a more emotional relationship with the nation during the nationalist period. See Gikandi, "Realism, Romance, and the Problem of African Literary History," 320; Chakrabarty, *Provincializing Europe*, 151–55.

21. The phrase "cult of experience" was coined in Rahv, "The Cult of Experience in American Writing." Rahv, the editor of the American journal *Partisan Review*, was drawing on what was for him a specifically American emphasis in its culture and politics on experience over logic or authority; see Jay, *Songs of Experience*, 267. In the context of Verma's writing, it is unclear whether he is drawing more from Rahv or applying this concept to a critique of 1950s literature, with its emphasis on the importance of individual experience.

22. Verma, "Muktibodh kī gadya-kathā," 4.

23. Verma, "Muktibodh kī gadya-kathā," 4.

24. I will discuss *Pūrvagraha*, and their reception of Muktibodh, in the conclusion. *Pūrvagraha* began publishing in the early 1970s, and quickly established itself as one of the most prominent journals of the decade, although one that was frequently a target of the left.

25. Verma, "Muktibodh kī gadya-kathā," 8.

26. Verma, "Muktibodh kī gadya-kathā," 8.

27. As I have noted elsewhere, the cities in which Muktibodh lived, such as Ujjain, Jabalpur, Indore, or Nagpur, are far from qasbahs—indeed, they were then and are now some of the largest cities in Central India. But in his reception, and arguably in his own writing, Muktibodh presented them as limited, marginalized places, in ways that became archetypes for the small city. Arguably, this bifurcation can be read as the elevation of Delhi as capital following independence, so that other cities, regardless of how prominent they were prior, become gradually "qasba-ized," as it were. On the growth of Delhi and its gradual domination in Hindi letters, see Sadana, *English Heart, Hindi Heartland*, 23–26.

28. The *Pañcatantra* is a collection of animal fables, existing in multiple versions across languages, that are intended to illustrate moral maxims—traditionally as a means of teaching kingship to princes. See Vishnusharman, *Five Discourses of Worldly Wisdom*.

29. Muktibodh, "Pakṣī aur dīmak," 4:159.

30. Muktibodh, "Pakṣī aur dīmak," 4:163–64.

31. Chevrolet appears elsewhere in Muktibodh's work; in his poem, "Maiṃ tum logoṃ se dūr hūṃ" (I Am So Far from You All), the speaker claims he will "lie underneath the wheels of a Chevrolet." See Muktibodh, *Muktibodh samagra*, 2:255.

32. Muktibodh, "Pakṣī aur dīmak," 4:166.

33. Unmentioned in the short story is the caste status of the narrator, but anxiety regarding Brahmin status arguably animates the narrator's horror and disgust at his position. On caste in the modern Indian university, see Thomas, "Brahmins as Scientists and Science as Brahmins' Calling."

34. It is noteworthy that this resentment does not take into account anyone but the protagonist—his wife, for instance, is portrayed as failing to understand his specific struggle. A great number of Muktibodh's writings feature domestic tension, meant to illustrate the poverty and stress of lower-middle-class life. In the first chapter, for instance, I discussed the moment in which Muktibodh, in a diary entry, compares himself to a Brahmarakshas, upon feeling humiliated by a female coworker at his place of employment. See Muktibodh, *Muktibodh Samagra*, 5:192.

35. Muktibodh, "Pakṣī aur dīmak," 4:167.

36. Muktibodh, "Pakṣī aur dīmak," 4:169.
37. Muktibodh, "Pakṣī aur dīmak," 4:171.
38. Muktibodh, *Racnāvalī*, 3:130.
39. For an analysis of the hierarchical form of the bureaucracy, and the way in which it can be explored through narrative, see Levine, *Forms*.
40. Muktibodh, *Racnāvalī*, 3:139.
41. Muktibodh, *Racnāvalī*, 3:140.
42. Muktibodh, *Racnāvalī*, 3:140.
43. Muktibodh, *Racnāvalī*, 3:149.
44. Kafka, *Complete Stories*, 250–59.
45. Kafka, *Complete Stories*, 250.
46. Muktibodh, *Racnāvalī*, 3:140.
47. The CID is a state-level investigative agency; around this time, it was featured in a film, *CID*, released in 1956.
48. On the life of Claude Eatherly, see Harrington, "The Hiroshima Pilot Who Became a Symbol of Antinuclear Protest."
49. On the interrelated literary genealogies of both *tilismīya* and *jāsūsī* literature, see Orsini, *Print and Pleasure*, 237–47. On contemporary detective fiction, see Brueck, "Bhais Behaving Badly."
50. On *Candrakāntā*, see Orsini, *Print and Pleasure*, 198–225. Muktibodh frequently mentions the *tilism*, an enchantment common to the *dāstān* through which someone might be trapped in a magical world.
51. Muktibodh, "Klauḍ ītharlī," 4:171–72.
52. Muktibodh, "Klauḍ ītharlī," 4:175.
53. Muktibodh, "Klauḍ ītharlī," 4:177.
54. On the history of India during the Cold war, see Bhagavan, *India and the Cold War*.
55. See Lal, *The Oxford Anthology of the Modern Indian City*, 1:xxiii.
56. On the history of *Seminar*, see the articles collected in its fortieth anniversary issue, no. 481 (September 1999).
57. In addition to the paranoia and surveillance described here, which also appears in works such as "Aṃdhere meṃ" (In the Dark), "Cāṃd kā muṃh ṭeṛhā hai" (The Moon Has a Crooked Face), and "Ek arūp śūnya ke prati" (To a Formless Void), friends and acquaintances described Muktibodh's increasing paranoia in the final decade of his life, as he felt increasingly under surveillance as a suspected Communist. See Varma, *Lakṣit muktibodh*, 153.
58. Muktibodh, "Klauḍ ītharlī ītharlī," 4:173.
59. Muktibodh, *Muktibodh Samagra*, 2:122–23.
60. Muktibodh, "Klauḍ ītharlī ītharlī," 4:174.
61. Muktibodh, "Klauḍ ītharlī ītharlī," 4:176–77.
62. Muktibodh, *Racnāvalī*, 3:368.

63. Muktibodh, "Klauḍ ītharlī ītharlī," 4:179.

64. Muktibodh, "Klauḍ ītharlī," 4:179.

65. Muktibodh, "Klauḍ ītharlī," 4:179.

66. Muktibodh, *Racnāvalī*, 3:164.

67. New Wave science fiction typically refers to writers, such as Philip K. Dick, who emphasized a fragmented individual subjectivity and paranoia, and who question the technocratic optimism of early science fiction. See Vint, *Science Fiction*, 65–67.

68. Verma, "Muktibodh kī gadya-kathā," 8.

69. Verma, "Muktibodh kī gadya-kathā," 9.

70. Śukla, *Dīvār meṃ ek khiṛkī rahtī thī*, 48–49.

Chapter Four

1. Joshi, *Ek kavi kī noṭbuk*, 12.

2. See Jackson, *Dickinson's Misery*; Jackson and Prins, *The Lyric Theory Reader*, 1–8; Prins, "What Is Historical Poetics?"

3. On the social content of the lyric, see Kaufman, "Lyric Commodity Critique, Benjamin Adorno Marx, Baudelaire Baudelaire Baudelaire." See also Culler, *Theory of the Lyric*, 248–96.

4. On the *ghazal*, see Mufti, "Towards a Lyric History of India."

5. Quoted in Vajpeyi, "Muktibodh Ke Sāth Sāṭh Sāl," 71.

6. Singh, *Racnāvalī*, 3:245.

7. Singh, *Racnāvalī*, 3:246.

8. Although Benjamin's work on the dialectical image preceded Shamsher's writing, I use "looking forward" in the sense that Benjamin's reception in Hindi would not occur until the 1970s. Benjamin's idea of a constellation of disparate elements that fuse together into a new image, as described in *The Arcades Project* and "Theses on the Philosophy of History," bear a strong resemblance to Muktibodh's own conception of the image. See Benjamin, *The Arcades Project*, 462; N2a, 3. On the concept of the dialectical image, see Pensky, "Method and Time."

9. Singh, *Racnāvalī*, 3:246.

10. Singh, *Racnāvalī*, 3:247.

11. Singh, *Racnāvalī*, 3:247.

12. Shamsher's comment on the Mexican muralists is somewhat obscure; interestingly, he does not explicitly compare Muktibodh to the contemporary painters, such as M. F. Husain, with whom both writers associated. Ironically, one could argue that Shamsher's comparison gained further relevance unintentionally through the support of Muktibodh's writing by the state of Madhya Pradesh in the 1980s (I discuss this in

the conclusion). Absent other evidence, however, I interpret Shamsher's comment as gesturing towards the capacity of the mural to create narrative through collective allegory and myth, within the space of a single image. On the Mexican muralists, see Coffey, *How a Revolutionary Art Became Official Culture.*

13. Singh, *Racnāvalī,* 3:246.

14. Shamsher's seeming—or performed—discomfort around the difficulty of Muktibodh's works would carry through to his most well-known piece of criticism on Mutkibodh, the long introduction to *Cāṃd kā muṃh ṭeṛhā hai.* By then, as he notes, Muktibodh had become an "event" (Singh, "Ek Vilakṣaṇ Pratibhā," 11). Whereas the chief object in analysis in the earlier essay was "Brahmarākṣas," here Shamsher focuses on "Aṃdhere meṃ" (In the Dark), the poem that is most well-known today. Shamsher, citing Prabhakar Machwe's comparison of "Aṃdhere meṃ" to Picasso's *Guernica* in its encompassing canvas of a violent society, views this poem as the culmination of Muktibodh's work: "Here the people and the individual are fused together in a strange and startling form" (25). Perhaps unlike the tragic web of "Brahmarākṣas" and other works, Shamsher saw "Aṃdhere meṃ" as a fusion of personal imagination and societal critique.

15. Singh, "Ek Vilakṣaṇ Pratibhā," 20.

16. Singh, "Ek Vilakṣaṇ Pratibhā," 25.

17. Singh, "Kālbaddh Aur Padārthmay," 30.

18. *Bhūrī bhūrī xāk dhūl,* published in 1980 just prior to the release of the first edition of Muktibodh's collected works, focused on shorter poems and works that otherwise contrast with the poems collected in *Cāṃd kā muṃh ṭeṛhā hai.* See Muktibodh, *Bhūrī bhūrī khāk dhūl.*

19. Singh, *Kavitā ke naye pratimān,* 231–52.

20. As I will discuss in the conclusion, Kedarnath's treatment echoes a pattern in literary criticism in which Muktibodh's literature is seen as a reflection of his personal life. However, Kedarnath Singh's interpretation should also be seen in the context of *Pūrvagraha,* for which he wrote, which often emphasized a new relationship with cultural authenticity. As I will discuss in the concluding chapter, this position was often contrasted to that on the left, which over the 1970s had increasingly become influenced by Maoist concepts of peasant revolution and the Naxalbari movement.

21. Muktibodh, "Ek lambī kavitā kā ant," 173.

22. Muktibodh, "Ātma-vaktavya," 313.

23. On Mahadevi Varma, see Schomer, *Mahadevi Varma.*

24. The dichotomy would not be out of place with the statements made by other progressive writers in the late 1930s and early 1940s, not

least that made by Premchand in "The Aims of Literature," which I discussed briefly in the previous chapter.

25. Muktibodh, "Ātma-Vaktavya," 315.

26. Especially because the only example he gives of the "world of beauty" is Mahadevi Varma, who was particularly skilled with adapting tropes from Brajbhasha poetry, it is difficult to decide precisely how Muktibodh is here defining this old tradition. Arguably, he is also invested in his own poetic education, particularly the influence of Makhanlal Chaturvedi (1889–1968), with whom he interacted as a teenager. On Makhanlal Chaturvedi, see Caturvedī, *Mākhanlāl caturvedī racnā-sañcayan.*

27. The textbook, along with documents relating to the court case, are collected in Muktibodh, *Bhārat.* The case indicates the power of the Hindu Right in Central India more generally; beyond the foundation of the RSS in Nagpur, the Hindu Mahasabha achieved early success in this region among disaffected, formerly aristocratic landholders. See Jaffrelot, *The Hindu Nationalist Movement in India,* 109–14.

28. Muktibodh, "Ātma-Vaktavya," 319.

29. On Viśāl bhārat and its editor, Banarsidas Chaturvedi, see Parson, "The Bazaar and the Bari," 57–58; Mukul, *Gita Press and the Making of Hindu India,* 199–200. Chaturvedi was particularly notable for his advocacy for indentured laborers in Fiji.

30. Muktibodh, "Ātma-Vaktavya," 321.

31. Muktibodh, "Ek Lambī Kavitā Kā Ant," 165.

32. Muktibodh, "Ek Lambī Kavitā Kā Ant," 173.

33. Muktibodh, "Ek Lambī Kavitā Kā Ant," 173.

34. Muktibodh, "Ek Lambī Kavitā Kā Ant," 173.

35. Muktibodh, "Ek Lambī Kavitā Kā Ant," 173.

36. The essay is also anthologized as Gupt, Caturvedi, and Sahi, "Arth kī lay."

37. "Arth kī lay," 1:108. The original poem "Vijñāpan," from the 1955 collection Atimā, is collected in Pant, *Granthāvali,* 3:389.

38. For an overview of the problems of meter in modern Hindi, see Schomer, *Mahadevi Varma,* 78–82.

39. On Braj poetry, see Busch, *Poetry of Kings.*

40. See Pant, *Pallav,* 51.

41. Urdu, which was and is grammatically identical to modern Hindi, drew its own metrical system from Persian Arabic, which departed from that of Sanskrit in significant ways, although it also featured a system of long and short syllables and moraic meters. On Persian and Urdu meter, see Pritchett and Khaliq, *Urdu Meter;* Thiesen, *A Manual of Classical Persian Prosody.*

42. On the *payār* meter, see Seely, *A Poet Apart*, 89.

43. Meter in Hindi is the subject of a well-known debate between Sumitranandan Pant and Nirala; see Nirala's essay, "Pantjī aur pallav,"in Nirala and Sharma, *Nirālā racnāvalī*, 5:173–217.

44. This point is made in Ahmad, *Muktibodh ke māhaul meṃ*, 30.

45. See Muktibodh, *Samagra*, 8:372.

46. Singh, "Kālbaddh Aur Padārthmay," 34.

47. On this milieu, see Jain, *Mahāguru Muktibodh Jummā Taiṇk Kī Sīḍhiyoṁ Par*. The multilinguistic environment of Central India requires further study.

48. On meter in Marathi, in English, see Engblom, "Keshavsut and Early Modernist Strategies for Indigenizing the Sonnet in Marathi"; Deśpāṇḍe and Rājādhyakṣ, *A History of Marathi Literature*, 15–16. In Marathi, a crucial and monumental study of meter is the out-of-print Paṭvardhan, *Marāṭhī Chandoracnā*.

49. Although this translation is my own, a selection of Tukaram's verses are translated by the Marathi poet Dilip Chitre in Tukārām, *Says Tuka*.

50. On Arun Kolatkar, see Nerlekar, *Bombay Modern*; Zecchini, *Arun Kolatkar and Literary Modernism in India—Moving Lines*. Mardhekar is translated in Chitre, *An Anthology of Marathi Poetry, 1945–65*, 53–81.

51. See Deshpande and Rajadhyaksh, *A History of Marathi Literature*, 143. A limited selection of translations from Mardhekar is available in Chitre, *An Anthology of Marathi Poetry, 1945–65*; as well as Dharwadker, "The Future of the Past," 1:64–76.

52. Mardhekar, *Marḍhekarāñcī kavitā*, 36.

53. See Deśpāṇḍe, *Bhagnamūrti*, 87–94.

54. Deśpāṇḍe, *Bhagnamūrti*, 25. I have added a solidus in the Marathi to show the division between feet in the line.

55. Muktibodh, *Racnāvalī*, 2:327.

56. Muktibodh, *Navī Malvāṭ*, 106.

57. Muktibodh, *Navī Malvāṭ*, 106.

58. On Sharachchandra Muktibodh, see Joshi, *Sharachchandra Muktibodh*.

59. See Rosenstein, *New Poetry in Hindi*, for a study of the background of this work, and selected translations of poems from the *Tār saptak* poets.

60. Muktibodh, *Racnāvalī*, 1:110.

61. Muktibodh, *Racnāvalī*, 1:158.

62. Muktibodh, *Racnāvalī*, 1:374.

63. On the political resonances of "The Mask of Anarchy," see Borushko, "Violence and Nonviolence in Shelley's 'Mask of Anarchy'"; Kaufman, "Legislators of the Post-everything World."

64. Muktibodh, "Aṃdhere meṃ," 2:375.

65. Muktibodh, "Aṃdhere meṃ," 2:375.

66. On *Candrākāntā*, see Orsini, *Print and Pleasure*, 198–225. In the novel, an *ayyār*, a combination of magician and spy, kidnaps his victim and traps him in a cave created by his *tilism*, or magical amulet.

67. I have rendered the stressed syllables in bold.

68. Muktibodh, "Aṃdhere meṃ," 2:375–76.

69. Muktibodh, "Aṃdhere meṃ," 3:382.

70. This aspect of Muktibodh's life and work is discussed extensively in Lotz, "Long Poem or Unending Poem?"

71. Muktibodh, "Aṃdhere meṃ," 2: 383–84.

72. For a description of the growth of the motorable road in the Central Provinces, see Baker, *Changing Political Leadership in an Indian Province*, 49.

73. Muktibodh, "Aṃdhere meṃ," 2:396–97.

74. See Muktibodh"Aṃdhere meṃ," 2:411.

75. Muktibodh, "Aṃdhere meṃ," 2:415–16.

76. A useful overview of this issue can be found in Rai, *Hindi Nationalism*.

Conclusion

1. See *Times of India*, "Troops Move in as Calcutta Riots Continue"; *Times of India*, "Railway Sentry Fires on Mob of Best Workers"; Jain, "A Letter from London."

2. *Times of India*, "Chinese Reds Are Censured."

3. Parker, "Moscow Fortnight."

4. *Times of India*, "Nehru Tired and Weak, Is Advised Rest."

5. On the history of the CPI and its offshoots, see Chandavarkar, "From Communism to 'Social Democracy'"; Raza, *Revolutionary Pasts*.

6. On Ginsburg's visit to India, see Baker, *A Blue Hand*. For a representative example of the mockery of *akavitā*, see Chauhan, *A-Bodhatā*.

7. Anant, "From the Archive, 28 May 1964."

8. In Hindi, this moment is inseparable from the change in status of the Hindi language and its increasing marginalization, but a range of challenges became apparent in the years following Nehru's death that would impact Hindi literary culture, most prominently the advent of Naxalites and the declaration of Indira Gandhi's Emergency. On the Naxalites, see Sen, Panda, and Lahiri, *Naxalbari and After*. On the Emergency, see Jaffrelot and Anil, *India's First Dictatorship*; Plys, *Brewing Resistance*.

9. Much of these events are described in a contemporary article, Machwe, "Dillī Meṁ Muktibodh."

10. Joshi, "Pukār kho gayī kahīṃ!"

11. Muktibodh's death is discussed in many sources; one of them, intriguingly, is Husain, *Where Art Thou*, xviii. Husain helped to carry the bier at Muktibodh's funeral, and claims that this is the occasion upon which he ceased to wear shoes. See also Dalmia, *The Making of Modern Indian Art*, 156.

12. Husain, *Where Art Thou*, xviii.

13. See Singh, "Ek vilakṣaṇ pratibhā," 2.

14. Among the pieces published by his friends after Muktibodh's death, one of the most prominent is Parsāī, "Muktibodh."

15. Although he published sparingly, Shamsher was one of the most important critics and poets in twentieth-century Hindi, responsible not only for the early reception of Muktibodh's work, but also for one of the first and most prominent reviews of *Tār saptak*; translating selections of Louis Aragon into Hindi in the 1940s; and, through translation and criticism, serving as a bridge between Hindi and Urdu after the languages became increasingly separated. In English, Shamsher is discussed in Rosenstein, *New Poetry in Hindi*, 53–65.

16. Singh, "Ek vilakṣaṇ pratibhā," 25.

17. See *Ālocnā* 18, no. 6 (1968).

18. Namvar Singh's major works include Singh, *Chāyāvād*; Singh, *Kavitā ke naye pratimāna* (1968); Singh, *Dūsrī paramparā kī khoj*; Singh, *Kahānī*. See also Mani, *The Idea of Indian Literature*, 105–6. On his legacy, in English see Kumar, "Namvar Singh's Peerless Contribution to Hindi Literature Will Endure."

19. The four poets most associated with *chāyāvād*—Sumitranandan Pant (1900–1977), Suryakant Tripathi "Nirala" (1896–1961), Mahadevi Verma (1907–1987), and Jaishankar Prasad (1889–1937)—are collectively associated with a new paradigm of Hindi poetry. The term *chāyāvād*, which literally means "shadowism," is often framed as a romantic, or neoromantic, movement in literature, and the *chāyāvād* poets emphasized a personal response, relative freedom from poetic norms, and an indirect approach towards the questions of national reform that seemed to define the surrounding ecosystem of Hindi poetry. On *chāyāvād*, in English see Rubin, *Of Love and War*; Pauwels, "Diptych in Verse"; Tiwari, *Beyond English*, 63–88. The term "neoromantic" is drawn from Sahota, *Late Colonial Sublime*, 67. The literature on *chāyāvād* in Hindi is vast. Key texts include Singh, *Chāyāvād*; Sharma, *Nirālā kī sāhitya sādhanā*. Sharma's biography of Nirala is one of the most important works of cultural history written in Hindi and contains a wealth of material on the period.

20. Singh, *Kavitā ke naye pratimāna* (1968), 8.

21. At stake, for Singh's critics, was whether the New Criticism that he was citing contradicted his Marxism and constituted a "formalist

turn." Defending his choices in the second edition to the book, Singh acknowledged that the criticism he was using was written by critics opposed to Marxism, writing, "The question is why is it that that Marxist criticism was defeated in the struggle of ideas?" See Singh, *Kavitā ke naye pratimāna* (1990), 11.

22. The concept of the *laghū mānav* is discussed in the introduction to this book.

23. Singh, *Kavitā ke naye pratimāna* (1968), 24.

24. Singh, *Kavitā ke naye pratimāna* (1968), 78.

25. Singh, *Kavitā ke naye pratimāna* (1968), 34.

26. Singh, *Kavitā ke naye pratimāna* (1968), 34.

27. Singh, *Kavitā ke naye pratimāna* (1968), 221–22.

28. Singh cites these reviews in the preface to a revised edition; see Singh, *Kavitā ke naye pratimāna* (1990), 9–10.

29. See Jain, *Janāntik*, 157–64.

30. On Ram Vilas Sharma's career in the AIPWA, see Coppola, *Urdu Poetry, 1935–1970*, 23–249. For a modern assessment of Ram Vilas Sharma's position on Muktibodh, see Apūrvānand, "Rāmvilās Śarmā Kā Vijetā Mārksvād Aur Muktibodh-Kṣaṇ."

31. Sharma, *Nayī Kavitā Aur Astitvavād*, 88.

32. Sharma creates a parallel between an initial progressive *chāyāvād* poetry and its descent solipsism, and what he sees as the existentialism of *nayī kavitā*. See Sharma, *Nayī Kavitā Aur Astitvavād*, iv.

33. Sharma, *Nayī kavitā aur astitvavād*, 88.

34. Ram Vilas Sharma, despite his hostility to Muktibodh, still engaged more deeply with his work than many more sympathetic critics. For instance, he was one of the first critics to analyze the role of the guru in Muktibodh's work; see Sharma, *Nayī Kavitā Aur Astitvavād*, 208–9.

35. Sharma, *Nayī kavitā aur astitvavād*, 54.

36. Sharma, *Nayī kavitā aur astitvavād*, 107. Sharma faults in particular the poets Sarveśvardayāl Saksenā, GirijākumĀr Māthur, Rājkamal Chaudharī, Jagdīś Caturvedī, Lakṣmīkānt Varma, Vijaydev Nārāyaṇ Sāhī, and Aśok Vājpayī.

37. Singh, *Kavitā ke naye pratimāna* (1968), 231–52.

38. See Singh, *Kavitā ke naye pratimāna* (1968), 245–46.

39. Singh, *Kavitā ke naye pratimāna* (1968), 231–32.

40. Singh, *Kavitā ke naye pratimāna* (1968), 240.

41. Singh, *Kavitā ke naye pratimāna* (1968), 252.

42. See Sharma, *Nayī kavitā aur astitvavād*, 216–23.

43. Sharma, *Nayī kavitā aur astitvavād*, 217.

44. See Pandey, "Muktibodh kā ālocnātmak-saṅgharṣ," 186.

45. On the Naxalite movement, see Sen, Panda, and Lahiri, *Naxalbari and After*; Shah and Jain, "Naxalbari at Its Golden Jubilee."

46. See Kumar, "The Poet's Corpse in the Capitalist's Fish Tank."

47. See, for instance, the early work of Uday Prakash, such as Prakash, *Tirich*.

48. Although *Kaṇk*, in its irregular publication schedule and low budget, fits the mold of a little magazine, both *Kaṇk* and *Pūrvagraha* were ultimately quite similar in terms of their content and formal structure, including a similar balance of special issues. On the little magazine, see Bulson, *Little Magazine, World Form*; Nerlekar, *Bombay Modern*. Crucially, in this instance, both magazines, although theoretically opposed in their politics and networks, were clearly in communication with each other, and were published within a day's journey of each other in the same state.

49. Early issues of *Kaṅk* featured an emphasis on small-town, lower-middle-class writers akin to Muktibodh, but by the end of the 1970s the journal was increasingly associated with the Maoist, Naxalbari left, and would eventually release an important special issue on *janvādī* (people-ism), the term that came to replace the older *pragatiśāl* (progressive). See Sharma, "Samkālīn janvādī kavitā."

50. See Sharma, "Samkālīn Janvādī Kavitā." Critics for *Kaṅk* often defined *janvādī* in opposition to *pragativād*, but primarily because it had become discredited through its use as a derogatory term.

51. These poets took up a more directly aggressive stance and wrote poetry that was more harsh in its depiction of everyday life. Dhumil, in particular, became known for shorter lyrics; but Alok Dhanwa and Chandrakant Devtale followed more directly in the style of Muktibodh, with Devtale eventually writing a book of criticism on Muktibodh; see Devtale, *Muktibodh: kavitā aur jīvan-vivek*.

52. On Nagarjun, see Trivedi, "Bābā nagarjun."

53. Chauhan, "Ḍo. rāmvilās śarmā aur muktibodh kā punarmūlyāṅkan," 82–83.

54. Sharma, "Bātcīt 4," p. 217.

55. See, for instance, Joshi, *Ek kavi kī noṭbuk*, 12. Although Rajesh Joshi's interpretation of Muktibodh goes so far as to claim that Muktibodh's fantasy was the most effective way to pierce the "heavy curtains" of postindependence India.

56. The 1970s saw a rapidly expanding literary globe, as translation increasingly expanded beyond both the Anglo-American signifiers of literary modernism and the Soviet-affiliated writers that were more common up to this point. However, as Francesca Orsini points out in her article on the subject, these translations were most often performed through a prior English translation; see Orsini, "Literary Activism," 120.

57. Sharma, "Bātcīt 2," 128.

58. Sharma, "Bātcīt 2," 226.

59. Cauhān, "Muktibodh," 69.

60. On Shrikant Verma, see Sawhney, *Modernity of Sanskrit*, 54–56; Roadarmel, *A Death in Delhi*, 210.

61. The special issue was later compiled as a book, which does not include this final description. See Sharma, *Muktibodha*.

62. Mani Kaul's film on Muktibodh's works is discussed in Dadawala, "Gajanan Madhav Muktibodh and the Passing of Soviet India."

63. Sharma, "Muktibodh prasaṅg."

64. On Ashok Vajpeyi, see Sadana, *English Heart, Hindi Heartland*, 86–93. Ashok Vajpeyi, over the course of his long career, has held a range of positions in the institutions for the arts in India. Most important of these was his role in the establishment of Bharat Bhavan, an arts center in Bhopal that included not only writers, but painters and other artists, and had a hand in a great number of important art movements in the 1970s and 1980s.

65. On Bharat Bhavan, see Dutta, *Invisible Webs*, 106–22.

66. For an overview of Vajpeyi's career, see Sadana, *English Heart, Hindi Heartland*, 86–91.

67. Vinod Kumar Shukla's first novel, *Naukar kī kamīz* (The Servant's Shirt), was originally published in *Pūrvagraha*, no. 46–47 (1981).

68. See Dalmia, "The Heart of The Matter."

69. For an introduction to and selection of Nirmal Verma's short stories, see Verma, *Indian Errant*. A biography of Verma has recently been released; see Gill, *Here and Hereafter*.

70. Varma, "Ek Ādhūnik Klāsik Kā Sākṣātkār."

71. See Shah, "Upanyās Aur Muktibodh," 6.

72. In the fall of 2015, several prominent literary figures returned awards given to them by the Sahitya Akademi. See "Sahitya Akademi May Frame Policy on Returning Awards."

73. See, for instance, Apoorvanand, "Rāmvilās śarmā kā vijetā mārksvād aur muktibodh-kṣaṇ"; Kumār, "hindī kā mārksvād." Both of these examinations of Marxist thought in Hindi draw in large part from analyses of Muktibodh's thought.

Appendix

1. Domaji Ustad was most likely a reputed gangster and quasi-political figure in 1950s Nagpur. Balban could be Ghiyas ud din Balban, a ruler in the Mamluk dynasty of Delhi during the thirteenth century.

2. The myth of Ajigarta and Shunahshepa is discussed in Shulman, *The Hungry God*, 87–107.

3. The original line is *pradīpt jyoti kā ras bas gayā hai.* Rather than leave the notoriously difficult term *rasa* untranslated, I have taken the liberty of changing the line to emphasize both the liquid, flowing quality of *rasa* and the aesthetic quality of *rasa* as a derived essence.

4. There are several extant editions of Muktibodh's most famous poem; this translation is drawn from the newest version, collected in *Muktibodh Samagra,* which is based upon both the published versions and manuscript editions. The poem has been translated as Muktibodh, *In the Dark.* In my translation, even more so than with "Brahmarākṣas," I have attempted to preserve the syntax (including the meaning of individual line breaks and enjambment) and rhythm of Muktibodh's free verse, which builds up over many lines, along with the sudden, jolting breaks to that rhythm. As a result, this translation is both more and less literal than that by Krishna Baldev Vaid, hopefully conveying the many different registers that Muktibodh plays with, as well as the interpolation of a range of genres and modes. I have also referred to the translation in Germany by Barbara Lotz, found in *Poesie, Poetik, Politik,* 190–240. These two careful translations have guided me in my own interpretation of this singular, monumental poem, which I hope is distinct enough to avoid redundance.

Works Cited

Adorno, Theodor W. "Translator's Introduction." In *Aesthetic Theory*, edited by Gretel Adorno and Rolf Tiedeman, translated by Robert Hullot-Kentor, xi–xxi. Minneapolis: University of Minnesota Press, 1997.

Ahmad, Sultān. *Muktibodh ke māhaul meṃ*. New Delhi: Prakāśana Saṃsthāna, 2020.

Althusser, Louis. "Darśan: ek krāntikārī astra ke rūp meṁ (luī altuser se ek bātcīt)." Translated by Gopāl Bhārdvāj. *Ālocnā*, no. 53 (1971): 8–13.

Anant, Victor. "From the Archive, 28 May 1964: The Death of Nehru." *Guardian*, May 28, 2013.

Anderson, Benedict R. O'G. *Imagined Communities: Reflections on the Origin and Spread of Nationalism*. London: Verso, 1991.

Anjaria, Ulka. *Realism in the Twentieth-Century Indian Novel Colonial Difference and Literary Form*. New York: Cambridge University Press, 2012.

Apoorvanand. "The Worker of Poetry." *Indian Express*, n.d. Accessed December 9, 2015.

Apūrvānand, Sañjīv. "Rāmvilās śarmā kā vijetā mārksvād aur muktibodh-kṣaṇ." In *Hindī-Ādhūniktā: Ek Punarvicār*, edited by Abhay Kumār Dube, 2:395–421. New Delhi: Vani Prakashan, 2014.

Arnold, David. "Nehruvian Science and Postcolonial India." *Isis* 104, no. 2 (2013): 360–70.

Avasthī, Rekhā. *Pragativād aur samānāntar sāhitya*. 2nd ed. New Delhi: Rajkamal Prakashan, 2012.

Bachelard, Gaston. *The Poetics of Space*. Boston: Beacon, 1994.

Baker, D. E. U. *Changing Political Leadership in an Indian Province: The Central Provinces and Berar, 1919–1939*. Delhi: Oxford University Press, 1979.

Baker, Deb. *A Blue Hand: The Tragicomic, Mind-Altering Odyssey of Allen Ginsberg, a Holy Fool, a Lost Muse, a Dharma Bum, and His Prickly Bride in India*. New York: Penguin, 2008.

Bakhtin, M. M. *The Dialogic Imagination: Four Essays*. Austin: University of Texas Press, 2010.

Behl, Aditya. *Love's Subtle Magic: An Indian Islamic Literary Tradition, 1379–1545*. New York: Oxford University Press, 2012.

Benjamin, Walter. *The Arcades Project*. Cambridge, MA: Belknap Press of Harvard University Press, 1999.

Bhagavan, Manu Belur. *India and the Cold War*. Chapel Hill: University of North Carolina Press, 2019.

Blackburn, Stuart, and Vasudha Dalmia, eds. *India's Literary History: Essays on the Nineteenth Century*. Delhi: Permanent Black, 2004.

Bloch, Ernst, Theodor W. Adorno, Bertolt Brecht, and György Lukács. *Aesthetics and Politics*. London: Verso, 2007.

Borushko, Matthew C. "Violence and Nonviolence in Shelley's 'Mask of Anarchy.'" *Keats-Shelley Journal* 59 (2010): 96–113.

Bose, Buddhadeva. *Modern Poetry and Sanskrit Kavya*. Translated by Sujit Mukherjee. Modern Poetry and Sanskrit Kavya. Calcutta: Writers Workshop, 1997.

Bourdieu, Pierre. *Distinction: A Social Critique of the Judgement of Taste*. Cambridge, MA: Harvard University Press, 1984.

Boyk, David. "Collaborative Wit: Provincial Publics in Colonial North India." *Comparative Studies of South Asia, Africa and the Middle East* 38, no. 1 (2018): 89–106.

Brecht, Bertolt. "Notes on the Realist Mode of Writing, 1940." In *Brecht on Art and Politics*, edited by Tom Kuhn and Steve Giles, 242–62. London: Methuen, 2003.

———. *Schriften zur Literatur und Kunst*. Edited by Werner Hecht. Frankfurt: Suhrkamp, 1967.

Bronner, Yigal, David Shulman, and Gary A. Tubb. *Innovations and Turning Points: Toward a History of Kāvya Literature*. South Asia Research. New Delhi: Oxford University Press, 2014.

Brown, Nicholas. *Utopian Generations: The Political Horizon of Twentieth-Century Literature*. Princeton, NJ: Princeton University Press, 2005.

Browne, Paul. "An Unclaimed Legacy: Caudwell's Marxist Dialectics." *Science and Society* 48, no. 2 (1984): 192–210.

Brueck, Laura. "Bhais Behaving Badly: Vernacular Masculinities in Hindi Detective Novels." *South Asian Popular Culture* 18, no. 1 (2020): 29–46.

Bulson, Eric Jon. *Little Magazine, World Form*. New York: Columbia University Press, 2016.

Busch, Allison. *Poetry of Kings: The Classical Hindi Literature of Mughal India*. New York: Oxford University Press, 2011.

Chakradhar, Ashok. *Muktibodh kī kāvyaprakriyā: muktibodh ke cintan ke sandarbh meṃ unke kāvya kī racanāprakriyā aur arthaprakriyā kā adhyayan*. New Delhi: Macmillan Company of India, 1975.

Chaturvedi, Makhanlal. *Mākhanlāl caturvedī racnā-sañcayan*. Edited by Kṛṣṇadatt Pālīvāl. Prathama saṃskaraṇa. New Delhi: Sahitya Akademi, 2014.

Chauhan, Chanchal. "Ḍo. rāmvilās śarmā aur muktibodh kā punarmūlyāṅkan." In *Muktibodh: samagra Muktibodh-sāhitya Par Ālocanātmak Nibandhoṃ Kā Saṅgraha*, edited by Nirmal Śarmā, 1. saṃskaraṇa, 79–95. Ratlam, Madhya Pradesh: Trayī prakāśan, 1980.

Chauhan, Karansingh. "Muktibodh: mūlyāṅkan kī samasyā." In *Muktibodh: samagra muktibodh-sāhitya par ālocanātmak nibandhoṃ kā saṅgraha*, edited by Nirmal Śarmā, 1. saṃskaraṇa, 67–78. Ratlam, Madhya Pradesh: Trayī prakāśan, 1980.

Chakrabarty, Dipesh. *Provincializing Europe: Postcolonial Thought and Historical Difference*. New ed. Princeton, NJ: Princeton University Press, 2008.

Chandavarkar, Rajnarayan. "From Communism to 'Social Democracy': The Rise and Resilience of Communist Parties in India, 1920–1995." *Science and Society* 61, no. 1 (1997): 99–106.

Chandra, Nandini. *The Classic Popular Amar Chitra Katha, 1967–2007*. New Delhi: Yoda, 2008.

Chaudhuri, Supriya. "Modernisms in India." In *The Oxford Handbook of Modernisms*, edited by Peter Brooker, Andrzej Gąsiorek, Deborah Longworth, and Andrew Thacker. Oxford: Oxford University Press, 2012. https://doi.org/10.1093/oxfordhb/9780199545445.013.0053.

Chauhan, Herman. *A-Bodhatā* [Nonknowledge]. Jodhpur: Racnā prakāśan, 1968.

Cheah, Pheng. *What Is a World? On Postcolonial Literature as World Literature*. Durham, NC: Duke University Press, 2016.

Chelnokova, Anna, and Liliia Streltcova. "Brahmarakshasa in Modern Hindi Literature." *Rupkatha Journal on Interdisciplinary Studies in Humanities* 8, no. 4 (2017): 139–47.

Chitre, Dilip. *An Anthology of Marathi Poetry, 1945–65*. Bombay: Nirmala Sadanand, 1967.

Clark, Katerina. *Eurasia without Borders: The Dream of a Leftist Literary Commons, 1919*. Cambridge, MA: Harvard University Press, 2021.

———. "Indian Leftist Writers of the 1930s Maneuver among India, London, and Moscow: The Case of Mulk Raj Anand and His Patron Ralph Fox." *Kritika: Explorations in Russian and Eurasian History* 18, no. 1 (2017): 63–87.

———. "The Soviet Project of the 1930s to Found a 'World Literature' and British Literary Internationalism." *Modern Language Quarterly* 80, no. 4 (2019): 403–25.

Cleary, Joe. "Realism after Modernism and the Literary World-System." *Modern Language Quarterly* 73, no. 3 (2012): 255–68.

Coffey, Mary K. *How a Revolutionary Art Became Official Culture: Murals, Museums, and the Mexican State*. Durham, NC: Duke University Press, 2012.

Coppola, Carlo. *Urdu Poetry, 1935–1970: The Progressive Episode*. Oxford: Oxford University Press, 2018.

Culler, Jonathan D. *Theory of the Lyric*. Cambridge, MA: Harvard University Press, 2015.

Dadawala, Vikrant. "Gajanan Madhav Muktibodh and the Passing of Soviet India." *South Asia* 44, no. 6 (2021): 1090–1113.

Dalmia, Vasudha. *Fiction as History: The Novel and the City in Modern North India*. Ranikhet: Orient Blackswan, 2017.

———. *The Nationalization of Hindu Traditions: Bhāratendu Hariśchandra and Nineteenth-Century Banaras*. Delhi: Oxford University Press, 1997.

Dalmia, Yashodhara. "The Heart of The Matter." *Times of India*, January 4, 1981.

———. *The Making of Modern Indian Art: The Progressives*. New Delhi: Oxford University Press, 2001.

Daniyal, Shoaib. "At Delhi University's Vedic Chronology Seminar, Discussions on Flying Chariots, Mahabharat-Era TV." *Scroll.in*, October 1, 2015. http://scroll.in/article/759001/at-delhi-universitys-vedic-chronology-seminar-discussions-on-flying-chariots-mahabharat-era-tv.

Deshpande, Atmaram Raoji 'Anil'. *Bhagnamūrti*. 3rd ed. Pune: Venus, 1995. Originally published 1940.

Deshpande, Kusamavati, and Mangesh Vitthal Rajadhyaksh. *A History of Marathi Literature*. New Delhi: Sahitya Akademi, 1988.

Deshpande, Satish. "Mapping the 'Middle': Issues in the Analysis of the 'Non-poor' Classes in India." In *Contested Transformations: Changing Economies and Identities in Contemporary India*, edited by Mary John, Praveen Kumar Jha, and Surinder Jhodka, 215–36. New Delhi: Tulika, 2006.

Devtale, Chandrakant. *Muktibodh: kavitā aur jīvan-vivek*. New Delhi: Radhakrishna, 2003.

Dharwadker, Vinay. "The Future of the Past: Modernity, Modern Poetry, and the Transformation of Two Indian Traditions." PhD thesis, University of Chicago, 1989.

Dickie, Margaret. *On the Modernist Long Poem*. Iowa City: University of Iowa Press, 1986.

Djagalov, Rossen. "Progress Publishers: A Short History." In *The East Was Read: Socialist Culture in the Third World*, edited by Vijay Prashad, 79–86. New Delhi: LeftWord, 2019.

Dneprov, Vladimir. "In Defence of the Aesthetic of Realism." *Soviet Literature*, January 1958, 170–86.

———. "Method and Style in Art." *Soviet Literature*, March 1958, 139–47.

Dostoevsky, Fyodor. *A Writer's Diary*. Evanston, IL: Northwestern University Press, 2009.

Dubrow, Jennifer. "The Aesthetics of the Fragment: Progressivism and Literary Modernism in the Work of the All-India Progressive Writers' Association." *Journal of Postcolonial Writing* 55, no. 5 (2019): 589–601.

———. *Cosmopolitan Dreams: The Making of Modern Urdu Literary Culture in Colonial South Asia*. Honolulu, HI: University of Hawai'i Press, 2018.

Dutta, Amit. *Invisible Webs*. Shimla: Institute for Advanced Studies, 2018.

Ebeling, Sascha. *Colonizing the Realm of Words: The Transformation of Tamil Literature in Nineteenth-Century South India*. Albany: State University of New York Press, 2010.

Ehrenreich, Barbara. *Fear of Falling: The Inner Life of the Middle Class*. New York: Pantheon, 1989.

Engblom, Philip C. "Keshavsut and Early Modernist Strategies for Indigenizing the Sonnet in Marathi: A Western Form in Indian Garb." *Journal of South Asian Literature* 23, no. 1 (1988): 42–66.

Engell, James. *The Creative Imagination: Enlightenment to Romanticism*. Cambridge, MA: Harvard University Press, 1981.

Esty, Jed. "Realism Wars." *Novel* 49, no. 2 (2016): 316–42.

Esty, Jed, and Colleen Lye. "Peripheral Realisms Now." In "Peripheral Realisms," edited by Colleen Lye, Jed Esty, and Joe Cleary, special issue, *Modern Language Quarterly* 73, no. 3 (2012): 269–88.

Fārūqī, Shamsurraḥmān. *Early Urdu Literary Culture and History*. New Delhi: Oxford University Press, 2001.

Felski, Rita. "Nothing to Declare: Identity, Shame, and the Lower Middle Class." *PMLA* 115, no. 1 (2000): 33–45.

Foot, Paul. *Red Shelley*. London: Sidgwick and Jackson in association with Michael Dempsey, 1980.

Friedman, Susan Stanford. "When a 'Long' Poem Is a 'Big' Poem: Self-Authorizing Strategies in Women's Twentieth-Century 'Long Poems.'" *LIT* 2, no. 1 (1990): 9–25.

Gajarawala, Toral Jatin. *Untouchable Fictions: Literary Realism and the Crisis of Caste*. New York: Fordham University Press, 2012.

Gautam, Sanjay Kumar. "Conflict of Callings: Literature, Politics, and the Birth of Pain in the Poetry of Muktibodh (1917–1964)." PhD thesis, University of Chicago, 2005.

Ghosh, Pothik. *The Deed of Words: Two Considerations on Politics of Literature*. Delhi: Aakar Books. 2016.

Gikandi, Simon. "Realism, Romance, and the Problem of African Literary History." *Modern Language Quarterly* 73, no. 3 (2012): 309–28.

Gill, Vineet. *Here and Hereafter: Nirmal Verma's Life in Literature*. New Delhi: Penguin Random House India, 2022.

Gillott, Brendan C. *Reading the Modernist Long Poem: John Cage, Charles Olson and the Indeterminacy of Longform Poetics*. New York: Bloomsbury, 2020.

Gopal, Priyamvada. *Literary Radicalism in India: Gender, Nation and the Transition to Independence*. London: Routledge, 2012.

Gupt, Jagadis, Ram Svarup Caturvedi, and Vijayadev Narayan Sahi. "Arth kī lay." In *Nayī kavitā*, 24–32. Ilahabada: Lokabharati Prakasana, 2000.

Harrington, Anne I. "The Hiroshima Pilot Who Became a Symbol of Antinuclear Protest." *New York Times*, August 6, 2020.

Hošek, Chaviva, Patricia A. Parker, and Patricia Lee Parker, eds. *Lyric Poetry: Beyond New Criticism*. Ithaca, NY: Cornell University Press, 1985.

Husain, Maqbul Fida. *Where Art Thou: An Autobiography* Mumbai: M. F. Husain Foundation, 2002.

Jackson, Virginia Walker. *Dickinson's Misery: A Theory of Lyric Reading*. Princeton, NJ: Princeton University Press, 2005.

Jackson, Virginia Walker, and Yopie Prins. *The Lyric Theory Reader: A Critical Anthology*. Baltimore: Johns Hopkins University Press, 2014.

Jaffrelot, Christophe. *The Hindu Nationalist Movement in India*. New York: Columbia University Press, 1996.

Jaffrelot, Christophe, and Pratinav Anil. *India's First Dictatorship*. New York: Oxford University Press, 2021.

Jain, Girilal. "A Letter from London: Britain and East Africa." *Times of India*, January 25, 1964.

Jain, Kantikumar. *Mahāguru muktibodh jummā taiṇk kī sīḍhiyoṁ par*. New Delhi: Sāmayik Prakāśan, 2014.

Jain, Nemicandra. *Janāntik*. Hāpuṛ: Sambhāvanā Prakāśan, 1981.

Jalil, Rakhshanda. *Liking Progress, Loving Change: A Literary History of the Progressive Writers' Movement in Urdu*. Delhi: Oxford University Press, 2014.

Jameson, Fredric. *Allegory and Ideology*. London: Verso, 2020.

———. "Antinomies of the Realism-Modernism Debate." *Modern Language Quarterly* 73, no. 3 (2012): 475–85.

———. *Archaeologies of the Future: The Desire Called Utopia and Other Science Fictions*. London: Verso, 2007.

Jay, Martin. *Marxism and Totality: The Adventures of a Concept from Lukács to Habermas*. Berkeley: University of California Press, 1984.

———. *Songs of Experience: Modern American and European Variations on a Universal Theme*. Berkeley: University of California Press, 2005.

Jeffrey, Craig. *Timepass: Youth, Class, and the Politics of Waiting in India.* Stanford, CA: Stanford University Press, 2010.

Jones, John Paul, Helga Leitner, Sallie A. Marston, and Eric Sheppard. "Neil Smith's Scale." *Antipode* 49, no. S1 (2017): 138–52

Jones, Rodney W. *Urban Politics in India: Area, Power, and Policy in a Penetrated System.* Berkeley: University of California Press, 1974.

Joshi, Ashok. *Sharachchandra Muktibodh.* Makers of Indian Literature. New Delhi: Sahitya Akademi, 1997.

Joshi, Manohar Shyam. "Pukār kho gayī kahīṃ!" *Dharmyug,* September 26, 1964.

Joshi, Priya. *In Another Country: Colonialism, Culture, and the English Novel in India.* New York: Columbia University Press, 2002.

Joshi, Rajesh. *Ek kavi kī noṭbuk.* New Delhi: Rajkamal Prakashan, 2004.

Joshi, Sanjay. *Fractured Modernity: Making of a Middle Class in Colonial North India.* New Delhi: Oxford University Press, 2005.

———. "India's Middle Class." *Oxford Research Encyclopedia of Asian History,* April 26, 2017. https://doi.org/10.1093/acrefore/9780190277727.013.179.

Kafka, Franz. *Complete Stories.* Edited by Nahum N. Glatzer. Centennial ed. New York: Schocken, 1983.

Kalliney, Peter J. *The Aesthetic Cold War: Decolonization and Global Literature.* Princeton, NJ: Princeton University Press, 2022.

Kantor, Roanne L. "South Asian Magical Realism." In *The Palgrave Handbook of Magical Realism in the Twenty-First Century,* edited by Richard Perez and Victoria A. Chevalier, 83–100. Cham, Switzerland: Palgrave Macmillan, 2020.

Kapur, Geeta. *When Was Modernism: Essays on Contemporary Cultural Practice in India.* New Delhi: Tulika, 2000.

Kaufman, Robert. "Legislators of the Post-everything World: Shelley's 'Defence of Adorno.'" *ELH* 63, no. 3 (1996): 707–33.

———. "Lyric Commodity Critique, Benjamin Adorno Marx, Baudelaire Baudelaire Baudelaire." *PMLA* 123, no. 1 (2008): 207–15.

———. "Red Kant, or the Persistence of the Third 'Critique' in Adorno and Jameson." *Critical Inquiry* 26, no. 4 (2000): 682–724.

Kaviraj, Sudipta. *The Unhappy Consciousness: Bankimchandra Chattopadhyay and the Formation of Nationalist Discourse in India.* Delhi: Oxford University Press, 1995.

Khan, Maryam Wasif. "The Oriental Tale and the Transformation of North Indian Prose Fiction." *Modern Language Quarterly* 78, no. 1 (2017): 27–50.

Khan, Pasha M. *The Broken Spell: Indian Storytelling and the Romance Genre in Persian and Urdu.* Detroit: Wayne State University Press, 2019.

Kidambi, Prashant. "Consumption, Domestic Economy, and the Idea of the 'Middle Class' in Late Colonial Bombay." In *The Middle Class in Colonial India*, edited by Sanjay Joshi, 132–56. New Delhi: Oxford University Press India, 2010.

King, Christopher Rolland. *One Language, Two Scripts: The Hindi Movement in Nineteenth Century North India*. New Delhi: Oxford University Press, 1999.

Kumar, Amitava. "The Poet's Corpse in the Capitalist's Fish Tank." *Critical Inquiry* 23, no. 4 (1997): 894–909.

Kumar, Sanjeev. "Namvar Singh's Peerless Contribution to Hindi Literature Will Endure." *The Wire*, February 26, 2019. https://thewire.in/books/namvar-singhs-peerless-contribution-to-hindi-literature-will-endure.

Lal, Vinay. *The Oxford Anthology of the Modern Indian City*. New Delhi: Oxford University Press India, 2013.

Leffler, Melvyn P., and David S. Painter. *Origins of the Cold War: An International History*. 2nd ed. London: Routledge, 2005.

Levine, Caroline. *Forms: Whole, Rhythm, Hierarchy, Network*. Princeton, NJ: Princeton University Press, 2015.

Lotz, Barbara. "Long Poem or Unending Poem? On the Emergence of Muktibodh's 'Andhere Mein.'" *Hindi: Language, Discourse, Writing* 2, no. 1 (2001): 91–108.

———. "Poesie, Poetik, Politik: Engagement und Experiment im Werk des Hindiautors Gajanan Madhav Muktibodh (1917–1964)." PhD thesis, Universität Heidelberg, 2000.

———. "Rāhoṁ Ke Anveṣī: The Editor of the Saptak-Anthologies and His Poets." In *Hindi Modernism*, edited by Vasudha Dalmia, 125–46. Berkeley: Center for South Asia Studies, University of California, Berkeley, 2012.

———. "Romantic Allegory and Progressive Criticism." In *Narrative Strategies: Essays on South Asian Literature and Film*, edited by Vasudha Dalmia and Theo Dansteegt, 211–28. New Delhi: Oxford University Press, 1998.

Löwy, Michael. "The Current of Critical Irrealism: 'A Moonlit Enchanted Night.'" In *Adventures in Realism*, edited by Matthew Beaumont, 193–207. Malden, MA: Blackwell, 2007.

Lukács, György. *The Theory of the Novel: A Historico-philosophical Essay on the Forms of Great Epic Literature*. Cambridge, MA: MIT Press, 1974.

Lutgendorf, Philip. *The Life of a Text: Performing the Rāmcaritmānas of Tulsidas*. Berkeley: University of California Press, 1991.

Lye, Colleen. "Afterword: Realism's Futures." *Novel* 49, no. 2 (August 2016): 343–57.

Machwe, Prabhakar. "Dillī meṃ muktibodh." *Dharmyug*, July 19, 1964.

———. *From Self to Self: Reminiscences of a Writer*. New Delhi: Vikas, 1977.

Mandhwani, Aakriti. "Saritā and the 1950s Hindi Middlebrow Reader." *Modern Asian Studies* 53, no. 6 (2019): 1797–1815.

Mani, Preetha. *The Idea of Indian Literature: Gender, Genre, and Comparative Method*. Evanston, IL: Northwestern University Press, 2022.

———. "What Was So New about the New Story? Modernist Realism in the Hindi Nayī Kahānī." *Comparative Literature* 71, no. 3 (2019): 226–51.

Mardhekar, Bal Sitaram. *Marḍhekarāñcī kavitā*. 6th ed. Mumbai: Mauj Prakashan Grha, 1994.

Mayer, Arno J. "The Lower Middle Class as Historical Problem." *Journal of Modern History* 47, no. 3 (1975): 409–36.

McGregor, Stuart. "The Progress of Hindi, Part 1: The Development of a Transregional Idiom." In *Literary Cultures in History*, edited by Sheldon Pollock, 912–57. Berkeley: University of California Press, 2003.

McHale, Brian. *The Obligation toward the Difficult Whole: Postmodernist Long Poems*. Tuscaloosa: University of Alabama Press, 2004.

———. "Telling Stories Again: On the Replenishment of Narrative in the Postmodernist Long Poem." *Yearbook of English Studies* 30 (2000): 250–62.

McKeon, Michael. *The Origins of the English Novel, 1600–1740*. Baltimore: Johns Hopkins University Press, 2002.

Menon, Dilip M. *Being a Brahmin the Marxist Way: E. M. S. Nambudiripad and the Pasts of Kerala*. New Delhi: Centre for Contemporary Studies, Nehru Memorial Museum and Library, 1998.

Menon, Nikhil. *Planning Democracy*. Cambridge: Cambridge University Press, 2022.

Metcalf, Barbara D., and Thomas R. Metcalf. *A Concise History of Modern India*. 3rd ed. Cambridge: Cambridge University Press, 2012.

Mody, Sujata S. *The Making of Modern Hindi: Literary Authority in Colonial North India*. New Delhi: Oxford University Press, 2018.

Moe, Lukas. "Elegy's Generation: Muriel Rukeyser, M. L. Rosenthal, and Poetry after the Left." *Modern Language Quarterly* 80, no. 2 (2019): 195–219.

Mufti, Aamir. *Enlightenment in the Colony: The Jewish Question and the Crisis of Postcolonial Culture*. Princeton, NJ: Princeton University Press, 2007.

———. "Towards a Lyric History of India." *Boundary 2* 31, no. 2 (2004): 245–74.

Mukherjee, Meenakshi. *Realism and Reality: The Novel and Society in India*. Delhi: Oxford University Press, 1985.

Mukherjee, Upamanyu Pablo. *Final Frontiers: Science Fiction and Technoscience in Non-Aligned India*. Liverpool: Liverpool University Press, 2019.

Muktibodh, Gajanan Madhav. "Aṃdhere meṃ" In *Muktibodh Samagra,* 2:375–416.

———. "At Every Step." Translated by Arvind Krishna Mahrotra. *Journal of South Asian Literature* 10, no. 1 (1974): 42–43.

———. "Ātma-vaktavya: cār" In *Muktibodh Samagra,* 6:321–22. New Delhi: Rajkamal Prakashan, 2019.

———. "Ātma-vaktavya: ek" [Personal Statement: One]. In *Muktibodh Samagra,* 6:313–15. New Delhi: Rajkamal Prakashan, 2019.

———. "Ātma-vaktavya: tin:" [Personal Statement: Three]. In *Muktibodh Samagra,* 6:317–21. New Delhi: Rajkamal Prakashan, 2019.

———. *Bhārat: itihās aur sanskṛti.* Delhi: Rajkamal Prakashan, 2009.

———. *Bhūrī bhūrī khāk dhūl.* 1. saṃskaraṇa. New Delhi: Rājakamala Prakāśana, 1980.

———. "Brahmarākṣas." In *Muktibodh samagra,* 2:368–75.

———. "Brahmarakshas." Translated by Nikhil Govind. *Almost Island,* no. 6 (2011). https://www.almostisland.com/winter-2011/poetry/brahmarakshas.

———. "Ek lambī kavitā kā ant" [The End of a Long Poem]. In *Muktibodh Samagra,* 5:164–73. New Delhi: Rajkamal Prakashan, 2019.

———. "The Error." Translated by Arvind Krishna Mahrotra. *Journal of South Asian Literature* 10, no. 1 (1974): 39–40.

———. *In the Dark.* Translated by Krishna Baldev Vaid. Noida: Rainbow Publishers, in collaboration with Mahatma Gandhi Antarrashtriya Hindi Vishwavidyalaya, 2001.

———. "Kāmāyanī: ek punarvicār." In *Muktibodh Samagra,* edited by Nemicandra Jain, 5:205–400.

———. "Klauḍ ītharlī." In *Muktibodh Samagra,* 4:171–81. New Delhi: Rajkamal Prakashan, 2019.

———. *Muktibodh samagra.* Edited by Nemichandra Jain and Ramesh Muktibodh. New Delhi: Rajkamal Prakashan, 2019.

———. "Pakṣī aur dīmak" [The Bird and the Weevil]. In *Muktibodh samagra,* 158–71. New Delhi: Rajkamal Prakashan, 2019.

———. *Racnāvalī.* Edited by Nemichandra Jain. 2nd ed. 2007.

———. "Tīsrā kṣaṇ." In *Muktibodh samagra,* 5:80–102. New Delhi: Rajkamal Prakashan, 2019.

———. "Vīrkar." In *Muktibodh samagra,* edited by Nemicandra Jain, 5:68–75. New Delhi: Rajkamal Prakashan, 2019.

———. "The Zero." Translated by Arvind Krishna Mahrotra. *Journal of South Asian Literature* 10, no. 1 (1974): 41.

Muktibodh, Ramesh Gajanan, and Rajesh Joshi, eds. *Tummeṃ maiṃ satat pravāhit hūṃ.* 1st ed. Lokodaya Granthamālā 1434. New Delhi: Bhāratīya Jñānapīṭha, 2020.

Muktibodh, Sharachchandra. *Navī malvāṭ*. 3rd ed. Mumbai: Mauj Prakashan Grha, 1987.

Mukul, Akshaya. *Gita Press and the Making of Hindu India*. Noida: Harper Collins India, 2015.

———. *Writer, Rebel, Soldier, Lover: The Many Lives of Agyeya*. Gurugram: Penguin Random House India, 2022.

Nandy, Ashis. *Alternative Sciences: Creativity and Authenticity in Two Indian Scientists*. New Delhi: Oxford University Press, 1995.

Naval, Nand Kishor. *Ādhunik hindī kavitā kā itihās*. New Delhi: Bhāratīya Jñānapīṭha, 2012.

———. *Muktibodh, jñān aur saṃvedanā*. New Delhi: Rājakamala Prakāśana, 1993.

Nemade, Bhalachandra. *Nativism*. Shimla: Indian Institute of Advanced Study, 2009.

Nerlekar, Anjali. *Bombay Modern: Arun Kolatkar and Bilingual Literary Culture*. Evanston, IL: Northwestern University Press, 2016.

Nirala, Suryakant Tripathi, and Ramvilas Sharma. *Nirālā racnāvalī*. Delhi: Rajkamal Prakashan, 2009.

O'Hanlon, Rosalind. "Letters Home: Banaras Pandits and the Maratha Regions in Early Modern India." *Modern Asian Studies* 44, no. 2 (2010): 201–40.

Orsini, Francesca. *East of Delhi: Multilingual Literary Culture and World Literature*. New York: Oxford University Press, 2023.

———. *The Hindi Public Sphere, 1920–1940: Language and Literature in the Age of Nationalism*. New Delhi: Oxford University Press, 2002.

———. "Literary Activism: Hindi Magazines, the Short Story and the World." In *The Form of Ideology and the Ideology of Form: Cold War, Decolonization and Third World Print Cultures*, edited by Francesca Orsini, Neelam Srivastava, and Laetitia Zecchini, 99–136. Cambridge, UK: Open Book, 2022.

———. "The Multilingual Local in World Literature." *Comparative Literature* 67, no. 4 (2015): 345–74.

———. "Present Absence: Book Circulation, Indian Vernaculars and World Literature in the Nineteenth Century." *Interventions* 22, no. 3 (2020): 310–28.

———. *Print and Pleasure: Popular Literature and Entertaining Fictions in Colonial North India*. Ranikhet: Permanent Black, 2009.

———. "The Short Story as an Aide à Penser." In *Hindi Modernism: Rethinking Agyeya and His Times*, edited by Vasudha Dalmia, 103–23. Proceedings of the Berkeley Symposium February 11–13, 2011. Berkeley: Center for South Asia Studies, University of California, Berkeley, 2012.

———. "World Literature, Indian Views, 1920s–1940s." *Journal of World Literature* 4, no. 1 (2019): 56–81.

Pandey, Mainejar. "Muktibodh Kā Ālocnātmak-Saṅgharṣ." In *Muktibodh: samagra Muktibodh-sāhitya Par Ālocanātmak Nibandhoṃ Kā Saṅgraha,* edited by Nirmal Śarmā, 1. saṃskaraṇa, 104–39. Ratlam, Madhya Pradesh: Trayī prakāśan, 1980.

Pant, Sumitranandan. *Atimā.* 3. saṃskaraṇa., 1963.

———. *Pallav.* New Delhi: Rajkamal Prakashan, 1963. First published in 1926.

Parker, Ralph. "Moscow Fortnight." *Times of India,* January 19, 1964.

Parmar, Shyam. *Akavitā aur kalā-sandarbh.* 1. saṃskaraṇa. Ajamera: Krshṇā Bradarsa, 1968.

Parsai, Harishankar. *Inspector Matadeen on the Moon: Satires.* Translated by C. M. Naim. New Delhi: Katha, 2003.

———. "Muktibodh: ek sansmaraṇ" In *Racnāvalī,* edited by Kamlā Prasād, Dhanañjay Varmā, Śyāmsundar Miśra, Malayaj, and Śyam Kaśyap, 4: 410–17. New Delhi: Rajkamal Prakashan, 1985. Originally published 1964.

Parson, Rahul Bjorn. "The Bazaar and the Bari: Calcutta, Marwaris, and the World of Hindi Letters." PhD thesis, University of California, Berkeley, 2012.

Patel, Deven M. *Text to Tradition: The Naiṣadhīyacarita and Literary Community in South Asia.* South Asia across the Disciplines. New York: Columbia University Press, 2014.

Patel, Geeta. "Vernacular Missing: Miraji on Sappho, Gender, and Governance." *Comparative Literature* 70, no. 2 (2018): 132–44.

Patvardhan, Madhavrao. *Marāṭhī Chandoracnā.* 1937.

Pauwels, Heidi. "Diptych in Verse: Gender Hybridity, Language Consciousness, and National Identity in Nirālā's 'Jāgo Phir Ek Bār.'" *Journal of the American Oriental Society* 121, no. 3 (2001): 449–81.

Pensky, Max. "Method and Time: Benjamin's Dialectical Images." In *The Cambridge Companion to Walter Benjamin,* edited by David S. Ferris, 177–98. Cambridge: Cambridge University Press, 2004.

Perloff, Marjorie. "From Image to Action: The Return of Story in Postmodern Poetry." *Contemporary Literature* 23, no. 4 (1982): 411–27.

———. Review of *Theory of the Lyric,* by Jonathan Culler. *Nineteenth-Century Literature* 71, no. 2 (2016): 256–61.

Plys, Kristin Victoria Magistrelli. *Brewing Resistance: Indian Coffee House and the Emergency in Postcolonial India.* Cambridge: Cambridge University Press, 2020.

Pollock, Sheldon. *The Language of the Gods in the World of Men: Sanskrit, Culture, and Power in Premodern India.* Berkeley: University of California Press, 2006.

———. *A Rasa Reader: Classical Indian Aesthetics*. New York: Columbia University Press, 2016.

Popescu, Monica. *At Penpoint: African Literatures, Postcolonial Studies, and the Cold War*. Durham, NC: Duke University Press, 2020.

Prakash, Uday. *Tirich*. New Delhi: Vani Prakashan, 1989.

Pratt, Mary Louise. "The Short Story: The Long and the Short of It." In *The New Short Story Theories*, edited by Charles May. Athens: Ohio University Press, 1994.

Premchand. "Adab kī gharaz-o-ghayat'." In *Mazāmīn-i Prem Cand*, 234–52. Aligarh: Matba Muslim University, 1960.

———. "Sāhitya kā uddeśya." In *Premcand racanāvalī*, edited by Rāmavilās Śarmā and Rām Ānand, 7:499–510. New Delhi: Janvani Prakashan, 1996. Originally published 1936.

Prins, Yopie. "'What Is Historical Poetics?'" *Modern Language Quarterly* 77, no. 1 (2016): 13–40.

Pritchett, Frances W. *Nets of Awareness: Urdu Poetry and Its Critics*. Berkeley: University of California Press, 1994.

Pritchett, Frances W., and Khaliq Ahmad Khaliq. *Urdu Meter: A Practical Handbook*. Madison: South Asian Studies, University of Wisconsin, 1987.

Pue, A. Sean. "Ephemeral Asia: Position without Identity in the Modernist Urdu Poetry of N. M. Rashed." *Comparative Literature* 64, no. 1 (2012): 73–92.

Pullin, E. "'Money Does Not Make Any Difference to the Opinions That We Hold': India, the CIA, and the Congress for Cultural Freedom, 1951." *Intelligence and National Security* 26, no. 2–3 (2011):377–98.

Pyle, Forest. *The Ideology of Imagination: Subject and Society in the Discourse of Romanticism*. Stanford, CA: Stanford University Press, 1995.

Rahman, M. Raisur. *Locale, Everyday Islam, and Modernity: Qasbah Towns and Muslim Life in Colonial India*. Oxford: Oxford University Press, 2015.

Rahv, Philip. "The Cult of Experience in American Writing." *Partisan Review* 7, no. 6 (1940): 412–24.

Rai, Alok. *Hindi Nationalism*. Hyderabad: Orient Blackswan, 2001.

Rai, Amrit. *A House Divided: The Origin and Development of Hindi/Hindavi*. Delhi: Oxford University Press, 1984.

Ram, Harsha. "The Scale of Global Modernisms: Imperial, National, Regional, Local." *PMLA* 131, no. 5 (2016): 1372–85.

Ramaswamy, Sumathi. *Passions of the Tongue*. 1st ed. Berkeley: University of California Press, 1997.

Ramazani, Jahan. *Poetry in a Global Age*. Chicago: University of Chicago Press, 2020.

———. *A Transnational Poetics*. Chicago: University of Chicago Press, 2009.

Rao, D. S. *Five Decades: The National Academy of Letters, India: A Short History of Sahitya Akademi.* New Delhi: Sahitya Akademi, [2004].

Raza, Ali. *Revolutionary Pasts: Communist Internationalism in Colonial India.* Cambridge: Cambridge University Press, 2020.

Ritter, Valerie. *Kama's Flowers: Nature in Hindi Poetry and Criticism, 1885–1925.* Albany: State University of New York Press, 2011.

Roadarmel, Gordon C. *A Death in Delhi: Modern Hindi Short Stories.* Berkeley: University of California Press, 1972.

Robb, Megan Eaton. *Print and the Urdu Public: Muslims, Newspapers, and Urban Life in Colonial India.* New York: Oxford University Press, 2020.

Rooprai, Vikramjit Singh. *Delhi Heritage: Top 10 Baolis.* New Delhi: Niyogi Books, 2019.

Rosenstein, Ludmila L. *New Poetry in Hindi.* Delhi: Permanent Black, 2003.

Rubin, Andrew. *Archives of Authority: Empire, Culture, and the Cold War.* Princeton, NJ: Princeton University Press, 2017.

Rubin, David. *Of Love and War: A Chayavad Anthology.* Delhi: Oxford University Press, 2005.

Sadana, Rashmi. *English Heart, Hindi Heartland: The Political Life of Literature in India.* Berkeley: University of California Press, 2012.

Shah, Rameshchandra. "Upanyās aur muktibodh." *Pūrvagraha,* no. 46–47 (1981): 14–22.

Sahi, Vijayadev Narayaṇ. "Laghu mānav ke bahāne hindī kavitā par ek bahas." In *Chaṭhvāṁ daśak,* 259–321. Allahabad: Hindustani Ekedemi, 1987.

Sahota, G. S. *Late Colonial Sublime: Neo-epics and the End of Romanticism.* FlashPoints. Evanston, IL: Northwestern University Press, 2018.

Sarkar, Sumit. *Modern India, 1885–1947.* Delhi: Macmillan, 1983.

Sharma, Nirmal, ed. "Bātcīt 2." *Kaṅk,* no. 51–55 (1979): 120–32.

———, ed. "Bātcīt 4." *Kaṅk,* no. 51–55 (1979): 211–29.

———, ed. "Muktibodh prasaṅg: mezbān aur raham" [On the Occasion of Muktibodh: Hospitality and Mercy!]. *Kaṅk,* no. 51–55 (1979): 289–90.

———. *Muktibodh: Samagra muktibodh-sāhitya par ālocanātmak nibandhoṃ kā saṅgraha.* Ratlam, Madhya Pradesh: Trayī prakāśan, 1980.

———. *Nayī Kavitā Aur Astitvavād.* New Delhi: Rajkamal Prakashan, 1978.

———. *Nirālā kī sāhitya sādhanā.* New Delhi: Rajkamal Prakashan, 1969.

———. "Samkālīn janvādī kavitā: paramparā aur itihās-dṛṣṭi!" *Kaṅk,* no. 56–58 (1981): 5–21.

Sharma, Vishnuchandra. *Muktibodh kī ātmakathā.* New Delhi: Radhakrishna, 1984.

Saunders, Frances Stonor. *The Cultural Cold War: The CIA and the World of Arts and Letters.* New York: New Press, 2013.

Sawhney, Simona. *The Modernity of Sanskrit*. Minneapolis: University of Minnesota Press, 2008.

Schleifer, Ronald. *A Political Economy of Modernism: Literature, Post-classical Economics, and the Lower Middle-Class*. Cambridge: Cambridge University Press, 2018.

Schomer, Karine. *Mahadevi Varma and the Chhayavad Age of Modern Hindi Poetry*. Berkeley: University of California Press, 1983.

Scott, David. *Conscripts of Modernity: The Tragedy of Colonial Enlightenment*. Durham, NC: Duke University Press, 2004.

Scott-Smith, Giles. "The Congress for Cultural Freedom, the End of Ideology and the 1955 Milan Conference: 'Defining the Parameters of Discourse.'" *Journal of Contemporary History* 37, no. 3 (2002): 437–55.

Seely, Clinton B. *A Poet Apart: A Literary Biography of the Bengali Poet Jibanananda Das (1899–1954)*. Newark: University of Delaware Press, 1990.

Sen, Samar, Debabrata Panda, and Ashish Lahiri, eds. *Naxalbari and After: A Frontier Anthology*. Calcutta: Kathashilpa, 1978.

Shah, Alpa, and Dhruv Jain. "Naxalbari at Its Golden Jubilee: Fifty Recent Books on the Maoist Movement in India." *Modern Asian Studies* 51, no. 4 (2017): 1165–1219.

Shandilya, Krupa. *Intimate Relations: Social Reform and the Late Nineteenth-Century South Asian Novel*. Evanston, IL: Northwestern University Press, 2017.

Shankar, Subramanian. *Flesh and Fish Blood: Postcolonialism, Translation, and the Vernacular*. Flashpoints 11. Berkeley: University of California Press, 2012.

Shaw, Annapurna. *Indian Cities*. New Delhi: Oxford University Press, 2012.

Shridhar, Vijaydatt. *Bhāratīya patrakāritā*. New Delhi: Vani Prakashan, 2008.

Shringarpure, Bhakti. *Cold War Assemblages: Decolonization to Digital*. New York: Routledge, 2020.

Shukla, Vinod Kumar. *Dīvār Meṃ Ek Khiṛkī Rahtī*. New Delhi: Vani Prakashan, 1997.

Shulman, David. *The Hungry God: Hindu Tales of Filicide and Devotion*. Chicago: University of Chicago Press, 1993.

Singh, Charu. "Science in the Vernacular? Translation, Terminology and Lexicography in the Hindi Scientific Glossary (1906)." *South Asian History and Culture* 13, no. 1 (2022): 63–86.

Singh, Kedarnath. "Kālbaddh aur padārthmay." *Pūrvagraha*, no. 39–40 (1980): 29–35.

Singh, Namvar. *Chāyāvād*. New Delhi: Rajkamal Prakashan, 1979.

———. *Chāyāvāda: aitihāsika-sāmājika viśleshaṇa*.Banaras: Saraswati Press, 1955.

———. *Dūsrī Paramparā Kī Khoj* [The Search for Another Tradition]. New Delhi: Rajkamal Prakashan, 1982.
———. *Kahānī: nayī kahānī*. Allahabad: Lokbharati Prakashan, 1966.
———. *Kavitā ke naye pratimān*. New Delhi: Rajkamal Prakashan, 1968.
———. *Kavitā ke naye pratimān*. 4th ed. New Delhi: Rajkamal Prakashan, 1990.
Singh, Ravindra Pratap. *Geography and Politics in Central India: A Case Study of Erstwhile Indore State*. New Delhi: Concept, 1987.
Singh, Shamsher Bahadur. "Ek Vilakṣaṇ Pratibhā." In *Cānd Kā Muṃh Ṭeḍhā Hai*, 11–27. New Delhi: Bhāratīya Gyanpith Prakashan, 1964.
———. *Racnāvalī*. New Delhi: Shilpayan, 2017.
Siskind, Mariano. *Cosmopolitan Desires: Global Modernity and World Literature in Latin America*. Evanston, IL: Northwestern University Press, 2014.
Smith, Neil. "Scale Bending and the Fate of the National." In *Scale and Geographic Inquiry*, edited by Eric Sheppard and Robert B. McMaste, 192–212. Chichester, UK: Wiley, 2008.
Smith, Stan. "Balancing Accounts: Caudwell, Eagleton and English Marxism." *Critical Survey* 7, no. 1 (1995): 76–81.
Spivak, Gayatri Chakravorty. *Death of a Discipline*. New York: Columbia University Press, 2003.
Subramaniam, Banu. *Holy Science: The Biopolitics of Hindu Nationalism*. Seattle: University of Washington Press, 2019.
Tanoukhi, Nirvana. "The Scale of World Literature." *New Literary History* 39, no. 3 (2008): 599–617.
Terada, Rei. "After the Critique of Lyric." *PMLA* 123, no. 1 (2008): 195–200.
Thapar, Romila. *Early India*. Berkeley: University of California Press, 2003.
Thiesen, Finn. *A Manual of Classical Persian Prosody: With Chapters on Urdu, Karakhanidic, and Ottoman Prosody*. Wiesbaden: O. Harrassowitz, 1982.
Thiong'o, Ngũgĩ wa. *Decolonising the Mind: The Politics of Language in African Literature*. Nairobi: East African Educational Publishers, 1992.
Thomas, Renny. "Brahmins as Scientists and Science as Brahmins' Calling: Caste in an Indian Scientific Research Institute." *Public Understanding of Science* 29, no. 3 (2020): 306–18.
Thompson, E. P. "Christopher Caudwell." *Critical Inquiry* 21, no. 2 (1995): 305–53.
Times of India. "Chinese Reds Are Censured." January 1964.
———. "Nehru Tired and Weak, Is Advised Rest: Doctors Hopeful of Quick Recovery." January 1964.
———. "Railway Sentry Fires on Mob of Best Workers." January 1964.
———. "Troops Move in as Calcutta Riots Continue: Over 60 Dead; Curfew, Ban Orders in Many Areas." January 1964.

Tiwari, Bhavya. *Beyond English: World Literature and India*. New York: Bloomsbury, 2021.

Tripathi, Mrityunjay, and Shad Naved. *The Hindi Canon: Intellectuals, Processes, Criticism*. New Delhi: Tulika, 2018.

Trivedi, Harish. "Eliot in Hindi Modes of Reception." *Indian Literature* 32, no. 5 (1989): 140–53.

———. "The Progress of Hindi, Part 2: Hindi and the Nation." In *Literary Cultures in History*, edited by Sheldon Pollock, 958–1022. Berkeley: University of California Press, 2003.

Trivedi, Sunil. "Baba Nagarjun." *Indian Literature* 42, no. 6 (1998): 140–44.

Tukaram. *Says Tuka: Selected Poetry of Tukaram*. Translated by Dilip Chitre. New Delhi: Penguin Books India, 1991.

Vaitheespara, Ravi, and Rajesh Venkatasubramanian. "Beyond the Politics of Identity: The Left and the Politics of Caste and Identity in Tamil Nadu, 1920." *South Asia* 38, no. 4 (2015): 543–57.

Vajpeyi, Ashok. "Bhayānak khabar kī kavitā." In *Filhāl*. New Delhi: Rajkamal Prakashan, 1970.

———. "Muktibodh ke sāth sāṭh sāl." *Ālocnā*, no. 55 (2015): 69–80.

Varma, Dhananjay. "Ek ādhūnik klāsik kā sākṣātkār." *Pūrvagraha*, no. 42 (1981): 23–28.

Varma, Dhirendra. *Hindī Sāhitya Koś*. Benares: Gyan mandal, 1985.

Varma, Keshavchandra. *Parimal: smṛtiyāṃ aur dastāvez*. Allahabad: Lokbharati Prakashan, 2003.

Varma, Lakshmikant. *Nayī kavitā ke pratimān: pariprekshya, naye dharātal, mānavavād*. Allahabad: Bharati Press, 1957.

Varma, Moti Ram. *Lakṣit muktibodh*. New Delhi: Vidyarthi Prakashan, 1972.

Varma, Pramod. "Carcā." *Vasudhā*, no. 8 (1956): 59–60.

Verma, Nirmal. *Indian Errant: Selected Stories of Nirmal Verma*. Edited and translated by Prasenjit Gupta. New Delhi: Indialog, 2002.

———. "Muktibodh kī gadya-kathā." *Pūrvagraha* 7, no. 3 (1981): 3–9.

Vint, Sherryl. *Science Fiction*. Cambridge, MA: MIT Press, 2021.

Vishnusharman. *Five Discourses of Worldly Wisdom*. Translated by Patrick Olivelle. Bilingual ed. New York: Clay Sanskrit, 2006.

Wakankar, Milind. "The Moment of Criticism in Indian Nationalist Thought: Ramchandra Shukla and the Poetics of a Hindi Responsibility." *South Atlantic Quarterly* 101, no. 4 (2003): 987–1014.

Warwick Research Collective. *Combined and Uneven Development: Towards a New Theory of World-Literature*. Liverpool: Liverpool University Press, 2015.

Watt, Ian P. *The Rise of the Novel: Studies in Defoe, Richardson, and Fielding*. Berkeley: University of California Press, 1957.

Westad, Odd Arne. *The Global Cold War: Third World Interventions and the Making of Our Times*. Cambridge: Cambridge University Press, 2007.
Yadav, Rajendra. *Ek duniyā: samānāntar*. Delhi: Akshar Prakashan, 1966.
"Yah Aṅk." *Kalpanā*, August 1964.
Zaitseva, Lusia. "Gained in Translation: Faiz Ahmed Faiz's Soviet Travels." *Comparative Literature* 73, no. 1 (2021): 41–60.
Zecchini, Laetitia. *Arun Kolatkar and Literary Modernism in India—Moving Lines*. London: Bloomsbury, 2014.
———. "What Filters through the Curtain." *Interventions* 22, no. 2 (2020): 172–94.

Index

"A Report to the Academy," 115.
See also Kafka
Adorno, Theodor, 68
advaitā vedāntā, 84
Africa, 123
Agrawal, Kedarnath, 17
Agyeya (Sachchidananda Hirananda Vatsyayan), 5, 8, 18–19, 100
Ājkal, 77
akavitā, 79, 170, 256–257n48, 270n51
ālhā. See under epic
alienation, 175
All-India Medical Institute, 170
All-India Peasant's Union, 17
Allahabad, 75
allegory
  "Brahmarakshas" and, 59
  fantastic and, 116, 130–131
  Kāmāyanī and, 90
  Muktibodh's theorization of, 138–140
  mural painting and, 130
  narrative and, 109
  in poetry, 138–140
  postindependence nation and, 59, 116–117, 152, 163, 172, 175, 178
  realism and, 69
Ālocnā, 68
Aṃdhere meṃ, 152–167
āñcalik sāhitya. See under regional literature
Aṅgāre, 17
Anil (Atmaram Ravaji Deshpande), 146–147
Anjaria, Ulka, 97, 259n1
Apoorvanand, 271n73
Apte, Hari Narayan, 134

Bachchan, Harivansh Rai, 17, 170
Banaras, 75
Bangla language, 18, 143
Bengali. *See under* Bangla language
Benjamin, Walter, 68, 263n8
Bergson, Henri, 134
bhadratā, 78
Bharat Bhavan, 188
Bhārat: itihās aur sanskṛti, 94
bhāv and *vibhāv. See* rasa
"Bhaviśyadhārā," 120–121
Bhopal, 75
bhūkhī pīḍhī, 170
Bhūrī bhūrī khāk dhūl, 264n18
Blok, Alexander, 186
Brahmarakshas
  background in mythology, 40
  relation to political commitment, 33–34
  ritual impurity, 43

"Brahmarakshas," 129
Braj, 134, 143
Brecht, Bertolt, 68–71, 89
bureaucracy, 114, 262n39

Cāṃd kā muṃh ṭeḍhā hai
preface, 129, 172
Candrakāntā, 98, 118, 154
Carpentier, Alejo, 98
caste, 113–114
and brahmanical education, 41–43, 51–53
Brahmin status, 44–46, 261n33
Caste
and left politics, 34
and patronage networks, 113
Caudwell, Christopher, 87. See also *Illusion and Reality*
Central India, 261n27
Chaturvedi, Makhanlal, 265n27
Chauhan, Chanchal, 185
Chauhan, Prithvi Raj, 17
chāyāvād, 5, 15, 17, 32, 89, 134, 140–141, 178, 268n19
Cheah, Pheng, 99
Chevrolet, 107–108
China, 123
CID [Central Investigative Division], 117, 123
circus, 114–115
Civil Lines, 84
civilization, 72
Clark, Katerina, 9
"Claude Eatherly," 117–124
Cold War, 67, 246n34
literature and, 6–12, 244n21
Coleridge, Samuel Taylor
Biographia Literaria, 255–256n37
"The Rime of the Ancient Mariner," 131
Comintern, 8–9
Communist Party of India, 91
Congress for Cultural Freedom, 9, 19, 184
Congress Socialists. *See under* Socialist Party
criticism, 14, 44–46, 95, 185, 190
critique of realism, 67–68
Culler, Jonathan, 14
cult of experience, 78, 102, 260n21

Dange, Amrit, 91. *See also* Communist Party of India
Delhi, 75, 78
detective fiction, 118, 119
Devtale, Chandrakant, 184, 270n51
Dhanwa, Alok, 184, 270n51
Dharmyug, 170. *See also* Hindi journals
Dhumil (Sudama Panday), 184, 270n51
Dinkar, Ramdhari Singh, 32
Dinmān, 75. *See also* Hindi journals
disillusionment, 178
Dīvār meṃ ek khiṛkī rahtī thī, 125–126
"Dūr tārā," 148–149

Eatherly, Claude, 119, 262n48
Ek duniyā, samānāntar, 100
"Ek lambī kavitā kā ant," 133, 137–140, 148–149
Ek lekhak kī ḍāyarī, 74–75, 105
Emergency, 6, 182, 244n18. *See also* disillusionment
Enola Gay, 118
epic, 89, 166, 185
event [*ghaṭṇā*], 104
existentialism, 176–177

fable, 107
fantastic, the, 30, 44, 63–64, 97–100, 152–154, 163, 186, 247n44, 258n72. *See also*

allegory; fable; magic realism; parable
qissā-dāstān narratives, 55, 97
fantasy, 87–88, 94, 106, 258n66, 270n55. *See also* fantastic, the; romanticism
Felsky, Rita, 73
flowers, 37
Frankenstein, 163

genre, 3, 73, 105. *See also* novel; poetry; short story
ghazal, 128
Ginsburg, Allen, 170
Gorky, Maxim, 17, 176
Guernica, 265n14
Gunslinger, 31
Gupt, Jagdish, 140–143
guru
relationship to student, 38
Gyanpith Prakashan, 18

Hans
See Chauhan, Prithvi Raj
Hindi
āñcalik sāhitya, 255n27
Cold War literature and, 4, 8–11, 19, 195
history of, 16, 244n20, 248–249n62
khaḍī bolī, 16, 143
lower middle class, relationship with, 72–74
metrical traditions in, 142–143, 148
modernism, 82, 88, 141, 146, 173, 189
as national language, 15–16, 243n15
nayī kavitā, 5, 19, 71–72, 100–101, 173–174, 177, 182
nayī kavitā, critique of, 79
novel in, 249n63
postmodern poetry, 31
progressive poetry, 17, 79
and Progressive Writers Association, 16–17, 97, 249n67
relationship to novel, 14, 135, 189
relationship to prose, 2, 4, 77, 102–106, 124–126
relationship to Sanskrit, 55–56
relationship with Indian state, 18
social context of, 77
syntax, 251n4
translation, 25–26, 49
translation in the 1970s, 68
Hindi journals, 75, 77
Hindu Mahasabha, 94, 135
hungry generation. *See* bhūkhī pīḍhī
Husain, Maqbool Fida, 264–265n12, 268n11

identity, 178
Illusion and Reality. See Caudwell, Christopher
imagination, 81, 86–87
imprisonment, 112
Indonesia, 123
Indore, 77

Jabalpur, 75
Jackson, Virginia, 14
Jameson, Fredric, 242n6, 245n29
Jayshankar Prasad. See *Kāmāyanī*
Joshi, Rajesh, 89, 127, 258n72
Joshi, Sanjay, 73–74

Kafka, 112–117
Kalpanā, 56, 75
Kāmāyanai: ek punarvicār
critique of *Kāmāyanī,* 37, 94

Kāmāyanī, 15, 90, 166, 193
as allegory, 90
critique by Muktibodh (see *Kāmāyanī: ek punarvicār*)
as neo-*kāvya*, 32
relationship to mythical past, 37
Kāmāyanī: ek punarvicār, 89–95. *See also* Kāmāyanī
Kaṅk, 183–187, 270n49. *See also* Hindi journals
Kantor, Roanne, 98–99
Kaul, Mani, 187–188
kavitā. *See* poetry
Kavitā ke naye pratimān, 173–176, 178
kāvya, 3, 13–14, 15, 32, 141
khaḍī bolī. *See* Hindi
Khatri, Devkinandan. See *Candrakāntā*
kṣaṇvād, 79, 88

laghu mānav, 19–21, 72
Lohia, Ram Manohar, 19–20. *See also* Socialist Party
long poem. *See* poetry
Lotz, Barbara, 243n17
Lucknow, 74
Lukács, György, 68–69, 178, 247n46, 253–254n3
Lumumba, Patrice, 123
lyric, 2–4, 31–32, 64–65, 127–128, 131, 137–138, 150, 248n58, 263n3. *See also* poetry
formation as genre, 14
in relation to the novel, 12–15
theorization, 127–128
in world literature, 12

magic realism, 98. *See* realism
mahākāvya, 166
Maharashtrian Brahmans, 41
Mani, Preetha, 100–101, 248n53
Manto, Saadat Hasan, 99
Mao Zedong, 183
Marathi, 5, 21, 128, 134, 144, 148, 167. See also *muktachanda*
Mardhekar, Bal Sitaram, 145–146
Marx, Karl, 51, 271n73
Economic and Political Manuscripts, 178
Mayakovsky, Vladimir, 17, 189
meter, 142–143, 149–150
middle class, 15
and the Brahmarakshas, 45
lower middle class, 71–76, 102
Midnight's Children, 99
modernism, 250–251n84
mohbhaṅg, 189
Mukherjee, Meenakshi, 13, 249n63, 259n1
muktachanda, 128, 145–151, 153–154
Muktibodh, Gajanan Madhav
family background, 41
film, response to, 257n53
history textbook case, 94
Marathi-speaking background, influence of, 132, 144, 167
posthumous reception, 4, 243–244n17
"Muktibodh kī gadya kathā," 101–106
Muktibodh, Sharachchandra, 136, 147–148
mural, 129, 130

Nagarjun, 185
Nagpur, 5, 147, 157–158
naī kahānī, 74, 101, 124–125
narrative, 4, 30–32, 81, 104–106, 125, 130. *See also* allegory
poetry and, 24–25, 137
prose and, 102
Nationalism. *See under* Tagore, Rabindranath

Navī maḷvaṭ, 147–148
nayī kavitā. *See* poetry
Nayī kavitā aur astitvavād, 176–181
Nayī kavitā kā ātmasaṅgharṣ, 71
Nehru, Jawaharlal
  Death, 170–171, 242n15
  Relation to science and the expert
    1950s and, 58
Neue Sachlichkeit. *See* magic realism
New Delhi. *See under* Delhi
New Left Review, 68
Nirala (Suryakant Tripathi), 134, 144, 154, 157
non-poetry. See *akavitā*
novel, the, 249n63, 259n1. *See also* allegory, narrative
  contrast between poetry and, 2, 80–81, 134–135
  long poem, relationship with, 189
  popular fiction and, 120–121
  relation to *dāstān* narratives, 13
  relation to short story, 13, 100
  relationship to realism in South Asia, 97–98
  short story and, 2
  world literature, position in, 12

ovī-abhaṅga, 145–148

"pakṣī aur dīmak," 106–111
Pallav, 142. *See also* chāyāvād
Panchatantra, 109. *See also* fable
Pant, Sumitranandan, 130, 141
parable, 106, 110
Parimal group, 19–20
Parsai, Harishankar, 18, 75, 169
Paterson. *See under* Williams, William Carlos
Persian, 155
poetry
  See also *akavitā; chāyāvād; mahākāvya; ovī–abhaṅga*
  anxiety over length, 136–137
  Braj poetic tradition, 128
  emergence in *khaḍī bolī*, 142
  free verse, 141, 144–151
  genre and definition, 12, 128
  ghazal, 128
  impact of *Tār saptak*, 17–18
  long poem, 3, 31–32
Popescu, Monica, 9
postcolonial literature, 9
pragativād. *See under* progressivism
Prakash, Uday, 89
Prasad, Jayshankar, 134, 193
Pratt, Mary, 248n53
Praxis, *33*
prayogvād, 18
prayogvād and *pragativād*, 8, 68, 78, 140
Premchand (Dhanpat Rai Srivastava), 81, 97–98, 100–101, 176, 181
Prins, Jopie, 14
progressivism, 3, 249n67
  changes in terminology, 19
  critique of modernism, 79, 176–177, 179
  critiques of, 20, 71–72, 185
  as literary movement, 5
  poetry, relationship to, 17, 149
  Soviet-aligned aesthetics, relationship to, 245–246n30
prose narrative, 3
Pūrvagraha, 101, 103, 183, 264n20. *See also* Hindi journals

qasbah, the 78, 102, 105

Rahv, Philip. *See* cult of experience

Rai, Dhanpat. *See* Premchand
Rajkamal Prakashan, 18
Rajnandgaon, 135
rasa, 81, 93, 95, 138–139, 141, 257n55
realism, 92, 105, 138
  Brecht's critique of, 69–71
  ideas of the *laghu mānav,* 19
  lower middle class and, 75
  magic realism, 89–100
  Muktibodh's critique of, 23
  and *nayī kavitā,* 73, 174
  novel and, 12–13, 259n1
  peripheral realism, 274n44
  prose narrative and, 105
  relation to literary genre, 15, 24, 64
  relationship to allegory, 89–93
  short story and, 100–101
  sympathy and, 81
realism-modernism debates, 3–4, 9–10, 178, 181
regional literature, 74
Renu (Phanishwar Nath Mandal), 74
romanticism, 39, 70, 87, 179, 254n9. See also *chāyāvād;* fantastic
  fantasy and, 87–89
  left critique of, 179–180
  nationalism and, 17
  poetics and, 91–92

Sagar, 75
Sahi, Vijaydevnarayan, 17, 19–20, 76. See also *laghu mānav*
Sahitya Akademi, 18
Samājvād. See under Socialist Party
"Samjhautā," 112–117
Sanskrit, 155
Sanskrit language, 46, 55–56, 155
Satah se uṭhtā ādmī, 188
science, 41
  as archaic modernity, 50
  Nehruvian science and, 50–51
  in popular narrative fiction, 55–56
science fiction, 122, 263n67
Scott, David, 242n6
Seminar, 120
Shah, Ramesh Chandra, 189
Shankar, 244–245n23
Sharma, Ramvilas, 17, 68, 74, 176–181, 186
Shastri, Lal Bahadur, 170
Shelley, 152, 179–180
short story, the, 248n51, 248n52, 248n53
  importance in Hindi literature, 100
Shringarpure, Bhakti, 9
Shukla, Ramchandra, 241n3
Shukla, Vinod Kumar, 89, 125–126, 188
Singh, Kedarnath, 132, 140, 264n20
Singh, Murli Manohar Prasad, 186
Singh, Namwar, 173–176, 186, 268n18, 268n21
Singh, Shamsher Bahadur, 79, 129–133, 140, 172–173, 264n14, 268n15
Socialist Party, 17, 19–20
Stepwells *(bāvṛī),* 28, 36
sthāyī bhāv. See rasa
style, 93

Tagore, Rabindranath, 94
Tamil, 244n20
Tār saptak, 5, 133–137, 148, 173, 176, 243n13
  influence of, 17–18
"The Aim of Literature." *See under* Premchand
The Changing Light at Sandover, 3, 31

"The Masque of Anarchy." *See* Shelley
The Maximus Poems, 3
The Wasteland, 3, 6
third world, 123
Third World, 9–11
Tilak, Bal Gangodhar, 161–163
Times of India, 170
"Tīsrā kṣaṇ," 83, 91, 106
"Toba Tek Singh." *See under* Manto, Saadat Hasan
Tolstoy, Lev Nikolayevich, 1–2, 134, 241n2
Tukaram, 145

Ujjain, 84
United States, 120
Urdu, 142
  meter, 265n41
Urvaśī, 32

Vajpeyee, Ashok, 6, 129, 186–188
Varanasi. *See under* Banaras
Varma, Lakshmikant, 21, 72
Varma, Pramod, 75, 78
Vasudhā, 18, 74, 83, 88. *See also* Hindi journals
Verma, Nirmal, 101–106, 108–109, 124–125
Verma, Shrikant, 186
Vernacular, 7–8, 244n22
"Vīrkar," 82, 91
Viśāl bhārat, 136–137. *See also* Hindi journals

Warwick Research Collective, 247n44
Williams, William Carlos, 3

Yadav, Rajendra, 72, 100–101
Yātrik, 148
Yoga, 85

Zhdanov, Andrei Aleksandrovich, 9, 69, 245–246n30

www.ingramcontent.com/pod-product-compliance
Lightning Source LLC
Chambersburg PA
CBHW030524230426
43665CB00010B/753
* 9 7 8 1 4 3 8 4 9 9 5 8 1 *